Lope de Vega

Lope de Vega

(Five Plays)

TRANSLATED BY JILL BOOTY

EDITED WITH AN INTRODUCTION BY

R. D. F. PRING-MILL

A MERMAID DRAMABOOK

HILL AND WANG · NEW YORK

A NOTE ON THE TRANSLATIONS

Miss Jill Booty would describe her translations as "acting versions," and this seems to me to be their great merit. If I am right that Lope's power as a dramatist lies precisely in the liveliness of his somewhat schematic characterization, the breathtaking pace of his actions, and the subordination of all other aspects of his drama to its theatrical efficacy, then a fresh and vivid acting version is going to be far more true to the spirit of his plays than any studiously scholarly rendering of their literal meaning. Miss Booty has had to sacrifice much Golden Age rhetoric in the interests of producing credible dialogue, but what has struck me time and again in the course of checking her translations is the way in which she has disclosed an immediately acceptable line of argument in what would strike most modern readers as an incredibly alembicated piece of sophistry. It is a great tribute to her ability that she should have been able to preserve the entire argument of a complex sonnet, for instance, and present it as a wholly acceptable prose soliloquy—but the fact that she should have been able to do so at all is also a tribute to Lope's instinctive feeling for what an actor can put over. The zest and liveliness with which she renders him owe not a little to the fact that she is herself a professional actress, and while her versions are in no sense a serviceable "crib," I think that it is not unfair to claim that they bring out the drive and import of each speech in a way which can illuminate both theme and action even for the scholar who is accustomed to working on the original texts.

R. D. F. P-M.

Caution: The translations in this volume are fully protected under the copyright laws of the United States, the British Empire including the Dominion of Canada, and all other countries of the Copyright Union, and are subject to royalty. All rights, including professional, amateur, motion picture, recitation, lecturing, public reading, and radio and television broadcasting, are strictly reserved. Particular emphasis is laid on the question of readings, permission for which must be obtained in writing from the Publisher. All inquiries should be addressed to the Publisher, Hill and Wang, Inc., 104 Fifth Avenue, New York 11, N.Y.

Contents

Contents

INTRODUCTION

THIS introduction is intended to put the five plays in this volume into the theatrical context of the Spanish Golden Age, and more particularly into the immediate context of Lope de Vega's own dramatic output. To this end, I have had to sacrifice any exposition of Lope's extremely adventurous life, as well as any attempt to discuss his non-dramatic works, and I have also excluded virtually all the references to versification which I should have made had I been presenting the Spanish texts. Readers who want to follow up these aspects will find adequate guidance in the *Bibliography*, which also gives the full titles and references of the various critical studies alluded to in the course of the introduction itself.

THE CONTEXT OF LOPE DE VEGA'S DRAMA

The great age of Spanish drama began in the 1580s, at about the same time as the first flowering of the Elizabethan theater in England. It lasted without interruption for about a hundred years and was dominated by two figures: Lope Félix de Vega Carpio (1562–1635), who created the Spanish *comedia*—a term used to denote any full-length secular play—and Pedro Calderón de la Barca (1600–1681), who brought it to a complex and highly stylized form of perfection. As in the English drama of the period, the pattern of society reflected in their plays was dominated by the notion of an absolute monarchy, with the sovereign seen as God's vice-regent—dispenser of justice, and the source of honor. The structure of this society was hierarchic, and related to a general world-picture by their interaction in a universal harmony. The whole universe depended on God's will, and nature—harmoniously ordered—was God's instrument. Human society reflected the structure of the natural order, based on numberless but closely linked degrees of being. There

vii

was a precise analogical correspondence not merely between society and nature, but also between the macrocosm and the microcosm (the "little world of man"), and therefore likewise between the individual human organism and the body politic.

The structuralized vision of Creation forms the background against which every play is enacted: the framework within which it is constructed and in terms of which it is articulated. The individual drama is related outward to the framework by subtle use of interlocking images which bring out the analogical correspondences, by mythological references endowed with an allegorical force, and by the constant use of generalized statements (*sentencias,* the Latin *sententiae*). This continual aphoristic formulation of moral and philosophical commonplaces should not be dismissed as platitudinous, but used as a key to the relationship between the general and the particular—between the abstract universal principle and the particular concrete situation facing the characters in the play. Within this universal structure, human motivation is governed by three things: the theory of the four "humors" (so prominent in Elizabethan drama); the systematic conceptions of Catholic moral theology (basically Thomist), exemplified both by the values which are admired and by the way in which the conduct of those who reject them is analyzed in terms of weakness and passion, and condemned for misuse of their free will; and, lastly, by the highly stylized code of honor. In a recent analysis of "The Uniqueness of the *Comedia,*" Reichenberger has described it as being firmly based on the two rocks of *la honra* and *la fe,* and while one may not agree with him in every other respect, this affirmation is beyond dispute.

In the plays which are included in this volume, *la fe* forms part of the background (the moral dimension which gives depth to personal dilemmas). *La honra,* however, is very much to the fore. Each of these five plays is deeply concerned with questions of honor, both of honor in the sense of social reputation (endangered by the actions of others, which are not within one's own control) and of honor in the sense of personal integrity and moral worth. In the latter sense, honor is wholly consonant with *la fe,* but the defense of reputation leads to the development of an apparently autonomous code of conduct often hard to reconcile with Christian morality. It is best regarded as a formalized embodiment of the demands made on the individual by the conventions of the society of which he is a member, and almost all Golden Age plays are in some way concerned with dilemmas facing individuals in their relationships with society as a whole—and, through society, with the basic structure of the universe itself.

These dilemmas were handled very differently by different Spanish playwrights, and there is a great gulf between Lope and Calderón in this respect. Calderón is more subtly casuistical in his approach, gravely concerned with moral issues, illustrating universal themes or principles in terms of carefully planned individual cases, which are meticulously worked out to their logical conclusion with strict subordination of action to theme. Lope is freer and fresher, less solemnly concerned, less obviously subtle and more supple. This difference is chiefly one of temperament, but Lope was also less rigid in his approach because he came earlier in the tradition. He was, indeed, its founder, responsible for the creation of the basic dramatic formula which all the later Golden Age dramatists were to employ. He used it himself with a light-hearted freedom and abandon which is more immediately delightful than the approach of other dramatists, but not necessarily any the less well planned for that.

Lope de Vega had a number of minor predecessors on whom he could draw, but none of them had succeeded in establishing a satisfactory formula (and in this respect Shakespeare, born only two years later, had the distinct advantage of being able to use an existing mold—however much he may have then gone on to change it). When Lope began writing plays, about 1580, there were three kinds of drama in existence in Spain: religious plays still conceived in a medieval tradition, plays for the gentry presented with some pomp, and popular plays presented as economically as possible, with hardly any scenery. These popular plays were put on in *corrales* of much the same kind as the Elizabethan playhouse: an open square or *patio* (mirroring the innyards in which the strolling players had been accustomed to perform), with the surrounding balconies and windows used as boxes, and with the groundlings (*mosqueteros*) in the open square, and the women "respectably" segregated in a separate section (the *cazuela*) at the back. The *mosqueteros* decided the fate of a play, and they were stanch supporters of the moral commonplaces which the plays upheld. They liked a swift and melodramatic action which held their attention, and Lope catered to this taste throughout his many hundred plays.

Three of Lope's predecessors deserve to be mentioned here, one from each of the three earlier generations of sixteenth-century playwrights: Bartolomé de Torres Naharro (*ca.* 1480–1530), Lope de Rueda (*ca.* 1510–1565?), and Juan de la Cueva (1550?–1610?). Torres Naharro belonged to the very first generation of Spanish secular dramatists, and he distinguished between documentary satires, which he called *comedias a noticia* ("plays of observation"), and romantic *comedias a fantasia* ("plays of invention")—tragicomedies with frequently very extravagant plots. One of the latter, the *Comedia Himenea*, is really a Lope de Vega "cloak and dagger" play in miniature, foreshadowing the seventeenth-century use of both the honor theme and the humorous subplot. Torres Naharro's plays—all of which were written in verse—were meant for a noble audience, and it took another generation before men like Lope de Rueda popularized the secular drama, under the influence of visiting Italian companies. Rueda was a professional actor-manager, touring the country with his own troupe of players, and though his own *comedias* were merely rather poor adaptations of Italian models, the farcical interludes (*pasos*) with which they are interspersed developed a gallery of comic types, many of whom were to have their place in Lope de Vega's plays.

Prose was normal in such interludes, which reached their peak in the *entremeses* of Cervantes (1547–1616), but whereas Rueda wrote his *comedias* in prose as well, this was abandoned once more by his successors. Cueva moved well away from Rueda in this respect, introducing different meters into a single play, and this device was to prove a potent means of creating atmosphere in the abler hands of Lope de Vega and Calderón, besides serving to mark the essential difference between the stage illusion and real life. Cueva was also the first to use Spanish epic material, in his *Siete infantes de Lara* (Seville, 1579), but his own plays were ill-knit and episodic—still epic rather than dramatic in construction. It was left to Lope de Vega to adapt this material effectively to the demands of the stage, and his use of epic history and ballads is one of the most distinctive features of his work—it is already there in his earliest surviving play (*Los hechos de Garcilaso de la Vega y Moro Tarfe*, written not later than 1585), and is to be seen in three of the five plays in this collection: *Peribáñez, Fuenteovejuna,* and *The Knight from Olmedo.*

Torres Naharro had used five acts (like the Elizabethans), but Cueva popularized the four-act play. Lope de Vega started by using this somewhat unstable form, but he soon adopted and perfected the three-act pattern, whose invention he attributed to Cristóbal de Virués (1550–1609). The shape which this gives to the unfolding of a plot brings the seventeenth-century *comedia* vastly closer to nineteenth- and twentieth-century drama than its English counterpart. Two other features foster this impression of modernity: firstly, the mixture of tragedy and comedy; and, secondly, the rejection of the unities, which were to dominate the French classical stage and which tended to foster an extreme degree of artificiality in plot construction. It is important, however, to realize that Lope de Vega's rejection of any rigid distinction between comic and tragic material and his modification of the unities did not constitute a revolutionary breach with previous practice, but merely a perpetuation of this in the face of the increasing intolerance of the neo-Aristotelian literary theorists. (Humanistic comedies and tragedies, when tried out by the erudite, had proved a failure, and the only noticeable classical influence on the seventeenth-century *comedia* is that of the Senecan tragedy, with its gory ending.)

Lope de Vega's position was, then, a very different one from that of the French and German Romantics, although they claimed him as their forerunner: so far from leading a revolt against an existing formula, he was constructing a pattern out of previously uncoordinated elements. It is important to bear this in mind when reading his *New Art of Writing Plays,* for this was far from being a consciously daring literary manifesto like Victor Hugo's *Préface de Cromwell* (1827), in which it is quoted.

The New Art of Writing Plays

A prose translation of the *New Art* is available in another volume in this series, with an introduction by Brander Matthews (see *Bibliography*). The original verse epistle, written when Lope already had "483 *comedias*" to his credit (probably in 1609), is less of a program for the future than a series of reflections on his own dramatic practice—a somewhat unmethodical summing up, prepared in no very serious mood for a literary academy which would be no more than a rather amateur gathering under the patronage of some lettered nobleman. If, indeed, it existed at all: J. S. Pons (1945) suggests that the "dedication" may be merely a convenient device, and puts forward the idea that the *New Art* was really a reply to Cervantes' criticisms of Lope in the first part of *Don Quixote* (1605).

The epistle is written in a highly ironical and offhand fashion, which led to its being sadly misinterpreted by its earliest modern critics. Even Chaytor in 1925 still called it "a half-hearted defense of Lope's dramatic methods, conceived in a tone of apology, written without apparent conviction and padded with a deal of second-hand and unnecessary pedantry." Romera-Navarro (1935) was the first person to perceive the broad irony with which Lope handles the classical erudition he displays, and Menéndez Pidal (whose study was delivered as a set of lectures the month before Romera-Navarro's book appeared) went over wholeheartedly to the view which most critics would accept today: namely, that, far from being a half-hearted apology, the *New Art* glories in the practical success of Lope's plays, mocks at the classicists, and establishes a genuine—if unsystematized—dramatic theory based on the constant subordination of art to nature.

Apart from the restatement of the classical precepts it rejects, the *New Art* contains a limited number of clues to Lope's general theory of dramatic art and a large number of practical hints on actual dramatic technique. On the theoretical side, the traditional "holding the mirror up to nature" enables him to advocate the mingling of comic and tragic elements on the grounds that variety is the key to natural beauty. There is also a continuous stress on verisimilitude, though this is never carefully examined, and I think it is clear that this is really closely bound up with his constant stress on popular appeal: his holding the mirror up to nature is something far removed from any type of literal realism, and his version of reality is calculated to appeal by showing life not as it is but as his audience would like to think it was. In the comic parts, this leads toward caricature, but in the treatment of the central situation it results in a simultaneous simplification and idealization both of the issues involved and of the characters themselves.

On the technical side, his advice can be swiftly and succinctly summarized. Let the *comedia* have three acts. Expound the situation in the first, develop it in the second, and bring it to its conclusion in the third (but keep the denouement for the final scene, lest the crowd—foreseeing the end—begin to leave). The thread must be continuous from start to finish: unity of action, avoiding side issues which are irrelevant to the thrust, and avoiding an episodic structure in which different scenes build up a unity of their own at the expense of the whole. Observe the unity of time in a modified form, by restricting the events of each act to a single day, but disregard the unity of place whenever necessary. Suit your verse form to the subject matter, and, as far as subjects are concerned, choose plots concerning honor. Equivocate, for this delights the public. Avoid impossibilities. As for style: be natural, and suit the speech to the person. In soliloquy, show the way an argument develops through the gradual changes in a person's mind, so that the audience may itself be convinced by the reasoning. Finally, be neither clear nor open in your satire, "since it is known that for this very reason comedies were forbidden by law in Greece and Italy." And Lope ends with another bantering apology for daring to give precepts which contradict the theorists and for allowing himself to be carried along by the vulgar stream, justifying his *comedias* with one final and outrageous thrust, saying that, though they would have been "better" if made differently, they would have been less pleasing, since "that which is contrary to what is just, for that very reason, pleases the taste."

INTRODUCTION

THE UNDERLYING PRINCIPLES OF THE SPANISH
GOLDEN AGE comedia

Out of these hints and technical devices, and out of the
very varied material offered by his predecessors, Lope succeeded in creating a well-knit and highly effective formula,
mixing his ingredients with supremely competent crafts-
manship and superb dramatic self-assurance. His greatness
lies at least as much in the formula itself as in any of his
individual plays, although these very frequently achieve a
high degree of technical mastery and poetic finish. His
plays are swift-moving and exciting, deft, tender, and lyrical (in many varying moods), lithe in plot and both
lifelike and witty in dialogue. Lope was a skillful professional playwright with a sure instinct for pleasing his
contemporary audience, and the sheer theatricality of his
invention holds the attention even of the modern reader
—although the latter might be inclined to say that Lope is
sometimes a trifle superficial in the treatment of his
themes, though not in his best plays.

A more important criticism would be that Lope's characterization can strike one as perfunctory, but here we
come up against a feature of Spanish Golden Age writing
which requires to be seen against a more general background if it is to be properly understood. The subordination of characters to action is neither a feature peculiar
to Lope nor yet necessarily a source of weakness in a play.
It is in fact a deliberate technique, and has rightly been
singled out as one of the salient traits of the plays of this
period by Professor A. A. Parker, in *The Approach to the
Spanish Drama of the Golden Age*. Parker has formulated
five general principles of dramatic construction (or, rather,
four principles of construction and one of interpretation)
whose operation can be observed throughout the period
—principles which apply with varying force to different
plays (and above all to different dramatists), but which
prove extremely useful tools when one approaches the
task of analyzing the works of any Golden Age playwright.

The first of these is "the primacy of action over character drawing," but it really depends for its theoretical
justification as a deliberate technique on the second: "the
primacy of theme over action." Whereas we are now
accustomed to seek the ideas of a play through the char-

acters, the Golden Age playwright linked his ideas directly
to the action itself, and the schematic nature of his characterization should not be allowed to delude us into thinking that there is no significant pattern of ideas. As Parker
says, what the dramatist has to offer us is "not a series of
complete characters, but a complete action," i.e., one
which discloses "a theme that can be taken out of the
action and universalized in the form of an important
judgment on some aspect of human life." Such themes
are likely to take the form of a moral commonplace when
detached from the action, and it is the business of the
action to embody them in a particular series of events in
such a way that the commonplace utterance is made
significant to the audience. The "moral" requires to be
taken very seriously, in other words, before it can take
on the weight of a profound moral statement—"an important judgment on some aspect of human life"—once
more.

When one applies these two interlocking principles to
Lope de Vega and to Calderón, one gets rather different
results, partly because they do seem to have a different
idea of seriousness in this connection, but largely because
the relationship between theme, action, and characters
is rather different in the two cases. Calderón generally
handles his themes with great gravity, and shapes his
actions to suit the demands of the dramatic demonstra-
tion with a minimum of autonomous theatricality, but
with Lope de Vega one often feels that the theme is
largely a pretext for the action: something whose implications in the given situation are being exploited chiefly for
their dramatic possibilities. His better plays—including
all those in this collection—do show him deeply interested
in the wider meaning of the action, but this interest is
never quite the overriding factor which it is for Calderón.

Theme and action are in fact equally balanced in Lope's
better plays: in *Justice without Revenge*, for instance,
while Lope is obviously fascinated by the ultimate moral
values at issue, he seems to me to be no less interested in
the illustration of the title proposition by means of a
highly melodramatic action, which is developed with at
least as great a concern for its theatrical as for its moral
potentialities at each turn of the plot. Far from being a
defect, this may well be Lope's saving grace, for while

Calderón has written many profoundly significant plays, they require a great deal of background knowledge on the part of the reader before he can appreciate their subtle casuistry; whereas Lope's plays are carried through with such zest that they make their primary appeal on purely theatrical grounds. They can be enjoyed in terms of the action, even though an understanding of the theme will increase one's enjoyment; whereas Calderón's subordination of action to theme is so marked that failure to grasp the theme leaves the reader, or the modern audience, completely bewildered by the action itself.

This different handling of Parker's second principle— "the primacy of theme over action"—naturally affects the relationship between action and characterization too. Although one might say that the subordination of characters to action was fully "justified" (the term is mine, not Parker's) by the subordination of action to theme in the case of Calderón, this is not strictly true of most of Lope's plays. In his case, the overriding importance attached to the action generally has to justify itself on its own terms: it is in fact so theatrically effective, and put over with such lyricism, that one is prepared to accept the lack of psychological subtlety. None of this means, however, that his characters fail to be alive: they are indeed quite startlingly vivid. But they are basically conventional in conception, and it is significant that all that Lope has to say about characterization in the *New Art* is that characters must always speak according to type. They are all "types": easy to recognize and to accept, given a very convincing measure of differentiation by the attribution of individual traits, but never seen in real depth. Nor, save for showing the effects of falling in love, do they ever develop in the course of a play. Their motives are certainly explored at length, but primarily so that these may also be exploited as sources of action in the construction of a breathless plot.

Parker's third principle is that the real unity of Spanish Golden Age plays is to be looked for in the theme rather than in the action, and in spite of my qualifications regarding the balance between these elements in Lope's plays, this principle too is useful in this connection. As we have already seen, Lope professes an apparently sincere belief in the unity of action, but it would often be hard to see how this could fit a given play without converting it into a unity of theme. Nor is this really splitting hairs, because I think that Lope had this kind of unity in mind but had simply not analyzed his plays with any great measure of critical acumen. He often uses secondary plots (like Aurora's love life in *Justice without Revenge*, or Marcela's in *The Dog in the Manger*), or "background" historical actions (as in *Fuenteovejuna*), and although these might seem to detract from the dramatic unity of a play, their division of the action is transcended by their integration on the level of the theme. Thus the affairs of Marcela and Aurora not only serve to keep the main action going, but are also used to bring out the significant features of the central characters and plot by contrast, while the background events in *Fuenteovejuna* are used to set the conduct of both the villagers and the "villain" (the Commander) in a proper perspective, providing a framework of social doctrine and pointing the central moral from a different angle.

Parker's fourth and fifth principles require to be considered as a pair, like his first and second. They are "the subordination of the theme to a moral purpose through the principle of poetic justice," and "the elucidation of the moral purpose by means of dramatic causality." The latter is an analytical technique, while the former is a principle of construction used by the dramatist himself. I would not fully agree with its phrasing, however: where themes are moral in nature, it is hard to distinguish between the purpose and the theme (they can certainly not be separated in the same way as action and theme, or character and action), and I should prefer to say that "the moral purpose inherent in the theme" is brought out "through the principle of poetic justice." This principle is clearly very important in Spanish drama, and can be shown to respond to a genuinely artistic need to have things work out as they "should." [1]

The task of working out its application in the less obvious cases brings in the last of those five principles.

---

[1] See A. A. Parker, "History and poetry: the Coriolanus theme in Calderón," in *Hispanic Studies in honour of I. González Llubera*, Oxford, 1959, an article in which Professor Parker was concerned to investigate the reasons for Calderón's deliberate distortion of historical material.

This involves "following the chain of causality" back from the denouement of a play, in a search for its "inner dramatic structure," until one discovers the individual responsible for initiating the whole sequence of events. My only reservation here is based on Professor Parker's own distinction between theme and action: the pursuit of causality will certainly disclose the structure of the action, but it does not necessarily follow that the causation of the action is in fact the theme of the play, nor yet that the initiator is the central character. The initiator may be there to pose a problem for the true protagonist, and the action may simply be designed to create the central situation through whose development the true theme and moral purpose may be expressed.[2] "Following the chain of causality" back from the denouement is, nonetheless, a most effective guide to the workings of poetic justice in any individual play. It must be said, however, that poetic justice itself applies with differing force in different instances, and that one cannot demand that the apportioning of punishment should always be strictly commensurate with the apportionable blame. The wrongdoers do get punished, but the less guilty may sometimes seem to suffer more than they deserve—true though it is that "even where the tragic character is the victim of a wrong done to him by another, it is almost invariably the case that he will have contributed to it by his own fault."

Within the general framework of Parker's principles— which are applicable in varying degrees to all the dramatists of the period—Lope's handling of his own formula for the *comedia* stands out by its constant exploitation of the dramatic possibilities of his material. The results of such an approach are, on their own terms, superb: actor's and producer's plays, guaranteed to hold interest, but which make no demands that could not be adequately met by any competent repertory company, although they are

---

[2] This point emerges more clearly when one examines Professor Parker's application of the principle to the plays of Calderón, but the discussion of that aspect of his article has no place here. I should, however, like to make two final comments on his study: firstly, that I have grossly oversimplified his arguments; secondly, that—despite my various reservations —I consider it to be by far the most stimulating introduction to the drama of the Spanish Golden Age I know.

at the same time capable of being presented at various levels of "significance" and therefore offer an exciting challenge to the modern producer.

THE CLASSIFICATION AND CHRONOLOGY OF LOPE'S *comedias*

Lope de Vega's output was enormous: about 470 of his plays survive, and we know the titles of roughly as many again, while he himself claimed to have written over 1500 dramatic pieces, between *comedias*, nativity plays, and *autos sacramentales* (allegories in a single act written for the Feast of Corpus Christi). When it comes to trying to place individual works in relation to the rest of such a vast production, classification becomes essential (though it always tends to stress differentiatory features at the expense of common elements), and Lope's *comedias* have been variously grouped according to subject matter and on a chronological basis.

In terms of subject, they fall into half a dozen categories, three of which are represented here: firstly, religious plays (on Old or New Testament subjects or based on the lives of saints or pious legends); secondly, a small group of pastoral plays; thirdly, another on mythological subjects; fourthly, historical plays such as *Peribáñez, Fuenteovejuna,* or *The Knight from Olmedo* (some based on classical antiquity and some on foreign themes, but the vast majority based on Spanish chronicles and ballads, as in the case of all our three examples); fifthly, "cloak and dagger" plays and *comédies de mœurs*, such as *The Dog in the Manger*; and, sixthly, novelesque plays such as *Justice without Revenge*, based either on the romances of chivalry or on later Spanish or (as in the case of *Justice without Revenge*) Italian prose fiction.

Chronologically speaking, Lope's output has been divided into three periods on the basis of developing technique and (in the last period) increasing use of rapidly improving stage machinery (*tramoyas*). None of the plays in this collection belongs to the "early" period, three (*Peribáñez, Fuenteovejuna,* and *The Dog in the Manger*) being "middle," and two (*The Knight from Olmedo* and *Justice without Revenge*) being "late." Of these, only *Justice without Revenge* can be precisely dated: the autograph manuscript was finished, and signed by Lope, on

August 1, 1631 (just over four years before his death), and the play was first published in 1634. *The Knight from Olmedo* was not published until 1641, but Morley and Bruerton attribute it to the period 1615–26, and say that it was probably written between 1620 and 1625.

Working backwards, we come to *The Dog in the Manger*, published in 1618 and attributed to the period 1613–15 by Morley and Bruerton, who say it was most probably written in 1613. *Fuenteovejuna* was published in 1619, but may have been written as early as 1611 (Morley and Bruerton place it between 1611 and 1618, and probably between 1612 and 1614), and I have decided to place it before *The Dog in the Manger* in this edition. *Peribáñez* could theoretically be later than *Fuenteovejuna* (Morley and Bruerton assign it to the years 1609–12, and say that they think it was probably written about 1610), but a case can be made out for dating it as early as 1605 (see note on p. 42), and it was actually published in 1614—four years before any of the other plays in this collection.

Peribáñez and the Commander of Ocaña

Peribáñez is a very good example of Lope's *comedias*: closely knit, with a clear-cut central theme and central plot, arising out of an active and dynamic situation which is swiftly established and rapidly developed, striking home to a neat and fitting climax, and given an unpredictable final twist (the reward paid to Casilda). The thematic significance of the events (the attempted seduction of Peribáñez's bride, Casilda, by his feudal overlord, whom Peribáñez kills—a crime for which he is ultimately pardoned by the king) is characteristically brought out both by the use of *sentencias* and allusions and by a highly lyrical network of associated images, and there is a very conscious use of irony. All these traits are to be found in every play in this volume, and *Peribáñez* is in fact uncharacteristic only in its lack of complications—there is neither a secondary plot nor a background of significant political events. It is very typical, too, in its use of a traditional ballad motif (see note on p. 34), and in the careful way in which Lope has established the "period" background—even though the period is not in itself particularly important in relation to the meaning of this play.

Peribáñez has been a favorite text with the critics. Menéndez y Pelayo (1899) discussed the use of the ballad motif and showed that Lope based his historical background directly on the chronicles. But he missed the irony in the Commander's ennobling of Peribáñez to get him away from Ocaña in charge of a local levy, so as to be able to seduce Casilda in his absence. By so doing, the Commander endows him with the social status which fully entitles him to avenge the insult and protect his reputation—as an equal. There is a first and fairly obvious level of irony in this, insofar as the Commander is giving "honor" in order to be able to dishonor, only to be defeated by his own device. But there is also a second level, which depends on the twofold meaning of honor (honor as public reputation and honor as personal integrity): the Commander possesses the first, but his dishonorable intention shows that he lacks the second; Peribáñez possesses the second from the start, and what he receives is merely the first. The "honor" the Commander confers is in one sense a sham, a hollow mockery—and that is all that he intends it to be; but it does confer real rights within the social structure, rights which Peribáñez uses as they should be used—in defense of virtue rather than merely in defense of reputation. Lope clearly sees Peribáñez as being more "honorable" than the Commander throughout the play: the ambiguity of the latter's position shows that public honor is only meritorious when it is accompanied by personal integrity. It is important as a means of relating one to the ordered pattern of society, but only if one observes the spirit of that order—and the contrast between Peribáñez and the Commander shows just how much and how little it can be worth, at opposite ends of the scale of personal integrity.

Menéndez y Pelayo has been criticized for looking at both *Peribáñez* and *Fuenteovejuna* in the light of nineteenth-century ideas, and for trying to see them as democratic propaganda against the nobility. Aubrun and Montesinos (1943) were in fact the first critics to try to evaluate the social picture presented by the play in seventeenth-century terms: what we have is not a play dealing with class conflict, but with class relationships within a given social structure. The structure and the social differences which it involves are never called in question, only the way the classes deal with one another—the conduct of individuals is being evaluated in terms of whether they observe the duties and obligations incumbent upon them in "that station of life to which it has pleased their God to call them." This revised view of the play forms the point of departure for one of the finest articles on any aspect of Lope's theater, "Images et structure dans *Peribáñez*" (1949), in which E. M. Wilson studies the continuous contrast between the peasants and the representative of the nobility through a close examination of the imagery. Agreeing with Aubrun and Montesinos that the Commander is not a monster of depravity (like the Commander in *Fuenteovejuna*) but a man bowled over by "une passion coupable"—who is thereby led to violate the obligations placed on him by his position—Wilson sees the dominant theme of the play as being the rewarding of virtue and the punishment of vice within the social context.

Subsequent critics have shed further light on the play from a number of different angles. Sánchez (1954) developed the theme of the dramatic irony with special reference to its theatricality, seeing the play as a complex structure based on the interaction between the personal conflict and the framework of social harmony. Dunn's article (1957, see note on p. 12), drew attention to the functional use of the sonnets within the structure of the play, while Correa (1958) has analyzed the irony of the honor problem in an intriguing study of the ambiguities in the Commander's conduct. The general tendency of all the modern critics has in fact been to show that the play is less simple than it seems at first sight. This is also true of the general trend of Lope criticism today, as we shall see in connection with most of the remaining plays in this volume.

Fuenteovejuna

Fuenteovejuna differs from *Peribáñez* in three important respects: there is a prominent historical background action, which amounts to a secondary plot; this wider historical action is closely and very significantly

linked to the central situation, which is itself firmly rooted
in history; and lastly, with the exception of the Commander—a typical villain—there is no dominant individual character (although Laurencia is given more
prominence than the other peasants). Instead of being
faced with an individual such as Peribáñez, the Commander is faced with the mounting rage of an entire
village, and so far from being to some extent excusably
"in love" with a single peasant woman like Casilda, he is
shown as a lustful tyrant who expects to be allowed to
have his will of any woman who takes his fancy. The
progressive unification of the villagers, as they are goaded
to the point of open rebellion, is brilliantly established
through a series of thumbnail sketches of different peasant
types, and Lope's technique of swift but superficial characterization is shown to its best advantage in such a context.

The nature of the central situation, in which the
villagers all join together to kill their tyrannous overlord
and are ultimately "justified" in their rebellion by receiving a free pardon from the king, has made this play
even more prone to modern political misinterpretation
than *Peribáñez*, and it does provide magnificent material
for a tendentious political production. Such a production,
however, has to minimize a number of important features
in the text, reducing the king's role to that of a formal
method of indicating Lope's sympathies with the under-
dog, underplaying the fact that it is the villagers' refusal
to name any individual culprit under torture which forces
the king to choose between a free pardon and a general
and unchristian massacre, and radically changing the
treatment of the Commander.

The Commander is not being held up as the typical
representative of a hated class, itself indicted in his
person, but as a man who has viciously disregarded the
obligations placed on him by his position, misusing the
powers with which he has been entrusted in a way which
is as politically unsound as it is morally reprehensible,
and shattering the harmonious order of society. Society itself finally eliminates the element of discord (although
by means which are themselves discordant with its normal
functioning), thereby re-establishing the preordained
harmony of its hierarchic structure. Looked at in this way,

the historical secondary plot becomes entirely comprehensible: the Commander's implication in a rebellion against the Catholic monarchs is the counterpart of his treatment of his inferiors, and the self-centered pride which lies behind all his actions is illuminated by seeing him not merely as a wicked overlord but also as an arrogant vassal. His remarks on courtesy in the first scene, which seem so ironic in the light of his own failure to observe the precepts he propounds, provide a key to the theme of the whole play.

Serious study of *Fuenteovejuna* again begins with a prologue by Menéndez y Pelayo (1899), who drew attention to Lope de Vega's use of the account of the rebellion given in Rades y Andrada's *Crónica de las tres Ordenes militares* (1572). Lope kept faithfully to his source, which supplied almost all the details of the Commander's murder in 1476 (right down to the fact that the women of the village had named their own officers and raised a standard), as well as of the villagers' courage under torture. It was this feature which had made the most lasting impression on the public imagination, becoming enshrined in a proverbial saying ("Fuenteovejuna lo hizo") recorded and discussed in Covarrubias' *Tesoro de la lengua castellana* (1611). The Commander's outrages also gave rise to popular ballads, four lines of which have probably been used as the opening quatrain of the song in Act Two —immediately prior to the Commander's interruption of the wedding. Lope has again been inspired by a popular ballad motif, in other words, which he has then worked up into a play by making full use of the historical material available.

Where Menéndez y Pelayo went wrong was again in the matter of interpreting the political significance of the play, which he saw as being not only profoundly monarchical (which is undoubtedly correct) but also profoundly democratic. While rejecting this political thesis, Aníbal (1934) was able to expand Menéndez y Pelayo's account of Lope's use of Rades' chronicle by showing that the "background" plot (regarding the taking of Ciudad Real by the forces of the Master of Calatrava) was also closely based on the same text. Lope tampered with the facts in order to give the two plots a common villain: so far from being the young Master's evil genius in the matter of the assault on Ciudad Real, the Commander is merely named as one of his allies by Rades, while the Master was really guided and urged on by his own ambitious relatives.

According to Miss Macdonald's study (1940), the play's message is that "the duty of all governments is to give to no man placed in a position of authority the opportunity to gratify his greed for power," and Lope was commenting on the social conditions of a bygone age in order to make "a constructive contribution towards the formation of a theory of the state." This seems to me to be making too much of the political angle, but while the reaffirmation of social harmony can hardly be regarded as a real innovation in the field of political theory —and hence as a polemical thesis—it can constitute an adequate dramatic theme. Miss Macdonald's article did, however, clarify two other aspects of the play, by her discussion of "courtesy" and by her discussion of the relevance of the long debate on love. Both the courtesy motif and the love motif play a prominent part in Casalduero's study (1943), although they are seen as minor features in a far more complex pattern whose elements are integrated by a rhythmical structure of Baroque parallels and contrasts, based on a restatement of the classical opposition between town and country.[3]

The Baroque aspect of Casalduero's attitude was taken up in Reaton's two discussions of the play (1952), which were a rather strained attempt to show that Wölfflin's principles of Baroque in the visual arts could be used to clarify the structure of Spanish seventeenth-century plays. This particular thesis led to the publication of a very significant reply by Parker (1953). Parker suggested that the dominant theme was honor, with the peasants "vindicating their right to possess this against the contemptuous refusal of the Commander to recognize their claim," and he went on to show how the linking of the two plots was "part of a total thematic unity":

The political rebellion of the Comendador against the Sovereigns and his insolent treatment of the villagers are two

[3] Just as Wilson's study of *Peribáñez* is a model for all future analyses of the structural function of imagery in Lope's plays, Casalduero's study of *Fuenteovejuna* is a masterly example of how an analysis of the varying metrical structure of a play can clarify its underlying thematic pattern.

aspects of the same thing: of an overweening pride by which one individual can venture to assert himself against the community. The Comendador is guilty of a crime against a village, but also of a crime against the State. This puts village and State on the same level: the dishonour of one villager is the dishonour of the whole village, and this in its turn is the dishonour of the whole nation. . . . Treason and rape are dramatically unified in *Fuenteovejuna* because they are morally akin—aspects of an individual will to social disorder.

Parker's discussion of the play, however, took up a mere two pages of a review-article, and it was left to Ribbans (1954) to combine this line of approach with that of Casalduero by analyzing the play in terms of a fundamental contrast between "the way of life of the nobility and that of the peasantry."

The most recent contribution begins by summarizing and—broadly speaking—accepting all the main lines of interpretation proposed by Casalduero, Parker, and Ribbans, and then drawing attention to the importance of "the relationship between love and musical harmony." As Spitzer's title—"A Central Theme and Its Structural Equivalent" (1955)—suggests, his study is concerned with the relationship between theme and action, but he has approached this in an entirely new way by examining both aspects in terms of the continuous allusions to the subject of world harmony, and has found these reflected in structurally "musical" interactions between the constituent parts of the drama.

The Dog in the Manger

After the wealth of interpretations accorded to *Peribáñez* and *Fuenteovejuna*, it is refreshing to turn to a play which has received only cursory critical attention. As far as I know, the one serious discussion of *The Dog in the Manger* is to be found in the introduction to Kohler's edition (1934; revised 1951), and this is limited to a detailed synopsis and a few brief comments on the characters, written primarily from a naturalistic point of view. Lope's own attitude to characterization, with its exploitation of psychology in the interests of action, emerges very clearly from this play. It is perhaps more obvious precisely where it might seem less likely, since the action does stem from a psychological postulate.

The heroine, Diana, is a noblewoman who falls in love with her secretary, Teodoro, but her sense of honor prevents her from admitting her infatuation even to herself except under the stress of jealousy. Whenever she sees him courting his erstwhile sweetheart, Marcela, her self-dominion slackens and she begins to show her love, but this turns to disdain once more as soon as he responds to her half-hinted courtship. Whence the title, *El perro del hortelano*, which is based on the Spanish equivalent of the English saying about the dog in the manger, to the effect that "the orchard-keeper's dog neither eats nor lets one eat." The play chronicles Diana's growing love, and ends with the invention of a noble pedigree for Teodoro—a pedigree which she knows to be false, but which allows her to marry him without affecting her honor (in the sense of public reputation).

The conflict between Diana's love and her sense of duty to her station could have given rise to a truly profound scrutiny of her mentality, but while Lope has given a great deal of attention to her development—and portrayed this with real insight into feminine psychology—it is nonetheless clear that his primary interest as a dramatist lay in seeing how many baffling changes of direction could be successfully imposed on the rush of the action by her changes of mood. The central ebb and flow has been complicated by a number of side currents. The first of these involves two noble suitors, Ricardo and Federico—two of them so that they can talk things over with each other—who not only comment on Diana's growing infatuation but also take a hand in the action by plotting Teodoro's murder. Still on her social plane, there is Count Ludovico, who is tricked into accepting Teodoro as his long-lost son. Then there is a host of servants and lackeys, representing Teodoro's world, one of whom—Fabio—is gradually built up as a suitable match for Marcela when Teodoro finally marries Diana. And threading his way through all the concomitant plots there is the figure of Tristán, Teodoro's comic servant—perhaps the finest of all Lope's *graciosos* and truly comparable with Figaro. Tristán not only plays the role of Teodoro's confidant but also manages to get himself taken on by Ricardo and Federico in the guise of a hired bravo, to murder his own master, and finally devises the plot to provide Teodoro with a noble father—

passing himself off most comically as a Greek merchant in order to "sell" the story to Count Ludovico. As Kohler has rightly said, Tristán is a true Spanish *pícaro*, and he brings to his part not merely the *pícaro's* quick-wittedness in emergencies but also his genuinely humorous zest in improvisation.

Kohler has, however, completely missed the delicious irony of the ending, seeing the "solution" offered as being merely a dramatist's way out of an insoluble dilemma, using the classical device of *anagnorisis* (or recognition) with a mere minor twist—the fact that it is faked. Surely the whole point of it is that it is faked: on the one hand, there is the fun of the wonderfully successful parody of a traditional happy ending (at its best in the handling of Ludovico's "recognition" of his "son"); and, on the other hand, the use of a faked solution is part of Lope's comment on honor. The point is that honor, in the sense of public reputation, *is* satisfied by the fake, and that since such a conception of honor can be satisfied by a sham that conception of honor is itself hollow. Diana's honor in the other sense was neither threatened at any stage nor yet prejudiced by the outcome: her love was natural, and it develops into a sincere passion (which is yet never allowed to overwhelm her reason). Since it is in no sense morally "dishonorable" to love either above or below one's station, all that requires to be protected is the external fabric of society. The solution adopted both "keeps up appearances" and offers a wittily ambiguous comment on just how much, or little, such "appearances" are worth.

The Knight from Olmedo

After *The Dog in the Manger*, *The Knight from Olmedo* seems—despite significant differences—to be a reversion to the *Peribáñez* type of play. So it is, in many ways: there is the same use of a popular motif (see note on p. 222), and the same use of historical sources as a means of building up both the background and the general atmosphere, and—as in *Fuenteovejuna*—the central event is based on a historical happening, although this is modified even more radically than the Ciudad Real plot of *Fuenteovejuna*. Historically, the knight from Olmedo —whose name was not Don Alonso but Don Juan de

Vivero[4]—was murdered not by a rival for his lady's hand but as the result of a quarrel over the possession of some greyhounds, and the change in motivation was of course required in order to provide a more romantic story with a love interest (similarly, the fact that his murderer escaped execution had to be altered in the interests of poetic justice). But *The Knight from Olmedo* differs from both *Peribáñez* and *Fuenteovejuna* in two important respects: firstly, it is not concerned with relationships between different social classes, nor with the question of whether peasants have a right to protect their honor, and, secondly, it has a tragic—not a happy—ending.

Paradoxically, the first two acts are—at least on the surface—far gayer and more lighthearted than the corresponding acts of the other two plays, and seem to belong rather to the field of romantic comedy, such as *The Dog in the Manger*. This conflict in tone was, however, designed to strike Lope's audience rather differently from the way in which it would strike a modern reader who had not been warned of the tragic outcome, because the comedy of the first two acts would have been overshadowed throughout—even for the first-night audience—by the foreboding induced by Lope's use of the theme of a popular song. No one could have been unaware that "the knight from Olmedo" would end up by being "killed in the darkness," and Lope has used this feature consciously throughout, taking advantage of the aura of tragic inevitability to give an added piquancy to the romantic comedy of the first two acts by the obvious element of dramatic irony, present throughout the earlier episodes.

Menéndez y Pelayo's prologue (1899) discussed both the use of the popular *cantarcillo*—the basic quatrain is not in ballad meter—and Lope's modifications of history. He also discussed the role of Fabia, the bawd (who is employed by Alonso as a go-between), pointing out that Lope's stress on her use of sorcery must have made her more of a tragic than a comic figure, despite her obviously comic function. This introduction of a supernatural ele-

[4] Miss Macdonald suggested that the hero's name might have been changed because the younger of two well-known actors called Alonso de Olmedo (father and son) may possibly have played the title role.

ment into the earlier acts links through to the ghostly overtones of the final tragedy, where Lope has intensified the horror of the killing by having Alonso meet his own specter and, subsequently, hear the tale of his own death sung immediately before he meets his murderers.

Miss Macdonald (1935) sees the whole "rhythm" of the play as based on *pundonor*. The murderer's offense, and the poetic justice of his execution, are too obvious to require further discussion, but the position of Alonso and Inés is more complex. In Alonso's case, Miss Macdonald sees the tragedy as the outcome of foolhardiness: Alonso is heedlessly in love, overbold, and overgenerous to an opponent whose malignity he refuses to suspect; he also goes the wrong way about gaining Inés' hand, and "the wrong methods cannot in the end be entirely successful." He is punished for employing Fabia, while the fact that her incantations do help to overcome Inés' natural reserve saves the latter from being willfully dishonorable. According to Miss Macdonald, then, the central tragic theme is not merely "that all our actions bring about inevitable consequences," but more specifically "that illicit actions undo their own ends." Sarrailh (whose study also appeared in 1935) adds two important features to this picture: on the one hand, Lope's significant contrast not merely between the comedy and tragedy but between the whole mood of darkness and the youth of the victims; and on the other, the importance of Lope's deliberate anachronism in antedating the murder from 1521 to the reign of Juan II (1406–1454), in order to take advantage of the aura of magic and sorcery attached to that period.

Most recently, Parker (1957) has brought the various threads of the previous discussion together in a way which not only serves to explain the tragic denouement in terms of poetic justice but also unifies the disparate elements of the action on the level of the theme. Seeking an explanation of the switch in mood in terms of his fourth principle, he proceeds from the assumption "that the death of the hero exemplifies poetic justice," and on finding insufficient reason for his death "in that part of the action that leads directly to [it]," he deliberately looks for the reason "in the comedy." It is here, in the underhand conduct of the lovers (Alonso's use of the bawd, and Inés' pretense that she wants to become a nun in order to stave off an unwelcome match), that Parker discovers "the moral dimension that justifies the tragedy . . . by disclosing the moral flaw in the hero's conduct"—a flaw "that makes his tragic death fitting and inevitable." This line of interpretation is implicit in Miss Macdonald's approach, but Parker's use of his own principles regarding the relationship between theme and action, and the function of poetic justice, seem to me to map out the internal structure of the play far more clearly than any previous critic had been able to do.

My only reservation concerns the way the emphasis is made to lie. As in the case of theme and action (where it seemed to me that the theme was often chiefly a pretext for the action, in Lope's hands), so it seems to me here that poetic justice has been worked into the story by way of an explanation for a denouement whose actualization was perhaps Lope's primary aim. Having decided to make use of the legend and to take advantage of its somber overtones, Lope—instinctively observant of poetic justice —has been at pains to work in some fault to justify Alonso's death. But it is not unimportant that he has done so without detracting from our sympathy for the lovers in any way, and we are perhaps also entitled to feel that this is one of the cases in which the punishments are not strictly commensurate with the blame.

For my own part, I should also like to draw attention to Lope's characteristic irony, present not just in the final scene (when Inés learns that the real tragedy of Alonso's death lies in the fact that all their efforts were unnecessary, since her father would willingly have given them his blessing), but more subtly in this whole question of the interaction between the tragic and the comic elements— the ironical fact that it is precisely the comic level which reveals the tragic flaw. There is room for further work on this play in the light of Parker's analysis, both with reference to the irony of its construction and with reference to the imagery, which does so much to determine and heighten (both by affirmation and by contrast) the mood suggested by the somber associations of the song.

Justice without Revenge

Irony, and the dexterous complication of what may at first sight seem to be a fairly straightforward honor plot,

are also prominent features of *Justice without Revenge*—
the latest and perhaps the most ambiguous of our texts.
The play deals with the events which lead up to the gory
climax to which the title refers. The Duke of Ferrara is a
rake with an illegitimate son, and he marries a young wife
—not for love, but in hopes of providing himself with a
legitimate heir. Federico and Cassandra meet by accident
before they are aware that she is going to be his stepmother, and their initial attraction is fostered by the
Duke's neglect of his wife and his continuing immorality
(Lope has been at great pains to show how Cassandra's
common sense is only gradually overcome by her outraged pride and by her mounting passion). The Duke's
absence at the papal wars gives the affair time to develop,
and he returns as an apparently reformed character. When
he learns of what has been happening, he is filled with
horror, seeing it as a punishment for his own past life. Fearful of the dishonor which would ensue should the story
become widely known, however, he devises a plot which
involves Federico in slaying Cassandra unwittingly, so that
he can then be killed in his turn for murdering his stepmother.

As Parker has shown, the Duke is the key to the whole
situation. Van Dam (who edited the autograph manuscript text in 1928) and Vossler (1932) had both taken
the Duchess to be the protagonist: van Dam had seen her
as a tragic heroine destroyed by an understandable but
guilty love, and found the Duke's conversion unconvincing and the ending repellent; Vossler saw the Duke as
bringing the protagonist to her tragic end in his capacity
as the instrument of heavenly justice, but thought that
the dignity of the play was marred by the fact that the
code of honor had involved the Duke in taking a secret
and atrocious private vengeance. But Parker (1957) shows
that the Duke "is the agent who determines the whole
course of the plot" by his own initial immorality, and that
everything that happens "follows from his own actions by
an unbroken chain of cause and effect whose first link
is forged by the type of conduct exemplified in the
very first scene." The application of the principle of
dramatic causality thus clearly reveals that

the Duke is not a secondary character, merely the external instrument of the peripeteia, but is more intimately connected

with the whole action than anybody else, since he is the agent who in the long run, unwittingly but directly, produces the catastrophe. Since his conduct that started the chain of causality was morally reprehensible, he must share the guilt for the evil and tragedy that ensue. This fact alters the traditional interpretation of the play, since it changes the Duke from the minister of the supposed justice of honour to the ironically pathetic victim of his own imprudence.

And although the Duke does not die, poetic justice does overtake him, insofar as his whole life "lies in ruins about him" by the end of the play. His final lamentable state is clearly a fitting punishment for his part in the causation of the tragedy, and part of the irony lies in the fact that he has to kill his wife and son for a wrong which is like the wrongs he has done himself.

The deeper irony of the piece, however, emerges from a study of the relationship between the play and its title (literally "punishment without revenge"), which focuses our attention on the nature of the ending. Van Dam attacked the title on the grounds that the "punishment" is not a punishment but a repulsive murder, which—far from being "without revenge"—constitutes a most treacherous form of vengeance, and he says that the ending is therefore really a "revenge without punishment." This is in fact one aspect of the "truth" about it, the private, inner truth: Federico is punished for a crime he did not commit in revenge for a crime which he did. But as far as "appearances" are concerned, he is killed for killing Cassandra, and although he is not morally guilty of the intention to do so (since he was told by his father that the bound and masked figure in the chair was a plotter against the state), he has in fact done so—therefore the title is in this sense publicly valid. Federico has, indeed, been tricked by the truth: he and Cassandra are both "plotters against the state" insofar as their affair is a direct threat to the harmony of government. It is not only the Duke (whose constant self-deception would lead us to doubt his judgment) who thinks that he is actually punishing a crime by his device: the Marquis of Mantua (who sees through the plot and understands just what is happening) vindicates and ratifies the killing—like the king in, say, *Peribáñez*. So there is both a sense in which justice is "seen to be done" when it is not really being done at all, and a real sense in which it is being done when it is not being seen to be done.

The ambiguities lie, as in *Peribáñez* and *The Dog in the Manger*, in the interplay between public and private honor—between honor as reputation, manifested in keeping up appearances, and honor as intrinsic virtue and personal integrity. And Lope seems to me to be showing once more—this time by means of a public "justice without revenge" which is privately a form of "revenge without justice"—the relative worth of the two sets of associated values. This is where the Duke's immorality comes in again: not only is it responsible for setting the whole play in motion (as Parker showed) but it makes him directly comparable to the figure of the Commander in *Peribáñez*, who prized reputation above virtue. The hollowness of the reputation which the Duke seeks to preserve is what makes his revenge without justice seem so monstrous. But there is another element of irony here, in that, while the Duke is not worthy of his position, his position does form part of the social fabric, and the latter must be preserved. Justice must be executed, and it is the fault of the private unworthiness of the instrument of public justice that social order is restored by unworthy means.

T. E. May (1960)—who sees the Duke's conversion as a pretense (making its unconvincing nature intentional on Lope's part)—sees the supreme irony as lying in the Duke's self-deception as a result of his self-love: "the Duke worships a God made in his own image" and builds up his image of himself until this illusion finally "requires him to fake a legal *castigo* so as to conceal his vengeance and thus preserve if he can a public image of his own unscathed dignity and righteousness, whilst at the same time, since he knows that this fake will be apparent to Heaven, Heaven is bidden to see here its own mysterious work alone . . . and thus to see in him its servant." I would see the supreme irony as going beyond this, and lying in the triple-take: morally speaking, we have revenge without justice; the Duke tries to pass this off as Heaven's justice without revenge; in actual fact, Heaven does see justice done (and not merely on the lovers, but also—as Parker has shown— on the Duke himself) without this mitigating the Duke's private guilt both for the immorality which initiated the whole sequence of events and for the barbarous way in which he brings the sequence to an end.

In the closed context of the Duke's own private fate, evil breeds evil, and he ends with his life "in ruins about him"; in the wider context of the social structure, good has paradoxically come from evil, and order has been restored by the purging of the lovers' crime and the chastisement of the Duke himself. Private virtue has had no place in the play (except among the secondary characters such as Aurora and the Marquis of Mantua, whose betrothal holds the promise of an ordered future), but public virtue emerges triumphant from the web of ambiguities surrounding both private vice and the hollowness of public reputations unsustained by personal integrity. Therefore I would agree both with Parker, who sees the play as the Duke's tragedy, and with Reichenberger (1959) insofar as he sees the ending as a restoration of order—although I cannot see why he should contend that this prevents the play from being a tragedy. A definition of tragedy that excluded the restoration of order would surely exclude the bulk of pre-Romantic tragic plays—including *Hamlet*.[5]

[5] The further ramifications of May's important but perplexing article are too involved to be gone into in detail here. His analyses of the three central characters are extremely illuminating, and I am fully convinced by his case for the irony of the whole conception, but I am very doubtful about his attempt to discern a latent form of inverted Christian allegory in the play: "At the abstract level," he says, "this means an analogy between Federico [who suffers for a crime he did not commit] and Christ; a typically conceptist analogy, since it embraces terms which are not only different, but violently opposed. No one could be less God-like than the Duke, but he claims to act for the Father; no one could be less Christ-like than Federico, but his role is like that of the Son." Much though this might have appealed to the mind of a later *conceptista* such as Baltasar Gracián (1601–1658), whose theory of the conceit has been so ably analyzed by T. E. May on other occasions (*Hispanic Review*, XVI [1948] pp. 275–300 and XVIII [1950] pp. 15–41), I find this way of thinking somewhat alien to the Lope de Vega one has come to know through the whole range of such plays as the five which have been chosen to represent him in this collection.

The presence of such thematic ambiguities, and the fascination of discussing them, should not, however, be allowed to detract from the sheer theatrical effect of the action itself. Complex though *Justice without Revenge* may be (and it is a very late play, showing Lope at his subtlest), it can make a direct and vivid impact on an audience—and one may wonder whether the full range of such equivocation could possibly be appreciated in the theater. The trend in recent criticism has certainly been to see Lope de Vega as more subtle than earlier writers thought he was, but I should be reluctant to sacrifice his freshness and spontaneity and the vigor of his exultant theatricality in order to turn him into something more akin to Calderón.

Both Lope de Vega and Calderón did what they did supremely well, but they did different things within the framework of the *comedia* which Lope had created, and they set about achieving their purposes in very different ways—Calderón with cerebral ingenuity, and Lope with a direct and keen-edged thrust which can get blunted by too detailed scrutiny. The old-fashioned contrast between them does deserve to be perpetuated, for it is much more than merely a convenient pedagogic device.

R. D. F. Pring-Mill
Lecturer in Spanish,
University of Oxford

October, 1960

SELECTED BIBLIOGRAPHY

NOTE. The works have been listed chronologically within each section to give a clear idea of the sequence of the various critical controversies involved.

A. BIBLIOGRAPHICAL WORKS

Rennert, H. A., "Bibliography of the Dramatic Works of Lope de Vega," *Revue Hispanique*, XXXIII (1915), pp. 1–282.

Morley, S. Griswold, and Bruerton, Courtney, *The Chronology of Lope de Vega's Comedias*. New York, 1940.

——, "Addenda to the Chronology of Lope de Vega's *Comedias*," *Hispanic Review*, XV (1947), pp. 49–71.

Simón Díaz, J., and Prades, J. de José, *Ensayo de una bibliografía de las obras y artículos sobre la vida y escritos de Lope de Vega Carpio*. Madrid, 1955.

B. BIOGRAPHICAL STUDIES

Rennert, H. A., *The Life of Lope de Vega* (1562–1635). Glasgow, 1904.

——, and Castro, Américo, *Vida de Lope de Vega*. Madrid, 1919.

Astrana Marín, L., *La vida azarosa de Lope de Vega*. Barcelona, 1935.

Entrambasaguas, J., *Vida de Lope de Vega*. Barcelona, 1936.

C. THE DRAMATIC BACKGROUND TO LOPE DE VEGA

Rennert, H. A., *The Spanish Stage in the Time of Lope de Vega*. New York, 1909.

Crawford, J. Wickersham, *Spanish Drama before Lope de Vega*. Philadelphia, 1922; revised edition 1937.

Valbuena, A., *Literatura dramática española*. Barcelona, 1930.

Juliá Martínez, E., "La literatura dramática en el siglo XVI," *Historia general de las literaturas hispánicas*, ed. G. Díaz-Plaja, Vol. III. Barcelona, 1953.

Parker, A. A., "The Approach to the Spanish Drama of the Golden Age." *Diamante* VI, published by the Hispanic and

Luso-Brazilian Councils, London, 1957; reprinted in *Tulane Drama Review*, IV (1959), pp. 42–59.

Reichenberger, Arnold G., "The Uniqueness of the *Comedia*," *Hispanic Review*, XXVII (1959), pp. 303–16.

D. THE CODE OF HONOR

Castro, Américo, "Algunas observaciones acerca del concepto del honor en los siglos XVI y XVII," *Revista de Filología Española*, III (1916), pp. 1–50.

Fichter, William L., *Lope de Vega's "El Castigo del Discreto" together with a study of conjugal honor in his theater.* New York, 1925.

Menéndez Pidal, R., "Del honor en el teatro español," a lecture delivered in 1937, printed in *De Cervantes y Lope de Vega*. Buenos Aires, 1940.

Jones, C. A., "Honor in Spanish Golden-Age Drama," *Bulletin of Hispanic Studies*, XXXV (1958), pp. 199–210.

Correa, G., "El doble aspecto de la honra en el teatro del siglo XVII," *Hispanic Review*, XXVI (1958), pp. 99–107.

Dunn, P. N., "Honour and the Christian Background in Calderón," *Bulletin of Hispanic Studies*, XXXVII (1960), pp. 75–105.

E. GENERAL STUDIES OF LOPE DE VEGA'S DRAMA

Vossler, K., *Lope de Vega und sein Zeitalter*. Munich, 1932; Spanish translation entitled *Lope de Vega y su tiempo*. Madrid, 1933.

Heseler, M., *Studien zur Figur des gracioso bei Lope de Vega und Vorgängern*. Hildesheim, 1933.

Montesinos, J. F., *Estudios sobre Lope de Vega*. México, 1951. Especially with reference to the *gracioso*.

Brenan, G., chapter on "Lope de Vega and the New Comedy," in *The Literature of the Spanish People*. Cambridge, England, 1951.

Arco, Ricardo del, "Lope de Vega," in G. Díaz-Plaja, ed., *Historia general de las literaturas hispánicas*, Vol. III. Barcelona, 1953.

Dunn, P. N., "Some Uses of Sonnets in the Plays of Lope de Vega," *Bulletin of Hispanic Studies*, XXXIV (1957), pp. 213–22.

Marín, Diego, *La intriga secundaria en el teatro de Lope de Vega*. Toronto, 1958.

F. LITERARY THEORY AND LOPE'S *New Art of Writing Plays*

Menéndez y Pelayo, M., *Historia de las ideas estéticas en España*, Vol. II. This first appeared in 1884, but should be consulted in the Edición Nacional, as revised by E. Sánchez Reyes. Santander, 1947.

Morel-Fatio, A., "L'Arte nuevo de hazer comedias en este tiempo de Lope de Vega," *Bulletin Hispanique*, III (1901), pp. 365–405. This includes an edition of the text, and excellent notes on its sources.

Matthews, Brander, introduction to *The New Art of Writing Plays* (1914), and William T. Brewster's translation of the text, in *Papers on Playmaking*, ed. Brander Matthews. Dramabooks, New York, 1957.

Chaytor, H. J., *Dramatic Theory in Spain*. Cambridge, England, 1925. This includes an edition of the Spanish text.

Entrambasaguas, J., *Una guerra literaria del Siglo de Oro: Lope de Vega y los preceptos aristotélicos*. Madrid, 1932.

Romera-Navarro, M., *La preceptiva dramática de Lope de Vega y otros ensayos sobre el Fénix*. Madrid, 1935.

Menéndez Pidal, R., "El Arte Nuevo y la Nueva Biografía," *Revista de Filología Española*, XXII (1935), pp. 337–98; reprinted in *De Cervantes y Lope de Vega*. Buenos Aires, 1940.

Pons, J. S., "L'Art nouveau de Lope de Vega," *Bulletin Hispanique*, XLVII (1945), pp. 71–78.

Entrambasaguas, J., *Estudios sobre Lope de Vega*, 3 vols. Madrid, 1946–58.

G. STUDIES OF PLAYS IN THIS COLLECTION

Peribáñez

Menéndez y Pelayo, M., *Estudios sobre el teatro de Lope de Vega*, Vol. V (pp. 67–86 of 1925 edition, pp. 35–55 of 1949 edition). These studies first appeared as prologues to the relevant plays in the Academia Española edition of the *Obras de Lope de Vega*. The prologues to *Peribáñez*, *Fuenteovejuna*, and *The Knight from Olmedo* were all first published in Vol. X of that edition. Madrid, 1899.

Aubrun, Ch.-V., and Montesinos, J. F., eds., *Peribáñez*. Paris, 1943. Contains an important introduction. Also see the review by Entwistle, W. J., *Modern Language Review*, XLIII (1948), pp. 281–83.

Blecua, J. M., ed., *Peribáñez*, in *Clásicos Ebro*, Zaragoza, 1944.

Wagner, C. P., "The Date of *Peribáñez*," *Hispanic Review*, XV (1947), pp. 72–83.

Wilson, E. M., "Images et structure dans *Peribáñez*," *Bulletin Hispanique*, LI (1949), pp. 125–59.

Loveluck, J., "La fecha de *Peribáñez* y el comendador de Ocaña," *Atenea*, XXX, (Concepción, Chile [1953]), pp. 418–24.

Sánchez, R. G., "El contenido irónico-teatral en el *Peribáñez* de Lope de Vega," *Clavileño*, V (1954), No. 29, pp. 17–25.

Dunn, P. N., article listed under (E) above.

Correa, G., "El doble aspecto del honor en *Peribáñez y el comendador de Ocaña*," *Hispanic Review*, XXVI (1958), pp. 188–99.

Fuenteovejuna

Menéndez y Pelayo, M., 1899 prologue, in *Estudios sobre el teatro de Lope de Vega*, Vol. V. (pp. 194–205 of 1925 edition, pp. 171–82 of 1949 edition).

Aníbal, C. E., "The historical elements of Lope de Vega's *Fuenteovejuna*," *Publications of the Modern Language Association*, XLIX (1934), pp. 657–718.

Macdonald, I. I., "An Interpretation of *Fuente Ovejuna*," *Babel*, I (Cambridge, England, 1940), pp. 51–62.

Casalduero, J., "*Fuenteovejuna*," *Revista de Filología Hispánica*, V (1943), pp. 21–44.

Reaten, D. H., and Sánchez y Escribano, F., *Wölfflin's Principles in Spanish Drama 1500–1700*. New York, 1952. The section on *Fuenteovejuna* was also summarized by D. H. Reaten as a short article in the *Bulletin of the Comediantes*, IV (1952), No. 1, pp. 1–4. Reviewed in the following article.

Parker, A. A., "Reflections on a new definition of 'Baroque' Drama," *Bulletin of Hispanic Studies*, XXX (1953), pp. 142–51.

García de la Santa, T., ed., *Fuenteovejuna*, in *Clásicos Ebro*. Zaragoza, 1954.

Ribbans, G. W., "The meaning and structure of Lope's *Fuenteovejuna*," *Bulletin of Hispanic Studies*, XXXI (1954), pp. 150–70.

Spitzer, Leo, "A Central Theme and Its Structural Equivalent in Lope's *Fuenteovejuna*," *Hispanic Review*, XXIII (1955), pp. 274–92.

Seifert, Eva, ed., *Fuenteovejuna*, in *Sammlung Romanischer Übungstexte* No. 37. Halle, 1956.

The Dog in the Manger

Kohler, E., ed., *El Perro del hortelano*, Publications de la Faculté des Lettres de l'Université de Strasbourg, *Textes d'étude* No. 4. Paris, 1934. The second edition, Paris, 1951, takes account of the strictures in W. L. Fichter's review, *Hispanic Review*, III (1935), pp. 261–64.

The Knight from Olmedo

Menéndez y Pelayo, M., 1899 prologue, in *Estudios sobre el teatro de Lope de Vega*, Vol. V (pp. 86–116 of 1925 edition, pp. 55–87 of 1949 edition).

Macdonald I. I., ed., *El Caballero de Olmedo*. (Cambridge, England, 1934). Contains excellent notes and appendices.

————, "Why Lope?" *Bulletin of Spanish Studies*, XII (1935), pp. 185–97.

Sarrailh, J., "L'histoire dans *El Caballero de Olmedo*," *Bulletin Hispanique*, XXXVII (1935), pp. 337–52.

Blecua, J. M., ed., *El Caballero de Olmedo*, in *Clásicos Ebro*. Zaragoza, 1943. Contains useful introduction.

Parker, A. A., article listed under (C) above.

Justice without Revenge

Castro, A., article listed under (D) above.

van Dam, C. F., ed., *El Castigo sin Venganza*. Groningen, 1928. Contains an important introduction.

Vossler, K., book listed under (E) above; see pp. 257–60 of the German edition, pp. 284–88 of the Spanish translation.

Alonso, A., "Lope de Vega y sus fuentes," *Thesaurus*, VIII (Bogotá, 1952), pp. 1–24.

Dunn, P. N., article listed under (E) above.

Parker, A. A., article listed under (C) above.

Reichenberger, Arnold G., article listed under (C) above.

May, T. E., "Lope de Vega's *El Castigo sin venganza*: the Idolatry of the Duke of Ferrara," *Bulletin of Hispanic Studies*, XXXVII (1960), pp. 154–82.

PERIBÁÑEZ

(Peribáñez y el Comendador de Ocaña)

CHARACTERS

KING HENRY III OF CASTILE
THE QUEEN
THE CONSTABLE
GÓMEZ MANRIQUE
THE COMMANDER OF OCAÑA, DON FADRIQUE
PEDRO IBÁÑEZ, *usually called* PERIBÁÑEZ
CASILDA, *his wife*
INÉS
COSTANZA
LUJÁN } *Servants of the* COMMANDER
MARÍN }
LEONARDO, *a Gentleman in the service of the* COMMANDER
A PAINTER OF TOLEDO
BÁRTOLO
BELARDO
ANTÓN
BLAS
BENITO } *Peasants of Ocaña*
LLORENTE
MENDO
CHAPARRO
FELIPE
A PRIEST

ALDERMEN, MUSICIANS, PAGES, GUARDS, COURTIERS, AND
     PEASANTS

The action takes place in OCAÑA and TOLEDO, in 1406.

PERIBÁÑEZ

ACT ONE

A *peasant wedding in* OCAÑA

INÉS. I wish you long life and happiness together.

Costanza. No! Life's too short. May you both be happy forever.

Casilda. You are very kind. I only hope I deserve your affection and good wishes.

Priest. I do not say it is wrong, but I do not think there is really any need for all this. Anyway, my children, you can give them no greater blessings than those I have given them in the Sacrament. Your nearest and dearest could not wish you more.

Inés. But, Father, I only said I wish them well.

Priest. May it be as God, who protects the good, wills. My niece is a sensible girl.

Pedro. Well, so long as she isn't a jealous wife. . . .

Casilda. That depends on you! If you never give me reason to be jealous, I am sure I never will be.

Pedro. I will never make you jealous, I promise.

Inés. They say it is Heaven's curse on love.

Priest. Take your places and let us celebrate this happy day in which you two are joined.

Pedro. I couldn't be any happier than I am with my lovely bride whom God has given me.

Priest. I am glad you give the credit to God. There is no beauty like Casilda's in all the kingdom of Toledo.

Casilda. Can I ever repay you for your love? If I could, I think you would be overpaid, I love you so much.

Pedro. Casilda, I cannot let you outdo me in love or words. I should like to place at your feet the whole town of Ocaña, and, beside that, all the land on either side of

the Tagus from here to Portugal. You are more beautiful
to me than an olive grove laden with fruit or a meadow
full of flowers at dawn on a May morning. No ripe red
apple can compare with you, nor can golden olive oil
gleaming in jars give me more delight. The scent of your
lips is sweeter to me than the breath of the best white
vintage wine. A courtier would compare you to a rose,
but to a peasant wine smells better! The vine roots which
I pull up in December, the newly pressed grapes in
October, soft showers in May, and the white grain in
August—all these are good, but with you in my house I
shall not mind what time of year it is or what the weather
is like. In you, Casilda, I have all that I desire. I have
made a place for you in my heart and there you shall
reign as queen, and, thanks to your love, I, a peasant, shall
be a king. May God give you such good fortune that all
who see you say, "That is the heavenly Casilda who has
the luck of the Devil!"

Casilda. How can I begin to tell you even the first of
all the things I love in you? No music that ever set my
feet tapping can thrill me as much as you do, however
hard the drummer beat his stick or blew on his pipe.
Myrtle and vervain were never so sweet, nor are the horses
whinnying on Midsummer morning as exciting to me as
the sound of your voice. What gay, tinkling tambourine
or psalm in church can equal you? A processional banner
with all its bobbles and shiny silk cord is not as fine as
you in your new red hat. Your love is better than clean
feet in new shoes. Out of a million boys you are the
Easter cake—covered all over with little chicks and sugar
eggs. You are like a young red bull in a green field or a
new white shirt in a golden basket with jasmine all
around it. You are like Easter candles and almond paste
at a christening. You are like— Oh! you are like yourself,
because there is no one like you!

Priest. Come now, that's enough! These young people
are impatient to dance.

Pedro. Please forgive us, ladies and gentlemen. We were
carried away!

A Peasant. Don't let us stop you!

Song and Dance.

Musicians:
Proud May shall bless you
With the fields, the rivers, and springs,
Green alders salute you
And the heavy almond bow down before you.
At every daybreak
Green spears of lilies shall pierce the ground,
And the flocks on the mountain
Shall find sweet thyme where the cold snow has
   melted.

[*dance*]

God bless the happy pair,
And the earth give them her blessing,
For today the two are one.

[*dance*]

Snow-capped mountains,
Pines on the high slopes, ancient oaks,
Make way for the waters
The rushing waters that run to the valleys.
Let the nightingale sing
And tell her love to the green myrtles.
With new-found craft
Let the birds for their young build intricate bowers.

[*dance*]

God bless the happy pair,
And the earth give them her blessing,
For today the two are one.

A loud noise is heard. Enter BÁRTOLO, *a peasant.*

Priest. What's that?
Bártolo. Can't you guess from the noise and shouting?
Priest. They're not bringing a bull in here?
Bártolo. A bull? More like three of them. One is a real
black devil full of Spanish fire and fight. It took them an
hour to get a rope on him. He chased Blas round the
meadow twice—kept him hopping about like an Italian
tightrope walker. He has already ripped the guts out of
Antón Gil's mare so you could see the grass she had been

eating—it looked like ragged parsley. It is no joke. He has had the pants off young Tomás—he will never have to grow a beard to show he is a man! And just now our overlord, the Commander of Ocaña, appeared, looking magnificent. He swooped down on the bull like a hawk—if they had not already got a rope on its horns, I think . . .

Priest. It cannot get in here, can it?

Bártolo. It can!

Priest. In that case, Pedro, I think I shall retire to the terrace.

Costanza. No, Father, you musn't go. Please say a prayer!

Priest. A prayer? What for?

Costanza. To protect us from the bull!

Priest. How would that help? I doubt if the bull knows Latin. [*He goes*

Costanza. He has gone to the terrace.

The shouting is getting louder.

Inés. Let's all go up there. For even though they have a rope on him, he will still be dangerous.

Bártolo. Keep out of the way of the rope, too! [*He goes*

Pedro. Shall I have a try?

Casilda. Oh, no, love! He is terrible!

Pedro. I do not care how terrible he is. I will seize him by the horns and have him down on the ground, and show them all how brave I am.

Casilda. No, it would not be right or proper on your wedding day. Besides a bull's horns are no place for a brand new husband.

Pedro. Very well, since you forbid it.

Shouting and noise.

Casilda. Good heavens, what is that?

Voices off. What a terrible accident! How awful! Oh, look out!

Casilda. He has done some damage by the sound of it.

Pedro. How can he have? We are both safe here.

Enter BÁRTOLO.

Bártolo. Oh God, if only they had never brought the brute out of the fields. So help me, no one will ever boast about this day to his children. God damn the bull! God damn you! I hope you never find green grass in a field again. I hope it's as dry as August even in April. When you meet a rival I hope he beats the daylights out of you and when you go bellowing through the woods, I hope you find the stream is dry. I hope you die mauled by the mob, cornered in a cheap bullring, and not at the hands of a gentleman with a sword or gold-handled knife. May a base lackey come up behind you and slash you with a rusty old sword, so you sink down on your knees and stain the dust with your evil blood.

Pedro. Do not stand there cursing your head off, Bártolo! Tell us what has happened.

Bártolo. The Commander of Ocaña, our noble lord, came riding out on his bay horse, with black flies swarming round its back and neck. Under the silver bridle you could see its fiery nostrils and on its back there was a green and red silk cloth which it bathed with white foam. Well, he was coming down the street when he saw them chasing after the bull. He pulled down his hat, threw back his cloak and spurred his bay, which went like the wind toward the bull. And then, in the midst of the shouting crowd, the rope caught round his horse's legs and he fell, right among them. It was a terrible fall. I think he's dying. But what am I doing standing here talking about it? Here they come with him!

Enter MARÍN, LUJÁN, *and* PEASANTS, *carrying the* COMMANDER—*he is unconscious.*

Marín. Where is the priest? He can administer the last Sacrament.

Inés. I think he went and hid somewhere.

Pedro. Go up to the terrace, Bártolo.

Bártolo. I will find him.

Pedro. Hurry.   [BÁRTOLO *goes*

Luján. We will go and fetch a litter to carry him in, if, by God's will, he dies.

Marín. Come, Luján, I fear the Commander is dead already.

Luján. I am afraid—my heart is pounding.   [*They go*

Casilda. I think he is coming around. Go and get some water for him, Pedro.

Pedro. If the Commander dies here, I will never live a moment longer in Ocaña, and I will curse my wedding day.

[*He goes*

Casilda. Oh! What a terrible thing to happen to such a man! The flower of Spain. So fine a gentleman and such a gallant soldier. Was it you who terrified the Moors in Granada? Was this the sword? Was it you who killed so many? And now death claims you with a rope. A rope! The fate of thieves! Though you never stole aught, unless it were the fame of those you vanquished.

Commander. Who is that? Who is there?

Casilda. He spoke! Thank God!

Commander [*groans*]. Oh! Oh! Who are you?

Casilda. It is only me, sir. Do not worry, you are among those who wish you well, as well as you wish yourself. The only thing you need be sorry for is that you went after that brute of a bull. You are as welcome in this house as if it were your own.

Commander. I was dead on the ground and then, when I awoke, I thought I was in Paradise. Tell me who you are or I can only think I am in Heaven where angels dwell.

Casilda. No, do not say such things or I shall fear you are really dying!

Commander. Why?

Casilda. Because you are seeing visions. If Your Lordship is pleased to shelter in my humble house—I would have you know that only today has it become mine.

Commander. Are you, then, the happy bride?

Casilda. I am the bride, but shall not be happy if anything happens to you, because I feel I am to blame for your accident.

Commander. So you are married?

Casilda. Yes.

Commander. And, but for my accident, you are happy?

Casilda. Oh, yes!

Commander. That is a rare thing for one so beautiful.

Casilda. Oh! I am very lucky.

Commander. What is your name?

Casilda. Casilda, if you please, sir.

Commander [*aside*]. She is perfect, even in a peasant's dress. A diamond set in lead. [*To* CASILDA.] He is a fortunate man who has won a lovely girl like you.

Casilda. Oh, no sir! I am the lucky one, believe me!

Commander. Casilda, you might be the wife of a noble-man. . . .

Enter PEDRO.

PEDRO. I can't find the priest! If anything should happen to . . .

Casilda. Stay here! It is all right. My lord Don Fadrique is recovering.

Pedro. Thank Heaven, and you, my love; you could charm anyone back to life.

Enter MARÍN *and* LUJÁN.

Marín. I think he has come around.

Luján. We have brought the litter, sir.

Commander. Do not bring it in. I do not need it.

Luján. Thank God for that!

Commander. I am grateful to you both for the kindness you have shown me. If I live, I swear it shall not go un-rewarded.

Pedro. If I could give my health for yours, sir, I would give it.

Commander. I believe you.

Luján. How do you feel, my lord?

Commander. Well, and yet my soul is sick.

Luján. I do not understand.

Commander. No matter!

Luján. But your fall, sir . . . ?

Commander. My body is well and yet my life is in danger from a wild dream I have.

       [*They go out, leaving* CASILDA *and* PEDRO

Pedro. He seems better now.

Casilda. I'm sorry it happened at all.

Pedro. I cannot help feeling that his fall was a bad omen. Oh, curse this day, the bull, and whoever roped it!

Casilda. He will be all right. He talked to me afterwards. Who knows, it may all be for the best. I am sure if ever we need help he will be good to us.

Pedro. Casilda, my love longs for its loving reward. Here we are in our own house and you are mistress of it and me. You must be good and obey me, Casilda, for God said when the world began that a wife should obey her husband, and so we shall have peace. You will turn all my troubles to glory.

Casilda. What must I do to be a good wife? [1]

Pedro. One—always have a good supper ready for me when I come in from the fields. Two—that you keep our house like a new pin. Three—that you mend my clothes when they need it, and, four—that you love me always.

Casilda. I promise, Pedro. I will always be a good wife provided you treat me properly!

Pedro. What must I do to be a good husband?

Casilda. One—you must never come home drunk. Two —you must never be mean about money. Three—remember my birthday every year. Four—never flirt with other women but love me always, and, five—we must have three boys and two girls.

Pedro. I promise. [*They kiss.*]

Casilda. And now dare I ask you a favor on the very first day of our marriage?

Pedro. How could I refuse you anything? We will do anything you wish.

Casilda. Well, listen then.

Pedro. Go on.

Casilda. The Feast of the Assumption is next week and I have always wanted to go to Toledo and see the procession and the images and all the saints and everything. Not just to amuse myself, but for devotion too.

Pedro. We will arrange a party! You can invite Inés and Costanza and we will decorate the cart and travel in style. Will that please you?

Casilda. There is nothing I should like more.

Pedro. And when we get there I am going to buy you a present. . . .

Casilda. What? Tell me!

Pedro. The most beautiful dress we can find.   [*They go*

1

The COMMANDER's house

Enter the COMMANDER, LEONARDO, *and a* SERVANT.

COMMANDER. Leonardo! Call Luján. Tell him I want him immediately.

[1] The following exchange, down to Pedro's "I promise," is a simplified version of two contrasting lovers' alphabets, only a few of whose items (such as "F for faithful") could have been translated as they stood.—ED.

Leonardo. I have told him twice but he answered rudely and said he would not come.

Commander. Call him again!

Leonardo. I will, my lord.

Commander. Run, man!

Leonardo. I know not what troubles him. Since he has recovered from his fall he seems to be worse, not better. He groans when he is not in pain and sighs all day. He is in love, I swear. [*He goes*

Commander. Oh! Beautiful Casilda! More lovely than the dawn dressed in sunlight or the high mountain snows. Dare I trespass there? Your hands are white flowers, fairer than those which Zephyrus engendered in Flora's lap. Hope grows in my heart, planted by your hands, Casilda. How can your peasant husband know the treasure he has harvested? When his beard is white as snow, your children will work his land. Will he know then? I doubt it. The golden sun would give you his coach to ride in, the North Star would make the Milky Way your highroad. For his spade I would renounce my golden sword, my castle for his cottage with the bright star that sleeps in it. For oh, how fortunate is he that finds such a treasure in his bed.

Luján. I am sorry to make you wait, my lord. Your bay horse needed my attention.

Commander. Oh! Luján! I fear I shall never recover from my fall. Death was near me then, but now love binds me.

Luján. Your feelings have not changed?

Commander. As fire must burn, so must I love. That cannot change. Tell me, Luján, how can I approach the peasant, Peribáñez? What should I say? Shall I command his presence here, to express my gratitude? What favor can I do him? I thank God he is not a courtier! At least his pride and honor cannot be offended.

Luján. If I were in your place, I should certainly try to win the husband before the wife. I know he is highly respected among his equals, but with a few favors and well-chosen gifts, I doubt not but he will turn a blind eye to one or two trifles touching his honor—or his wife's virtue. And what is more, he will not be the first!

Commander. What shall I give him as a first token of my gratitude?

Luján. Think, sir, it is a peasant you are approaching.

He will be just as pleased with a couple of mules as if you
had given him Ocaña. And I should say a pair of earrings
for the wife, for thus, the poet says, did Medoro win
Angelica:[1] while Roland and the great paladins toiled
in battle for Angelica, hacking and slaughtering for her
sake, Medoro offered her a pair of slippers and won her
heart with them:

> They knew the best delights of love
> In dim green bowers of elm or lime,
> On beds of thyme and thistledown.
> And thirteen months she dwelt with him.

And all on account of a pair of slippers!

Commander. The poet well knew the powers of bribery.

Luján. Be assured, sir, gifts are always the best and
quickest way—and may be given on the quiet. Personal
services or advancement are too blatant; everybody would
soon know that you loved Casilda. But they say an interest
expressed in terms of money has its feet wrapped in cotton.

Commander. Very well then. We will see if bribes will
serve.

Luján. They will work! Believe me.

Commander. Luján, since I first observed your courage
and steadfastness in battle in Andalusia I have been pleased
to acquaint you with my innermost secrets, because I know
that a discreet and honorable man can be trusted whatever
happens or wherever he may be. I shall advance you in my
service.

Luján. If I can please you in any way, command me,
and you will have proof of my devotion. I can offer you no
more.

Commander. Get Casilda for me!

Luján. I have told you the best way.

Commander. Come! We will find him the best two
mules he has ever seen.

---

[1] In the original, the rest of this speech takes the form of an
intricate and highly ironical mock-heroic sonnet. The sonnet is
not an acceptable dramatic form in English, and I feel that the
translator has been wise to attempt to render its effect by other
means, both here and in other places. For an analysis of the
dramatic function of the sonnet (which, incidentally, discusses
this example in detail), see Peter N. Dunn, "Some Uses of
Sonnets in the Plays of Lope de Vega," *Bulletin of Hispanic
Studies*, XXXIV, 1957, pp. 213–222.—Ed.

Luján. The mules will prepare the ground with Pedro, never fear; and then you will reap the harvest of his wife's devotion. After all, even love has its price.   [*They go*

1

A *room in* PEDRO's *house*

Enter CASILDA, INÉS, *and* COSTANZA.

CASILDA. We still have plenty of time.

Inés. It is a lovely day and the road is good all the way.

Costanza. I have heard that in summer you can get there in ten hours or less. What will you wear, Inés? Are you going to dress up?

Inés. No. I shall wear this dress.

Costanza. I shall wear my blouse with the silver embroidery.

Inés. It will show up beautifully with your jacket open.

Casilda. I shall wear velvet over a red petticoat. I think it is most suitable for a married woman.

Costanza. Antón's wife lent me a blue woolen skirt from Cuenca, I think that is where they make them, but Menga, Blasco's wife, said the color didn't suit me, so I gave it back to her.

Inés. I know who'll lend you a better one.

Costanza. Who?

Inés. Casilda.

Casilda. Yes, of course. My white linen one is nice, or you can have the green spotted one.

Costanza. It is most kind of you to offer, but Pedro might not like you to lend me your things. I don't want to cause any trouble between you.

Casilda. Oh, no! Pedro is not mean.

Inés. Does he love you very much?

Casilda. You do not imagine we are quarreling already, do you? There is not a couple in Ocaña more thrilled with each other than we are. We have not been married long, you know! We are still eating the leftovers from the wedding feast.

Inés. What does he say? Does he tell you how he loves you?

Casilda. He never says anything else. He makes me so happy that I do not know what I am doing most of the time. As soon as it is dusk and the glowworms come out

Pedro comes in from the fields hungry for his supper. I can feel in my bones when he is coming, and I throw down my work and run and open the door. He jumps down off his mule and I run into his arms. We stand there kissing and hugging until the poor old mule becomes impatient and starts to whinny. So then Pedro takes him to the stable and we feed the animals together. Pedro throws the hay in for them and I fetch the oats. He holds the sieve while I help him put it through. Then we both give the oats and bran a good stir around in the manger, and he kisses me again, among the animals. We go back to the house and there is the stew pot calling to us, bubbling up and down and rattling the lid like castanets. The smell of garlic and onions fills the kitchen! I spread a clean tablecloth on the table and serve it up properly. There are no silver plates, of course, but ours are very pretty—from Talavera—with carnations painted on them. He says his stew smells so good the Commander himself could not have better. But he picks out all the best bits and gives them to me! He goes on eating until there is just half left, then he gives the bowl to me and I finish it up. After that, I put a dish of olives on the table, if we have any, and if we have none, then we would just as soon go without. When we have finished we say grace together for what we have received, and go to bed. And when dawn finds us there, we part unwillingly.

Inés. How lucky you are to be married. It sounds wonderful. But come, we must hurry.

Enter PEDRO.

Casilda. Have you finished decorating the cart?

Pedro. I have done the best I can.

Casilda. May we go and look at it then?

Pedro. I have just seen Blas go by with his cart and his has an embroidered tapestry with a coat of arms on it. I wish we had one.

Casilda. You could ask one of the gentlemen to lend you one.

Inés. Why not ask the Commander?

Pedro. He was very kind to us when he was here. I think he would lend us a tapestry.

Casilda. You lose nothing by asking.

Pedro. Yes, you are right. We cannot go without one.

Inés. We must go and dress.

Casilda. There is something else you might ask him. . . .

Pedro. What, Casilda?

Casilda. Borrow one of his hats, Pedro.

Pedro. Oh, no! I could not do that.

Casilda. Why? It is not much to ask.

Pedro. Because if I start dressing like a gentleman you will only get conceited! And I will not look like a fool in borrowed plumes, even to please you!   [*They go*

The COMMANDER's *house*

Enter the COMMANDER and LUJÁN.

COMMANDER. Yes, indeed, they are excellent animals.

Luján. I have never seen better in my life, and I have known more than a few, believe me.

Commander. We must now get the earrings for Casilda.

Luján. The owner told me they would be three years old this spring and he said he bought them at Mansilla market a month ago for the same price I paid him. He said they are good either for saddle or packs.

Commander. Luján, tell me, how can we give them to her husband without arousing his suspicion?

Luján. Command his presence here and tell him how grateful you are for his kindness. But it amuses me to think that you should choose one such as me to be your assistant in affairs of the heart.

Commander. Why should you find it strange? Since the woman I court is of base parentage I find it most fitting that you should be my ambassador. Were she a lady, I should, of course, have employed my secretary or some gentleman of my household. These would have sought out jewels, diamond necklaces, clasps for her hair, pearls, damasks, fine woolen cloths, silks and velvets, or even gone to Arabia to catch the Phoenix for her. But since she is a peasant I am obliged to take you into my confidence. In you, Luján, I find the man fit to buy mules, and through you I deal with my love in its own currency.

Luján. Even if your love is ill-advised, the way you handle it is most wise!

Enter LEONARDO.

Leonardo. Peribáñez is here!
Commander. Who, Leonardo?
Leonardo. Pedro Ibáñez, my lord.
Commander. What did you say?
Leonardo. I said that Peribáñez asks to see you, my lord.
I think you know him. He is a farmer of Ocaña, of pure
Christian ancestry, a man highly respected among his fel-
lows. Indeed, if ever this town should have cause to rise
in arms, every man that follows a plow would choose him
as his leader. For though he is only a peasant, he is an
honorable man.
Luján. Why do you turn pale?
Commander. Even at the approach of the husband of
the woman I love I feel myself turn pale and tremble.
Luján. Do you fear to meet him?
Commander. Let him come in. They say the face of the
mistress may be sensed in speaking to the maid. So I hope
to see in the husband the beauty I long for in the wife.

Enter PEDRO. *He kneels before the* COMMANDER.

Commander. Pedro, a thousand times welcome. Rise
and let me embrace you.
Pedro. My lord, I do not deserve such courtesy. I am a
peasant and the humblest of your servants in Ocaña.
Commander. Pedro Ibáñez, you are not unworthy of my
embrace, for by your ancestry, intelligence, and way of
life, you have proved yourself a man of honor who, among
all my vassals, stands apart. I owe you my gratitude to the
extent of my life, which, but for you, I should surely have
lost. What would you in my house?
Pedro. My lord, I am, as you know, newly married, and
my wife has asked me to take her to see the Feast of the
Assumption celebrated in the Cathedral of Toledo, where
all the kingdom gathers. Her two cousins are coming with
us. We countrymen of the old families, though no courtiers, like to show a little gallantry on such occasions, but
in my house I have only a few mean cloths, no French
tapestries made of silk and silver thread, no draperies
painted with arms, nor crests with waving feathers and
noble mottoes. And so I have come to ask you, my lord,
if you would be so kind as to lend me a tapestry and a

painted cloth to adorn my wagon. I beg you to excuse my lack of manners, and to pardon me as a man in love.

Commander. Are you happy, Pedro?

Pedro. So happy that I would not change this rough cloak of mine for the noblest sash of knighthood that your lordship wears. I have an honorable wife, and not bad-looking either, who is a good Christian and who loves me —I would not say she loves me more than I love her, but more than any woman ever loved before.

Commander. It is right, both by human and divine law that you should love her who loves you. You, there! Give the Moroccan carpet to Peribáñez and eight of the finest cloths painted with my arms. And since I now have occasion to repay him for receiving me so hospitably in his house, give him the two mules I bought for his wagon, and take the earrings to his wife as soon as the smith has finished them.

Pedro. My lord, how can I thank you for even the smallest part of your goodness to me? My wife and I, always your vassals, may now be counted your slaves.

Commander. Go with him, Leonardo.

Leonardo. Follow me.   [LEONARDO *and* PEDRO *go*

Commander. Well, Luján, what think you?

Luján. That good fortune knocks at your door.

Commander. Saddle my horse. Not the bay, he is too well known and too easily recognized. Saddle the chestnut. I shall ride to Toledo incognito. For I must have her within my sight.

Luján. What, will you follow her?

Commander. I must. Love follows me, and drives me to her side.

Outside the Cathedral at TOLEDO

Enter the KING OF CASTILE, *the* CONSTABLE OF TOLEDO, *the* KING's *train and* TOWNSPEOPLE.

CONSTABLE. The city of Toledo is proud to welcome Your Majesty, whose presence here on the eve of our great feast day completes for us the happiness of the occasion.

King. Our own pleasure at being able to attend the ceremonies is no less than yours. I have long been the most ardent admirer of your great city.

Constable. Our city in all love and honor will attempt to show her gratitude and allegiance to Your Majesty.

King. She is the eighth wonder of the world, the crown of Castile, its best jewel and ornament. She is the head from which the limbs receive their life. Like Rome, she is built upon a hill, but now this one hill has more fame than all Rome's seven. I come from your great Cathedral full of wonder and of pride.

Constable. It is indeed a miracle, sir, which surpasses the Temple of Diana at Ephesus. We humbly ask if Your Majesty will deign to grace our procession tomorrow with your royal presence?

King. As a testimony of my faith I will follow the image of the Virgin, whom I will beg to intercede for me in my great undertaking.

Enter a PAGE *followed by two* ALDERMEN *of* TOLEDO.

Page. My liege, here are two officers of the city who come to pay homage to Your Majesty on behalf of the city's Governors.

King. Bid them approach.

First Alderman. Toledo prostrates itself at your feet, Your Majesty, and wishes to give an immediate answer to your just request for men and money. The nobles met and all agreed to offer for your campaign a thousand men from all the kingdom of Toledo, together with forty thousand ducats.

King. We sincerely thank Toledo for this, its latest proof of that loyalty in which it has never wavered. Tomorrow the Constable shall reward you before the people, so that all Toledo may know my gratitude to this city and its nobles.

Enter INÉS, COSTANZA, *and* CASILDA *dressed in the manner of peasants of* LA SAGRA *of* TOLEDO. PEDRO IBÁÑEZ *is with them. The* COMMANDER *is following, dressed for travel.*

Inés. Oh, I must see him! We have come just in time to see the King.

Costanza. He is magnificent!

Inés. He is called Henry III.

Casilda. But he is wonderful. Is he only the third?

Pedro. He is the son of King Juan I, which means he is

the grandson of Henry II, the one who killed Pedro the
Cruel.

Inés. Who's that stiff man he's talking to?

Pedro. Oh, the Constable, at least.

Casilda. Is he real then? Really flesh and blood?

Costanza. What did you think he was?

Casilda. Oh, damask or velvet or something.

Costanza. How stupid of you!

Commander. I am as close to that peasant girl as if I
were her shadow. I pray none of the King's people recognize me. Ah! now he goes to the castle.

Inés. Long live the King!   [*Exit* KING *and* NOBLES

Costanza. Oh! dear! I had no time to notice whether his
beard was fair or red.

Enter LUJÁN *with a* PAINTER.

Luján. There she is.

Painter. Which one?

Luján. Quiet! Sir, here is the painter.

Commander. My friend, you are welcome.

Painter. I am at your service.

Commander. Have you brought your paints and palette?

Painter. Knowing your desire, I have them with me.

Commander. You see those three peasant girls? I would
have a portrait of the one in the center. But it must be
done with the utmost secrecy. Follow them until you may
observe her without being seen.

Painter. That will be difficult, but I assure you it will
be a good likeness.

Commander. If your first miniature pleases me I shall
commission a full-scale portrait on canvas.

Painter. Is it to be full length?

Commander. No, three-quarter length. Paint her in the
dress she is wearing now, with all its details of adornment.

Luján. See! They are sitting down to watch the crowds.

Painter. We are lucky. I will paint the first sketch now.

Pedro. Casilda, we may sit here and watch the lights.

Inés. They say there are to be bulls outside the City
Hall tonight.

Casilda. No, let us stay here. We shall be able to see
them better here and it is safer.

Commander. Paint heaven on your canvas, and the
earth as well, covered in flowers.

Painter. She is most beautiful.

Luján. Too beautiful, if you ask my opinion.

Painter. The light is failing fast.

Commander. Do not fear, painter, another sun shines in her fair eyes. To you they may seem merely stars, but for me they are burning lightning!   [*They go*

ACT TWO

1

The Guild Room in OCAÑA. BLAS, GIL, ANTÓN, *and* BENITO *are having a heated discussion.*

BENITO. That is my opinion!

Gil. Sit down then, and make a note of it.

Antón. I consider that we should not hold this meeting when so few are present.

Benito. It was properly convened. Word was sent around yesterday.

Blas. This last festival was just not good enough.

Gil. Gentlemen, since the Procession was so well attended and the Saint so well honored, we, as members of such a notable Guild, should consider it a disgrace to ourselves not to remedy the situation. The lack of devotion shown by Ocaña is a disgrace to the whole of Spain. Every day we see in this very kingdom of Toledo more and more expressions of devotion, more and more processions in honor of our own Saint Roque, yet we seem to be afraid to go to the least expense. . . .

Benito. I think it is thoughtlessness rather than meanness, Gil.

Enter PERIBÁÑEZ.

Pedro. I hope I am not too late. . . . If I can be of any service now I am here . . .

Blas. Come in, Peribáñez, we need your good advice.

Pedro. I will try to make up for my lateness as best I can.

Benito. Come and sit here, next to me.

Gil. Where have you been?

Pedro. In Toledo. I went up with my wife to see the Festival.

Antón. Was it good?

Pedro. Gentlemen, I can only say that to go into the Cathedral was like walking into Heaven. And the image of the Virgin they have there could not be bettered unless angels who had seen the heavenly original should come down from Heaven to carve it in her likeness. The Procession was magnificent and full of dignity. They tell me it always is, but the King himself was there this year, on his way to Andalusia for his latest campaign against the Moors.

Gil. The Guild has needed your advice on many issues while you were away.

Pedro. I did intend to return some days ago to join in our own local feast of Saint Roque, but I could not persuade Casilda to leave until the octave was over.

Gil. The King was there, you say?

Pedro. Yes, and the Master of Alcántara and Calatrava too, so I was told. They are preparing a great campaign. Soon, there will not be a Moor left standing in Andalusia. But tell me, what were you discussing before I came?

Benito. Our Guild of Saint Roque. And your arrival, just at the moment when we were electing our leader, suggested to me that it should be you, Pedro.

Antón. The same thought was in my mind.

Blas. Are we all agreed?

Gil. I vote we elect him and give him charge of the next festival and make him responsible for what must be done.

Pedro. As a newly married man, perhaps I should refuse to accept the responsibility, but I will allow my devotion to overcome my prudence. I will undertake the office so that I may be of service to Saint Roque.

Antón. Yes, indeed! You are the right man for the job.

Pedro. What must be done?

Benito. I propose that we have a new Saint made. A bigger one that will show up better in the procession.

Pedro. A good suggestion. What do you say, Gil?

Gil. I agree. Our present one is far too small, and, besides, he is worn out.

Pedro. Antón?

Antón. Yes, we need a bigger one, and one which can really inspire devotion. The old Saint is all split and gaping open down one side, his dog looks like a lump of carrion, half the loaf of bread is gone. His gown hangs off him like a rag, and his two fingers which are supposed to be raised in blessing are broken off at the knuckles.

Pedro. What do you think, Blas?

Blas. I think that Pedro and Antón ought to go up to Toledo today and take our old Saint to some good restorer. There is no need to waste money on a great big new Saint when our old one can probably be renovated.

Pedro. Blas is right. Our Guild is poor. But how shall we get him there?

Antón. He will be safe enough on your mule, or mine, if we wrap him up in a sack.

Pedro. Well then, I think we have talked enough for today, if I am to go to Toledo.

Blas. I don't want anyone to think that my proposal was made out of meanness. I assure you that when Roque returns a new man I shall be more than willing to pay my share.

Gil. I feel sure we are all in agreement about that.

Pedro. Come, then, Antón, I must say good-bye to my wife.

Antón. I'll go and get the statue and then meet you.

Pedro. Even though this is Guild business, I am afraid Casilda will doubt my love that I should leave her so soon. She will be angry with me for leaving Ocaña at harvest time.

✓

A room in the COMMANDER'S *house*

Enter the COMMANDER *and* LEONARDO.

COMMANDER. Tell me everything that happened.

Leonardo. I have won over her cousin, Inés, if that is any help! It happened like this: she came back from Toledo with our peasant girl; if Casilda is like the sun, she is like the dawn, gentler and more approachable. As soon as she was back in Ocaña I made a habit of strolling up and down in front of her house, unobtrusively of course, because you cannot be too careful with these people—once they start to gossip. . . . Well, at last, in the evening, she came out; they were holding a dance in the village, so I made it my business to speak to her. I spoke of love and that kind of thing. She was a little coy and not very forthcoming, but the next day I saw her again on the way to the threshing yard. I caught up with her and told her a long story about my secret sorrow! This time she was more amenable and promised to return my love for her; because, of course, I had told her I would marry her. Though I think she rather doubted that—as well she might. However, I assured her that if you saw fit you could arrange the match; and so, my lord, I think I have prepared the way for you to approach Casilda.

Commander. Oh, Leonardo! If only it might prove an entrance to her heart. The nearer I approach, the more I sense her coldness to me.

Leonardo. She has shown no sign of relenting, then?

Commander. I went to Toledo, as you know, like a shadow following the sun. Then, finally, I let her see me. She looked at me as if she gazed on death itself. She turned pale with fear and then her color returned and her face flushed with anger. Our roles were reversed. She was the mistress, I her slave, as she must have seen if the smallest part of my feelings showed in my face. The scorn in her eyes as she looked at me only enhanced her beauty! While I was there, Leonardo, I commissioned an artist to make a sketch of her in all her beauty and disdain.

Leonardo. Was it a good likeness?

Commander. Excellent. And even now he is painting a life-size copy on canvas, so that I may hang it where she will always be before my eyes, to flatter me with her gaze. It should be finished today and you must go to Toledo to fetch it. If she herself is denied me at least I may live with her image.

Leonardo. I will do as you command. But I think you torture yourself unnecessarily. Once you have an opportunity to speak to her, she will change her tune, you'll see. Inés will arrange that, just leave it to me.

Commander. If she can, Leonardo . . .

Enter LUJÁN, *dressed as a harvester.*

Luján. Are you alone?

Commander. My good Luján! Yes, only Leonardo is here.

Luján. Then here is some news for you! I went to Peribáñez dressed as you see, ready for the harvest, and asked to be taken on as a day laborer on his farm. He did not recognize me, for appearances easily deceive, and engaged me at once. As from today I am a member of his household.

Commander. I wish I were with you, Luján.

Luján. Tomorrow at dawn the reapers, me included, will be going to the fields, but I think you will reap your harvest before then. Pedro has gone to Toledo, and his absence gives me my chance: his reapers will be sleeping near the front porch and, if you should happen to be passing at the time when all good peasants should be sound asleep, I will open the door and lead you to Casilda!

Commander. Luján, how can I ever repay you for your part in this?

Leonardo. I think your own imagination can soon supply the solution to that. Imagination is a great gift, sir.

Commander. You have smoothed my path, Luján, and opened the door to my dearest desire. Such good fortune is beyond belief! That he should not recognize you! And he is going to Toledo tonight! You observed the house carefully?

Luján. Nothing escaped me. I even entered her room and saw her sitting there.

Commander. You entered her room? What was she doing?

Luján. She was sitting on a leather chair, doing some embroidery. On the walls, all around her, hung the cloths you gave him, painted with your arms. I think they fancy themselves nobles, though of course it may be that they just want to keep out the draft—though I doubt that, in August! But, seeing them hanging there, I took them as an omen of your coming victory in that field!

Commander. No, my surrender, rather. But were each cloth my life, I would willingly give it a thousand times over and count it well lost for Casilda. But you must return to your peasant friends, you must not be seen about my house.

Luján. Will Leonardo be with you?

Commander. Yes. It is always wisest to have a friend at one's side.

✦

Outside the house of PEDRO IBÁÑEZ

Enter CASILDA *and* INÉS.

CASILDA. Don't go, Inés, stay with me tonight.

Inés. I am sorry, Casilda, but I cannot, truly I cannot. My parents would worry.

Casilda. We could send someone with a message. Besides, it is too late for you to go now.

Inés. Very well, Casilda, I will stay.

Casilda. Thank you, Inés, I cannot tell you how grateful I am. Besides, I love having you here.

Inés. You have lost the habit of sleeping alone and you are nervous now that Peribáñez is away. I am afraid I shall be a poor substitute for him! And if we hear any noises in the night, I shall be terrified, I warn you. I tremble if I see a sword in its sheath; unsheathed I faint on the spot!

Casilda. There is nothing to be afraid of. Pedro's reapers will be sleeping outside the door.

Inés. Oh! I see. You are afraid of being lonely inside, and you think that loneliness may keep you awake.

Casilda. Yes, you are right. I am afraid that if I lie awake I may worry about Peribáñez, for they say that wakefulness breeds jealous thoughts.

Inés. There is no reason to be jealous of Pedro because he has gone to Toledo.

Casilda. Jealousy, they say, is a wind that blows from every quarter.

Inés. The song says it comes from Medina.

Casilda. No doubt, but why should it not come from Toledo, too? So do please stay.

Inés. Very well. They say the girls are very pretty in Toledo, Casilda.

Casilda. Let us not think about them; come in and have supper, Inés.

Enter LLORENTE, MENDO, *and* PEASANTS.

Llorente. We must get a lot of sleep in tonight, we have to rise early tomorrow.

Mendo. Too true. I shall bed down as soon as I have had a bite of supper.

Casilda. The men are coming in already.

Inés. Come along then. Oh, and do not forget to tell Sancho to keep an eye on the orchard.

CASILDA *and* INÉS *go. Enter* BÁRTOLO *and* CHAPARRO.

Llorente. The missus has gone to lock up. She will be out in the morning, I know, chivvying us round, now Pedro's away.

Bártolo. I have to get the whole hillside cut before sunup.

Chaparro. Well, get some shut-eye then and stop talking about it! Goodnight Mendo, Llorente.

Mendo. There will not be much idling now he has put us on piecework.

Chaparro. That won't make any difference to the good workers.

Mendo. What about a song or a story before we go to sleep?

Bártolo. Hey, Llorente. You asleep?

Llorente. Oh, Christ, I wish there were only four mornings in a year!

Enter FELIPE *and* LUJÁN *as a harvester.*

Felipe. Is there room for two more?

Mendo. It's Felipe! Yes, there's room. You're welcome.

Luján. Is there room for me too?

Chaparro. Sure, you can bed down there by the door.

Bártolo. Llorente's going to give us a song.

Chaparro. And maybe a story.

Luján. I wish I knew one for you.

Chaparro. Hey, just a moment while I get my cloak off. Then I can listen in comfort.

Luján. Let us hear the song first, then I have a story I bet you haven't heard.

Mendo. Go on.

Llorente. All right, here goes.

Song

The clover, the clover,
The sweet-smelling clover,
Clover, clover
Growing in the dew.
There's clover for the good wife,
Clover, clover,
Clover for the wife
Who loves her husband true.
Clover for the maiden
Clover, clover,
Trusting her first love
That soon she will rue.
The clover, the clover,
The sweet-smelling clover
Clover, clover,

Growing in the dew.
There's clover for the old maid,
Clover, clover,
She'll never tell you
How many loves she's had.
Clover for the widow,
Clover, clover,
Her dresses may be black
But her petticoat is red.
The clover, the clover,
The sweet-smelling clover
Clover, clover,
The clover is my bed.

Luján. They are all asleep. You can stop singing now.
Llorente. Then I will join them. Though it is not exactly clover!
Luján. Now, why does he tarry? They are dead asleep and the night is made for love. Ah! That was his whistle. I will open the door. [*He opens the door.*]

Enter COMMANDER *and* LEONARDO.

Luján. Is that you, sir?
Commander. It is.
Luján. Come in quickly.
Commander. Is it safe?
Luján. They're like logs. You can step between them or on them if you like. A cart could rattle past and they would never notice.
Commander. Lead me to her room.
Luján. Leave Leonardo here.
Leonardo. As you wish.
Luján. Follow me!
Commander. Oh! God of Love. Give me good success.
[*They go in*

Llorente. Hey, Mendo!
Mendo. What?
Llorente. Ssh! There is someone in the house.
Mendo. Did you hear them, too? So did I. Are we not supposed to be guarding Pedro's honor while he is away?
Llorente. It is not ordinary people.
Mendo. How do you know?
Llorente. There was gold on his cloak.

Mendo. Gold? Christ! The Commander!

Llorente. Shall we call out?

Mendo. No, better keep quiet.

Llorente. I reckon you are right. How do you know it is the Commander?

Mendo. Nobody else in Ocaña would dare break in here —or even think of such a thing.

Llorente. That is what you get for marrying a beautiful wife.

Mendo. Maybe she is innocent.

Llorente. Maybe. Look out, they are coming back. Make out you are asleep.

Commander. Leonardo!

Leonardo. What is it, my lord?

Commander. I have lost the best chance I could have had.

Leonardo. How?

Commander. The inner doors are bolted.

Leonardo. Knock.

Commander. And wake the whole house!

Leonardo. They will not wake. They are peasants and it is harvest time. They are locked in sleep by two good bolts—wine and weariness! Listen! Someone is opening the window over the door.

CASILDA *looks out. She has a shawl around her.*

Casilda. What is it? Is it time to get up?

Commander. Yes, madam, it will soon be day and time to go to the fields. But when you rise we need no other sun, it is day already. It grieves us all to see you left alone like this. Your husband cannot love you when he goes to Toledo and leaves you here at night, all by yourself. If the Commander of Ocaña were in his place (and I have it on good report that he loves you to distraction, although you scorn him) he would not leave you, even though the King of Castile summoned him. He would feel the laws of love more binding than the laws of kings.

Casilda. You must have come from far away, stranger, your manners are different from ours! Have you come looking for work? If you have, you had better put on your boots, take off your coat, tuck your gloves in your belt and be off to the fields with your scythe on your shoulder. I advise you to be careful when you tie up the sheaves,

for Pedro will not thank you if you break the corn ears.
When the stars come out go to sleep and do not meddle
in matters which do not concern you. The Commander
of Ocaña does not consort with girls in linen smocks and
red flannel petticoats. He will court a high-born lady with
wavy hair and fine cambric ruff, who travels to church in
a coach or sedan chair lined with silk; not a girl in a
country cloak and hood who rides from the cornfields to
the vineyards on a farm cart among the spades and scythes.
He will woo her in courteous letters full of poetry and
compliments, not through a tramp aping the manners of
the court. His lady will smell to him of scented gloves,
ambergris, and perfumes, not of thyme and lavender, mint
and pennyroyal. And even if the Commander did love me
with all his soul, in defiance of all codes of honor and
virtue, I love Peribáñez in his old brown cape more than
the Commander of Ocaña in his cloak embroidered with
gold. I would rather see Pedro in his white shirt riding
toward me on his gray mare, with frost in his beard, his
crossbow over his shoulder, a brace of partridge or a couple
of rabbits hanging from his saddle, and the old dog running beside him, than see the Commander of Ocaña in
silks and diamonds. The stone cross in the chapel means
more to me than the red cross of Saint James he wears on
his doublet. Go back where you came from, stranger, and
may bad fortune go with you! Because if Peribáñez finds
you here, you will not live to see the dawn break!

Commander. Casilda, I am the Commander of Ocaña.
You shall be a lady; I shall give you ropes of pearls and
a chain of gold, inlaid with rich enamel, heavier and more
precious than my own. . . .

Casilda. Wake up, harvesters! It is dawn. The sun will
soon be up and you are still asleep! Come now, rouse
yourselves. Shake the straw out of your hair! I will give
Pedro's big straw hat, which he wears in the vineyards, to
the man who ties most sheaves today.

                              [*She goes into the house*

Mendo. Llorente, the missus is calling.

Luján. Quick, my lord. Get away before they see you.

Commander. Oh! Cruel lady! But I will conquer your
disdain and overrule your anger, though I throw away my
fortune, honor, and even my life!

                 [*The* COMMANDER, LUJÁN, *and* LEONARDO *go*

Bártolo. Get up, Chaparro, it is light already.

Chaparro. Hey, Felipe, we must be late.

Felipe. Yes, look at the mountains! The sun is on the peaks already.

Llorente. Come on then, let us get going. We cannot have the missus saying we are idle at our work when the master is out of sight.   [*They go*

↗

A *painter's studio in* TOLEDO

Enter PEDRO, *the* PAINTER, *and* ANTÓN.

PEDRO. There is one picture of yours I should like to see again. I may have liked it because it is a portrait and the subject a peasant, as I am. But even so, I thought it best of all your work, religious and otherwise. I wonder if I might have another look at it, now we are agreed about repairing Saint Roque?

Painter. You are right. She is a beautiful girl.

Pedro. Could you fetch it down for us? I should like to show it to Antón.

Antón. I saw the one you mean. But I do not mind waiting if you want to look at it again.

Pedro. Fetch it, I pray you.

Painter. I will.

Pedro. You will see an angel.   [*The* PAINTER *goes*

Antón. I know why you are so taken with the portrait.

Pedro. It is only the dress which interests me.

Antón. Did you not think it looked like your wife?

Pedro. Is Casilda as beautiful as that?

Antón. Oh, Pedro! You are her husband. It is your job to praise her, not mine!

Enter the PAINTER *with a large portrait of* CASILDA.

Painter. Here is your peasant girl.

Pedro [*aside*]. And the death of my honor.

Painter. What think you of her?

Pedro. It is a remarkable painting. Do you like it, Antón?

Antón. Anyone would like it. But I think it means more to you than to the rest of us.

Pedro. Antón, go ahead and saddle the horses. I will follow you.

Antón. I do not know much about painting but I do

know that it is Casilda. God help the man who faces
Pedro's anger!   [*He goes*

Pedro. I have never seen a more beautiful creature. Oh!
those eyes and that soft mouth. Where does she come
from?

Painter. You do not recognize her? Then I'm afraid it
must be a poor likeness, for she comes from around your
way.

Pedro. From Ocaña?

Painter. Yes.

Pedro. I do know a married woman who looks somewhat
like her. . . .

Painter. I do not know who she is myself. All I know is
that I was ordered to paint her without her seeing me.
Not like this, of course, but on a small block. This is a
copy I have made from it.

Pedro. I know who commissioned it. If I am right, will
you tell me?

Painter. Yes.

Pedro. The Commander of Ocaña.

Painter. Yes. I dare to tell you this because the girl
knows nothing of it. Think of it. She does not know that
one of the noblest men in Spain is in love with her!

Pedro. The girl knows nothing, you say?

Painter. She knows as little as you did until I told you.
I had such trouble doing my first sketch, I can tell you.
She is so completely devoted to her husband, it was dif-
ficult to get near her.

Pedro. Would you trust me with it? May I deliver it?

Painter. They have not paid me for it yet.

Pedro. I will give you the full price.

Painter. I dare not! What could I say to the Commander? I am expecting his servant to come for it tomorrow.

Pedro. Does this servant know about it?

Painter. Know about it? He is under orders to get her
for him.

Pedro. I saw the man you mean yesterday. I should like
to make his acquaintance.

Painter. Is there anything else I can do for you?

Pedro. While you are repairing the Saint, may I come
again? I must gaze on her picture a thousand times.

Painter. Just as you wish. Good day to you.   [*He goes*

Pedro. What have I seen? What have I heard? Heaven, is this your spite? And yet, he said Casilda was innocent. What must I do? Must I tell her? But why should I publish my jealousy and shame? Is it not enough that the Commander should love my wife and seek to snatch my honor and self-respect from me? A Knight Commander of Saint James bound by his vows to God to protect the lives and honor of his people! I am his vassal, he, my overlord. How dare he think he can disgrace me so? He shall die for it! The mere attempt is offense enough. Oh, what a fool I was to think that a beautiful wife would mean a life of peace and happiness! I said on my wedding day that rich men would envy me my fortune. I little thought that it would lead to this. Oh! A peasant is a fool to marry a beautiful wife. Even now, what self-respect is left me when Don Fadrique has already commissioned a portrait of her? My honor is as dear to me as life itself! If a painted Casilda can damage my reputation and my life, how soon will it be before the real Casilda does so? A poor man with a beautiful wife is easily hurt. How proud I was that day when I asked her to marry me. What shall I do? What can I do? If I shut myself away at home, everyone will gossip, assuming the worst. Oh! how can a peasant hope to keep a beautiful wife? Shall I leave Ocaña? No, the result would still be the same and my farm is my livelihood; I could never earn my keep elsewhere. There is no way out. I must speak to Casilda, before men sneer and say "There goes Peribáñez who married a beautiful wife."   [*He goes*

1

A *room in the* COMMANDER'*s house*

Enter COMMANDER *and* LEONARDO.

COMMANDER [*with a letter*]. The King demands men from Ocaña, Leonardo. I cannot refuse him his request.

Leonardo. How must it be done, my lord?

Commander. Proclamations must be made and two hundred men enlisted. They will be divided into two companies, a hundred peasants and a hundred nobles.

Leonardo. Would it not be better to send all nobles?

Commander. I see you do not understand me or grasp my meaning, Leonardo. I intend to make Peribáñez the

leader and captain of the hundred peasants and so be rid
of him.

Leonardo. A clever idea, my lord!

Commander. Love is a war and must be won by cunning. Has he returned from Toledo?

Leonardo. Luján says they expect him home this evening, and that Casilda is tearful and depressed. But Inés
told me that they have agreed to say nothing about last
night. They do not want to upset him.

Commander. Heaven curse the moment when I fell
from my horse!

Leonardo. Calm yourself, my lord. Troy was stronger,
but she was conquered and her walls thrown down. They
are only cowardly peasants who often deny what they
most desire, thinking themselves unworthy of it. Once
Peribáñez is away, serving his King, it will not be long
before you succeed.

Commander. May it be so. But I swear to you that I,
a Knight Commander of Saint James, am now afraid.

Leonardo. We ought to know exactly when Pedro is
expected.

Commander. Go, Leonardo, and find out from Inés.

[LEONARDO *goes*

Commander. Why do I tremble? What have I to fear?
Pedro will soon be gone and then the field is mine to
win or lose. Casilda, I will win your love. My will is iron
and no peasant girl shall break it.   [*He goes*

In the countryside

Enter PEDRO *and* ANTÓN.

PEDRO. You can leave me here, Antón. You go on home.

Antón. What about you? Don't you want to get back?

Pedro. I want to see how my men are getting on and
have a word with them. This seems a good moment, as
this is the boundary of my land.

Antón. I would have thought Casilda was a more attractive prospect!

Pedro. You're right, believe me. But I must give them
their orders for tomorrow. You get back to your wife, and,
if you will, tell Casilda I have stopped to take a look at
the fields.

Antón. As you wish. God be with you.

Pedro. And with you. [ANTÓN *goes.*] Why do I hesitate to see Casilda? I know she is innocent and yet. . . . Oh, Casilda. . . . And yet it is your loveliness which has brought this horror on me. Your beauty is the cause of my disgrace. These fields are mine but now I see them without joy. I had hoped to come out with a light heart to gather my harvest and fill my barns with grain. But now my name is lost and the richness of the harvest is only a mockery.

Voices off. The harvesters are heard talking and shouting as they work.

Mendo [*off*]. Buck up, Bártolo. The sun is going down fast.

Bártolo [*off*]. They say he eats well who works well. I reckon we've earned a good supper.

A Harvester [*off*]. Hand it over, Andrés. You've drunk nearly a pint!

Andrés [*off*]. What of it? It would be wasted on you!

Pedro. They're coming! I can't face them now.

The harvesters enter on the way home. PEDRO *remains onstage, unseen by them.*

Mendo. Give us a song, Llorente! The one about the Master's wife.

Pedro. Oh, Death! Strike me now!

Llorente [*sings*].
The wife of Peribáñez is as sweet as any dove,
The Commander of Ocaña sought her for his love.
I'll give you pearls and diamonds, if you'll be mine, he said,
But the lass is bold as beautiful and this is what she said:
  Chorus.
I love Peribáñez in his woolen cape so old,
More than the Commander in his cloak of shining gold.[1]

The harvesters join in the chorus as they go.

Pedro. Their song makes me hope again! They have given me proof of Casilda's innocence. Oh, what a blessing from heaven is a faithful wife! If Casilda had done wrong

[1] The quatrain which this couplet translates is a fragment of a popular ballad, and almost certainly provided the initial inspiration for the play. (Compare the case of *The Knight from Olmedo*, see note on p. 222.)—ED.

their song would have told me—they would have made no
bones about it—but even so a reputation, however good,
which is bandied about in songs is of doubtful honor.
May God give me strength to follow the right course!

[He goes

✓

A *room in* CASILDA'*s house*

CASILDA *and* INÉS *enter.*

CASILDA. I cannot believe my ears! To hear you talk such
nonsense!

Inés. Please! Listen to me!

Casilda. How do you expect me to listen to such stuff?

Inés. Casilda, you do not understand! Besides, it is only
that you are so in love with Pedro that makes you imagine
his honor is insulted. What I am trying to say concerns
me!

Casilda. You?

Inés. Yes!

Casilda. I do not know what I was thinking of. I must be
mad. Tell me what it is that concerns you.

Inés. Leonardo, the Commander's gentleman, loves me
and wants to marry me.

Casilda. Oh! Inés! Can you believe that? He is deceiving
you!

Inés. No, Casilda, I know he loves me more than his
life.

Casilda. Did no one ever tell you men are like sirens
who sing to deceive us?

Inés. But I have a letter from him.

Casilda. Words are like feathers, the wind soon blows
them away. There are many ladies of noble birth in Ocaña
with rich dowries, and you are neither rich nor of noble
birth.

Inés. But do you not see, Casilda? If you continue to
treat the Commander rudely he will forbid our marriage.

Casilda. Are you blind too? The very fact that Leonardo
says so proves he does not truly love you.

Inés. Just being polite to him cannot hurt you! I do
not ask you to open the door to the Commander or talk
to him from the balcony.

Casilda. Even if it were a matter of your life, Inés, I
would not give him countenance. I warn you, Inés, never

name the Commander again in this house or that will be the last time you come here. For seeing leads to hearing, and evil words lead to worse deeds!

Enter PEDRO, *carrying saddlebags.*

Pedro. Casilda!

Casilda. My love.

Pedro. Are you well?

Casilda. I am now you are home again! How are you?

Pedro. Seeing you, I am bursting with health! Inés!

Inés. Pedro!

Pedro. What more could I ask, than to find you both here together?

Casilda. Inés has been very kind. She has kept me company while you were away.

Pedro. We must see that she is the next to marry! We shall soon have to be buying our new shoes to dance at her wedding.

Casilda. What have you brought me from Toledo?

Pedro. All my love! With such a load as that there was no room for any gifts or jewels! But I did manage to squeeze in these new slippers for your pretty feet. Look— pearl buckles. And six new caps, crimped and pleated. Oh, yes! And two ribbon girdles with silver tags.

Casilda. Oh, Pedro! Thank you.

Pedro. It is a miracle I'm here at all. I had an accident on the way home.

Casilda. You frighten me! What happened? Quickly! Tell me!

Pedro. I fell from my bay horse onto some rocks when going up a steep hill.

Casilda. Oh, no! Are you hurt?

Pedro. If I had not commended my soul to Saint Roque, in whose service I was making the journey, I think I should be dead by now.

Casilda. Oh, Pedro!

Pedro. I promised to give him the most valuable thing there is in this house to adorn his chapel. So tomorrow I want to have those cloths and the tapestry taken down, and hang them in the chapel as a token of my gratitude.

Casilda. If they were rich silk tapestries from France covered in gold and pearls and precious stones I would not say a word.

Pedro. I think it is wrong for us to have such cloths hanging in our house, with someone else's arms on them. I would not have Ocaña whisper that a peasant surrounds his humble bed with noble hangings, covered with symbols of knighthood. Crests and plumes go ill with plows and shovels, forks and hoes. Our whitewashed walls should be decorated with crosses of straw and poppies, not with silks. How many Moors have I ever conquered to have castles and mottoes on my walls? Anyway, I think we should have only religious pictures here, the Annunciation, the Assumption, Saint Francis with his stigmata, the Martyrdom of Saint Peter, Saint Blas, and Saint Roque, or other sacred subjects. I did see a portrait I should have. . . . No, I would not. Let us have supper, Casilda; I am tired and need to sleep.

Casilda. Do you not feel well, Pedro?

Pedro. Oh, I am all right.

Enter LUJÁN.

Luján. There is someone wants to speak to you. A servant of the Commander.

Pedro. Of whom?

Luján. The Commander of Ocaña.

Pedro. What does he want with me at this time of night?

Luján. You will know when you speak to him.

Pedro. Are you the man I engaged yesterday?

Luján. Have you forgotten me already?

Pedro. I remember now.

Luján [aside]. I do not like the sound of this.

Inés [aside]. Pedro knows something.

Pedro [aside]. The Commander wants me? How shall I answer him and guard my name? Honor is like a brittle glass, the slightest touch can break it!   [*They go*

ACT THREE

1

The Square in OCAÑA

Enter the COMMANDER *and* LEONARDO, *with a scroll.*

COMMANDER. Tell me briefly, Leonardo, what is the news from Toledo?

Leonardo. What I have here will take some time, but I will be as speedy as possible.

Commander. Give me healing words! Remember I am mortally sick.

Leonardo [*reading a proclamation*]. "King Henry III—the Just, as he is called—in this year of grace 1406 being in the town of Madrid, letters came to him saying that the Moorish King of Granada had broken the treaty already made with him and had refused to render to the King the castle of Ayamonte, much less his lawful tributes. The King has determined to go to war against him, and so, in order that right may triumph as befits the great King of Castile, and so that his allies Aragon and Navarre should join him, the Council of War has been summoned in Toledo. Prelates and nobles have gathered there, representing many towns and cities, and now in the castle they debated the matter in just accord——"

Commander. Come, man. Read faster!

Leonardo. Very well, my lord! "There present are the Bishop of Siguenza, together with the Bishop of Palencia, Don Sancho de Rojas, clearly worthy of his great name, Don Pablo of Cartagena, the Count of Trastamara, already known as the Duke of Arjona to all at court, the noble Don Enrique, both these last being cousins to the King, and whose swords are feared from Seville to Africa, Juan de Velasco, the King's Lord Chamberlain, Great Gómez Manrique, Rodriguez of Salamanca, Periáñez——"

Commander. Stop! You said Peribáñez; at that name my blood turns to ice!

Leonardo. My lord, I read to you the names of the King's Counselors, not those of peasants. I said Periáñez.

Commander. I will hear no more! You have told me the cause and nature of the King's campaign, that was all I wished to know. If I have understood you, Leonardo, this means that the King, together with the bravest knights of Christian Spain, is leading a campaign against those southern towns, which, under the protection of the Moor of Granada, refuse to pay their tribute to the King?

Leonardo. That is so, my lord.

Commander. Then I would have you know—and this means more to me than all the kings in Christendom—that while you have been in Toledo, my design has begun to prosper. I spoke with Peribáñez and told him it was my wish to make him captain of a hundred yeomanry. He thought I did him great honor, as indeed I do, albeit it is an honor bestowed upon him with dishonorable intent. He is determined to live up to his new rank. My men report that he has spent his meager savings on new clothes, and that yesterday he drilled his company in the square. According to Luján, he is marching to Toledo today.

Leonardo. And so, Casilda is left to you? But still unyielding, still the stubborn peasant?

Commander. Long absence wears down love, as water wears a stone.

Drums are heard.

Leonardo. What drums are those?

Commander. His, Leonardo! Leonardo, it is time for you to buckle on your sword. Call out my company of knights, unfurl my standard! He will swell with pride at so noble a reception!

Leonardo. I go, my lord.   [LEONARDO *goes*

Enter PEDRO, *with sword and dagger, leading a company of* PEASANTS, *quaintly armed,* BLAS *and* BELARDO *among them.*

Pedro. I could not go without taking leave of you, my lord.

Commander. I thank you for your courtesy.

Pedro. I go to serve you, sir.

Commander. No, Pedro, to serve the King.

Pedro. The King, and you, my lord.

Commander. As you say, Pedro.

Pedro. It is my duty to serve the King, and also you, my lord, who have honored me so greatly. For what have I, a peasant, ever done with my spade or hoe to merit the name of captain, a noble sword and the banner of a King? The King to whose ear my name could never come, for his person is far beyond my ken. May God protect you, sir, for many years to come.

Commander. May he protect you, Pedro.

Pedro. Am I properly dressed?

Commander. Most suitably. I see no difference between us.

Pedro. There is one favor I would like to ask. . . . I do not know if it will please you. . . .

Commander. Speak and you shall know.

Pedro. I would count it a great honor if your lordship would buckle on my sword.

Commander. I will, Pedro. But, first, kneel down and feel the weight of mine. Now rise a knight, from whom great valor is expected.

Pedro. I cannot speak, my lord.

Belardo. Get down on your knees, Blas! They're making him a Knight!

Blas. Why? Is there something wrong?

Belardo. There'll be something wrong with you if you don't kneel down.

Blas. You are an old man, Belardo, you must know about these things. Is he going to hit him with it?

Belardo. Don't ask me! I know more about harnessing my dapple mule and buckling on his old pack saddle than arming knights of Castile.

Commander. There! I have put on your dagger and sword. Now wear them for me.

Pedro. What must I do?

Commander. Swear to use both in the service of God and King.

Pedro. I swear. Furthermore, I vow before God to defend my honor as befits a knight. Now that I am going to the wars at your command, my lord, I leave my honor, my wife, and house in your care, as our overlord in Ocaña. They mean more to me than life itself, but I know no man will harm them if you guard them well. You, as an honorable man, know best what honor means. This sword I wear, which you put on, now represents my new estate. I take my leave your equal. See that you protect my honor, or I shall hold you responsible and acquit myself according to the rules and code of your behavior.

Commander. I give you my word. If there is any treachery may I be held responsible.

Pedro. Now, soldiers! March! And may God uphold us in our rightful cause!

The PEASANTS *march away,* PEDRO *marching behind them, very proudly.*

Commander. His words were double-edged! Was he threatening vengeance? Or does my guilty mind find malice now in innocence? But even if I have interpreted

his words aright, no peasant would dare challenge me.
Tonight you will be mine, Casilda. I shall break your
peasant's pride, and death to him who seeks my life before
this night is passed.   [*He goes*

A street in OCAÑA, *outside* PEDRO's *house*

Enter COSTANZA, CASILDA, *and* INÉS *onto the balcony.*

COSTANZA. Your husband is going away?

Casilda. Yes, Pedro is going to the war, but I think it
would be better if he stayed at home and quelled the
turmoil in my breast.

Inés. Don't upset yourself, Casilda. He has been made
a captain, don't forget. That doesn't happen every day.

Casilda. Oh, Pedro, I wish you had never deserved the
title!

Costanza. You are right, Inés. I have never heard of a
peasant being given such a rank. It is always a gentleman
who is a captain. There is no need to worry, Casilda. I
have heard they are only sending them as far as Toledo.

Casilda. If he goes any farther away I think I shall die.

A drum is heard. Enter PEDRO *with his soldiers and a
banner.*

Inés. Listen, a drum. I wonder if it is he?

Costanza. You shouldn't be feeling sorry for yourself,
but for those who are going with him.

Belardo. Look, there they are, up on the balcony. It
makes me feel young again to see them, not that it makes
much difference, they don't go for me any more!

Pedro. Come, Belardo, surely you're not that old?

Belardo. I've lost the taste for it.

Pedro. I bet there's a bit of the old taste left under that
old brown cloak!

Belardo. I tell you, Captain, there was a time, out in the
sun and the open air, when I was quite a wit. I took any
old job, sometimes a shepherd, sometimes a sexton. Then
one winter we had a bad snow and I noticed my hair was
going gray, so I entered the Church!

Pedro. I don't believe a word of it! I'd put you at thirty-
nine.

Belardo. You're not far out. Add another three years

and you would be right! [1] Or so my old nurse always said, though she never had much of a memory. She said I cut my first tooth the day King Charlemagne was born.

Pedro. But that was five hundred years ago!

Belardo. I said she didn't have much of a memory.

Pedro. Did you ever go to school?

Belardo. Not for long, but I knew a lot in those days, though many people will tell you I don't know how to read. Be that as it may, I know how to write—like those people who can dance and sing without being taught. Yes, I write a lot, but reading, well . . . I won't commit myself.

Casilda. Oh! Gallant Captain of my sorrowful heart!

Pedro. Oh, Lady of the balcony whose banner I bear!

Casilda. Are you riding forth from Ocaña this day, sir?

Pedro. Lady, I am bound for Toledo and the ends of the earth, leading these my soldiers, who are known to all as the Guardians of my Honor.

Casilda. Then know, Sir Knight, your Honor will be safely kept by so gallant a band.

Pedro. Casilda, I've come to say good-bye and to tell you I leave you in your own charge while I am away. You

[1] Lope frequently introduced himself into his own plays in some minor part, often under his pen name of Belardo (see S. Griswold Morley, "The Pseudonyms and Literary Disguises of Lope de Vega," *University of California Publications in Modern Philology*, XXXIII, 1951, pp. 421-484). Such scenes frequently contain personal allusions which help to date the play in which they occur. If Lope was forty-two when he wrote *Peribáñez*, the play must have been written in 1604 or 1605. The only serious objection to this lies in the line "a la Iglesia me acogí" ("so I entered the Church" in the present translation), which has been taken to refer either to Lope's entrance into a religious confraternity in 1609, or to his taking minor orders (late in 1613?); his actual ordination as a priest in May, 1614, was subsequent to the compilation of the *Quarta parte* of his *comedias* (in which *Peribáñez* appeared in print for the first time), whose *aprobación* is dated December 20, 1613. In an article on "The Date of *Peribáñez*" (*Hispanic Review*, XV, 1947, pp. 72–83), C. P. Wagner argues that the disputed reference "is so out of line with the other data that it cannot be accepted as having autobiographical value," and establishes a convincing case for Lope's having written the play in Toledo in August, 1605. This has not, however, been universally accepted (see J. Loveluck, *Atenea*, XXX, 1953).—ED.

must be your own best guardian. And now I beg the favor all ladies give their knights before they go into battle, to return laden with spoil! How do you like me as a knight, Casilda? Are my speeches elegant enough for my Lady? Who would have thought when I was a boy paddling about in the wine press that one day I should speak to you, Casilda, as a soldier and a knight; with my banners flying and my sword of valor at my side? It is true, Casilda, I am a knight, thanks to the Commander of Ocaña, and I will be worthy of the title both in words and deeds. Be faithful, Casilda. For though the Commander has made me a captain of men, he does not love me.

Casilda. Oh, Pedro. I do not understand you when you talk like that. But I will give you your favor. Look, take this ribbon.

Pedro. A black one, Casilda?

Casilda. You are not superstitious, Pedro?

Pedro. It is not the right thing for a favor. It means mourning or exile.

Blas. Well, Lady Costanza, will you reward my devotion with a favor?

Costanza. Here's a dog collar, use it on a Moor if you're capable of catching one.

Blas. May the heathen cut me into ribbons if I don't kill every one that flees before us.

Inés. Don't you want a favor, Belardo?

Belardo. Ah! I reckon I deserve one, as an old soldier if not exactly a brand new lover.

Inés. Well, you bring me back a Moor first!

Enter the Company of NOBLEMEN *with* LEONARDO *as their captain.*

Leonardo. Company, halt! Stand at ease, stand easy.

Inés. What is this?

Costanza. It is the Company of Nobles.

Inés. I think our men look better.

Costanza. Their clothes may be finer, but the men inside them are not.

Pedro. Now then, brace up! Come on, Belardo, get in line. Let us show we're men of spirit.

Belardo. If those bastards think they're going to piss on our straw they have got another think coming!

Pedro. Come on, Belardo!

Blas. You heard what the captain said, Belardo. Show some spirit!

Belardo. All right, all right. Show some yourself!

The PEASANTS *begin to march off, very proudly.*

Leonardo. I see the peasants are competing with the gentlemen.

Belardo. Look at them. Run like greyhounds when they see a Moor, you wait.

Blas. Or hear one.

Belardo. Like they did that day when the bull was loose!

PEDRO *and his Company go.* CASILDA *and* COSTANZA *leave the balcony.*

Leonardo. They have gone at last, Inés!

Inés. Is that you, Captain?

Leonardo. Why have your cousins gone in?

Inés. Can you not guess? Casilda is as obstinate as a mule. She will be in a black mood tonight.

Leonardo. Surely the Commander may see her for a moment?

Inés. Sssh! I will let him in when she thinks it is Pedro come home for the night.

Leonardo. If you would please me, blind the eyes of this woman who watches her virtue so keenly. The Commander is impatient.

Inés. Tell him to come to the street door.

Leonardo. What signal?

Inés. I should know a good singer if I heard one.

Leonardo. Farewell.

Inés. Will you come with him?

Leonardo. Yes. I will leave these gallant men in the charge of my lieutenant and return to Ocaña and to you.

Inés. Farewell.   [*She goes from the balcony*

Leonardo. Two suns have set! Beat, drums and march!
                              [LEONARDO *and his Company go*

*

A room in the COMMANDER'S house

Enter the COMMANDER *and* LUJÁN, *now dressed in livery.*

COMMANDER. At last! You saw him leave?

Luján. I did. He rode out on a gray mare, well known

in these parts for her speed and quality. She will serve well in retreat. He will travel a good way before nightfall, and if you saw the way he commands his soldiers you would have no fear of his return. He takes it all with great seriousness.

Commander. He has made them into a fine company! But I care more for that of his wife.

Luján. Faint heart never won fair lady.

Commander. By midday tomorrow they will be in Toledo.

Luján. If they camp tonight, that is.

Commander. You think they will march straight on?

Luján. They are peasants, used to the open air, and it is but a short journey. They have their drum to march to —I would not be surprised if they marched to Granada without stopping!

Commander. How can I pass the time between now and eleven o'clock?

Luján. It is nearly nine already. Come, my lord, be patient, you are within a hairsbreadth of your goal. The wait should serve to whet your appetite.

Commander. My heart is too full for patience.

Luján. Must Leonardo come with us?

Commander. Haven't you understood, man? That is the agreement with Inés. She thinks he is to marry her, and she will open the door to us.

Luján. What signal shall you give?

Commander. We are taking two musicians. Their song will be the signal.

Luján. Will not that fright your quarry?

Commander. No. It will rather cover the sound of the door being opened to us.

Luján. Your arrangements all sound excellent! But I heard a story once about a wedding, where all the family and guests had gathered to dance and eat. Everyone was there, the priest, the bridegroom, the best man, and the bridesmaids; the musicians were playing the psalms as if their lives depended on it, but the bride, you see, she hadn't given her consent—she said it had all been done without consulting her. So in front of everyone the priest asked her three times and each time she said no, and the wedding was called off.

Commander. Are you suggesting that I must wait for a peasant's consent?

Luján. Casilda is a stubborn girl.

Commander. Since pleas cannot melt her heart we resort to cunning and deception.

Luján. You may be lucky, but I think you may get more than you bargained for.

Enter a PAGE *and two* MUSICIANS.

Page. The musicians are here, my lord.

First Musician. Lisardo and Leonide! At Your Lordship's service from now till daybreak.

Commander. My friends, you are to share my secret thoughts! I will pay you well.

Second Musician. Your Lordship is always most generous.

Commander. Is that eleven striking?

Luján. One, two, three! That's all.

First Musician. No, you're wrong. It struck eight o'clock.

Commander. Oh my God, why doesn't it strike more?

Luján. I'll strike three more if you like. It is all the same to me.

Commander. The hour's chimes are sweeter than your voice, Luján! I will wait.

Luján. I will get you something to eat.

Commander. Eat! Damn you, did you say eat?

Luján. Well, drink then.

Commander. What would you have me drink? Wine to heat my brain? Fire gnaws my soul and he bids me drink!

Luján. Perhaps water would quench it?

Commander. Get out of my sight! Boy, where's my cloak?

Page. Here, sir.

Commander. What is that?

Page. The felt one, sir.

Commander. Everything conspires to mock me! Do you laugh, too? Beasts, brutes! Will you dress me in mourning?

Page. Shall I fetch a colored cloak?

Luján. Oh, do! He is a wise man who goes on a dark errand in a colored cape! Just the thing to identify you in a court of law.

Commander. You forget yourself, mule. Bring me my cloak!

Page. Here it is, my lord.

Commander. Love, I go where you lead me. Give your slave good fortune.

Luján. Shall I come with you?

Commander. Yes, since Leonardo does not appear. Tune your instruments. Perhaps their music may resolve the discord in my heart.   [*They go*

✓

A *street*

Enter PEDRO.

PEDRO. I give Heaven thanks for my gray mare! What a gift from God is a good horse; with it a man may travel many miles, fast as the wind. I am back in Ocaña sooner than I dreamed was possible. I have heard it said that honor is like a reed, which can be bent or broken by any wind that blows. I know now how true the saying is—how short a time it flourishes, how easily its leaves can be stripped off and the stem broken. But I will cut you down, weak reed, before you break! To be here so soon! I shall never regret a grain of the many feeds I have given that mare. Some men take pride in a trusty sword or a fine coat of mail, some rely on highborn friends or money, but this beast of mine is worth all of these! Three leagues in an hour! What a mare! Pedro returns to defend his honor— you are a match for the wind, my girl, and if they paint the wind with wings, I'll see you have a pair after tonight! Ah! This is Antón's house, and the next is mine—those walls, I fear, are already bowed in grief at my dishonor. Hallo there! Is anyone at home?

Antón [*within*]. Wife, do you hear? There's someone at the door.

Pedro. Is anybody there?

Antón. Who is knocking at this time of night?

Pedro. It is me, Antón.

Antón. I'm coming! Though I can't hear what you say. [*He opens the door.*] Who is it?

Pedro. Hush, Antón, my friend. It is Peribáñez.

Antón. Who?

Pedro. Peribáñez, who this day was cursed of God!

Antón. I kept my clothes on because I have to be up before dawn. Now I am glad I did! What can I do?

Pedro. My dear Antón, I must enter my house by way of yours. I think you know . . . that day in Toledo . . .

Antón. Yes, Pedro, I understand, but I guessed you did not want to talk about it. I can assure you that Casilda . . .

Pedro. There is no need to say it. . . . I know Casilda is an angel.

Antón. Be kind to her, Pedro!

Pedro. Let me be, Antón.

Antón. Come in then. I will let you through because I know you will find Casilda innocent.

Pedro. I shall always be in your debt, for making me doubly sure.

Antón. Where have you left your soldiers?

Pedro. They are encamped for the night. My lieutenant is in charge. I have returned alone, but for my cares, which God knows are weight enough!

1

A *street outside* PEDRO'*s house*

Enter the COMMANDER, LUJÁN, *and two* MUSICIANS.

COMMANDER. Begin here. The wind will carry the sound of your song.

Second Musician. Very well, sir.

Commander. At last my heart begins to resolve itself to harmony.

Musicians [*singing*].

> The bull threw me down at your door
> Lovely lady,
> But you would not wish me well.
> The bull at your wedding cast me at your feet
> And the villagers laughed at my plight.
> But you who mock me still,
> Lovely lady,
> Cruel lady, you would not wish me well.

INÉS *opens a window in* PEDRO'*s house.*

Inés. Psst, psst. Don Fadrique, sir!

Commander. Is it Inés?

Inés. It is.

Commander. I come before my time. Forgive me, but to wait until eleven would have meant death to me. I came to avoid that fate.

Inés. Is Leonardo with you?

Commander. He went with Peribáñez. Let me in, Inés,

and bring me to that precious jewel. Leonardo will soon return.

Inés. Will he be long?

Commander. No, not long. I sent him so that his presence might reassure Ibáñez of my good intent. It was necessary to take precautions with such a jealous husband.

Inés. Never fear. He will be so eager to be seen in Toledo as a captain, that he will be almost there already.

Commander. I expect he is asleep. May I come in?

Inés. Oh! Come in. I was only keeping you waiting in the hope that Leonardo might come.

Luján. May not Luján come in? [*To a Musician.*] That will be all, Lisardo. Farewell till daybreak.

First Musician. Heaven grant you good success.

The COMMANDER, LUJÁN, *and* INÉS *go in.*

Second Musician. Where shall we go?

First Musician. To bed.

Second Musician. She looked all right.

First Musician. Do not you breathe a word about this.

Second Musician. I must confess I envy him.   [*They go*

A room in PEDRO'*s house*

Enter PEDRO.

PEDRO. I have entered my own house like a thief in the night! I climbed over Antón's wall into the orchard and found the yard door open. I thought I would hide for a while in the barn, but I feared that the cock who roosts there would be alarmed and start to crow. There he was sleeping among the hens. "How can you sleep," I thought, "among so many, while I am awake in fear of one?" I do not sleep! I cannot guard one wife. I fear a cock with a red crest on his doublet! As I crossed the yard the doves cooed and nestled together in the dovecote, the very image of love and trust, and I said: "God curse any man, whoever it may be, that tries to disturb the peace of our home, or come between us." The geese have wakened, the oxen are lowing, and, in the cause of honor, even the little donkey tied to the manger is awake and uneasy for me. The animals sense the rope as it tightens to choke their master. Oh, I could weep with anger. . . . To think that this could happen . . . What if Casilda is asleep? What's

that, voices? I must hide behind these sacks. If it is the
Commander he must think me far away. [*He hides.*]

Enter Casilda *and* Inés.

Casilda. I tell you I heard someone!

Inés. And I say you are wrong.

Casilda. You were talking to a man.

Inés. Who, I?

Casilda. Yes, you.

Inés. You say you heard me?

Casilda. I know someone is there. If it is not a plot,
then it must be thieves.

Inés. Thieves! You frighten me.

Casilda. Shout, then.

Inés. No.

Casilda. Then I will.

Inés. No, Casilda. You will wake the whole neighbor-
hood without any reason.

Enter the Commander *and* Luján.

Commander. Casilda, my passion can be quelled no
longer. I am the Commander, your lord and master.

Casilda. Only Pedro is master in this house.

Commander. I come as your slave, although I am your
lord. Take pity on me. Otherwise I will say I found you
with this lackey here.

Casilda. Fearing the lightning, I shall not fear the
thunder. You, cousin! You have sold me.

Inés. Casilda, it is madness for you, a peasant, to let a
prince die for love. Your virtue is not worth his life. Besides, Pedro is in Toledo.

Casilda. Oh, hateful cousin, I little thought that you
would be his bawd.

Commander. Leave me.

Luján. Let us go. He will persuade her when we're not
here.

Casilda. I am the wife of a captain, and you are a knight.
Come a step nearer and I'll kick and bite and——

Commander. Be silent. . . .

Pedro *appears.*

Pedro. What holds my hand? My honor cries for vengeance. . . . [*He advances with his sword drawn.*] For-

give me, Commander, that I, a peasant, should seek revenge. Only blood can assuage my wounded honor now!
[PEDRO *wounds the* COMMANDER.]

Commander. Oh, I am dead. . . . Casilda. . . .
Mercy. . . .

Pedro. Do not fear, my love. Come with me.

Casilda. I cannot speak. . . . [PEDRO *and* CASILDA *go*

Commander. Lord, through your Holy Blood, have
mercy on me, for my sin has brought me to crave pardon
from a vassal.

He sinks down. Enter LEONARDO.

Leonardo. What is happening? Inés, where are you?
Are you hiding? Inés!

Commander. Whose voice is that? Who calls?

Leonardo. Inés! It is I!

Commander. Leonardo!

Leonardo. My lord? What has happened?

Commander. I am dying, Leonardo. Killed by a peasant!
I have the just reward for my offense.

Leonardo. Wounded, my lord? By whom?

Commander. Be silent! I want no brawling or vengeance
now. I am dying, Leonardo. I can only beg mercy for my
soul. Bear me to the chapel to make confession for my
sins. Forget revenge, I pardon Peribáñez.

Leonardo. What, a peasant? And I may not revenge?

Commander. He is no peasant now. Remember, I
knighted him to further my black intent. It is fitting that
my blood should stain his sword.

Leonardo. I will fetch help, my lord.

Commander. There is none now but God.

LEONARDO *helps the* COMMANDER *away.* LUJÁN *and* INÉS
enter running, followed by PEDRO.

Pedro. Both of you shall die!

Inés. Oh, I am dead already!

Luján. Unlucky Luján! Where can you hide?

Pedro. There is no escape. Your death is certain.

Luján. Why, master Captain?

Pedro. For a false harvester.

Inés. But why kill me?

Pedro. As a traitor!

[*They go, wounded, followed by* PEDRO

Luján. Oh, I am killed!
Inés. Casilda! Cousin!

Re-enter CASILDA *and* PEDRO.

Pedro. They fell in the doorway.
Casilda. It was a just punishment, Pedro.
Pedro. Will you come with me?
Casilda. I am yours wherever you go and whatever happens.
Pedro. The mare will carry us. We will be in Toledo by sunrise.
Casilda. I would come, even on foot.
Pedro. Distance is the best truce in any quarrel.
Casilda. God be with the Commander. His presumption killed him.   [*They go*

✓

A gallery in the castle at TOLEDO

Enter the KING, CONSTABLE, *and* GUARDS.

KING. We are pleased to see how gladly Castile has answered our just demand for men and money in our great campaign.
Constable. My liege, our people hate the Moorish tyrant.
King. It is our purpose to free Andalusia before winter comes to cover the fields with frost and freeze the land. Juan de Velasco shall prepare the great assembly of troops I plan shall gather on the plains of La Vega, so that the fame and glory of our knights may be noised abroad. On those green plains a golden river shall appear and there we shall build a new Toledo with diamond walls and colored pavilions. Then let the bold Moor in Granada tremble at our blood-red banners! Then shall his rejoicing turn to wailing and to grief. Here comes my Queen, my adored helpmate.

Enter the QUEEN *with her train.*

Queen. If you are discussing matters of importance, I will not stay, my lord.
King. Madam, your presence is always welcome to me. In matters of peace I have always heeded your advice, why should I not in war? Your counsel is precious to me. How is my son, the Prince?

Queen. He weeps to see you, my lord.

King. May God protect him. He is a divine mirror in which may be seen, rather than those present, those past.

Queen. Prince Juan is your son, my lord. That is recommendation enough.

King. And yours, my Queen. He is compounded of all virtues.

Queen. May heaven make him the very image of you. If he had no other blessing, that alone would be all I could desire.

King. I know your love for us both.

Queen. Had he fifteen more years to add unto his two, I know how gladly he would follow you in your campaign.

King. I would he could, to magnify the glory of Christ.

Enter GÓMEZ MANRIQUE.

King. What drum is that?

Gómez. The Companies from La Vera and Extremadura, my lord.

Constable. And from Guadalajara and Atieza also.

King. And Ocaña?

Gómez. They are detained, my lord.

King. How?

Gómez. The most recent comers say that a peasant has assassinated Don Fadrique.

King. Don Fadrique? The greatest soldier the Order of Saint James has ever known?

Queen. Is it true?

Gómez. It is, madam.

King. What could have caused such an outrage?

Gómez. Love and jealousy.

King. Was it deserved? Was it just?

Gómez. It was madness.

Queen. Jealousy, sir, is rarely sane.

King. Has the peasant been arrested?

Gómez. He fled with his wife.

King. It was an act of shame! To be received in Toledo with such news. Is this how Spain respects my laws? Give out a proclamation in the city, and in Madrid, Segovia, Talavera and Ocaña, that I will give a thousand ducats to the man who finds them, alive or dead. Go, and say also that none shall protect them or give them food, on pain of death!

Gómez. I go, my lord. [*He goes*

King. May heaven receive the soul of our great warrior.

Queen. Be sure they will soon be discovered, once your promised reward is known.

Enter a PAGE.

Page. Arceo is here, my lord. The standard is completed.

King. Let me see it.

ARCEO, *a secretary, enters with a red standard. On it are the arms of Castile with a hand above holding a sword, placed beneath Christ Crucified.*

Arceo. Here is the standard, my lord.

King. Show me. Yes, it is good. He is indeed the Captain of my Redemption.

Queen. What does the Latin mean?

King. It means: "Judge thy cause, O Lord."

Queen. They are fearful words.

King. And rightly so.

Queen. What is shown on the lower half?

King. The Castle and the Lion, and the hand above already deals chastisement.

Queen. And the letters?

King. My name.

Queen. In what form?

King. Henry the Just. A form I prefer to Henry III. That it may strike more fear among my enemies.

Enter GÓMEZ.

Gómez. Your proclamation has gone out, my lord. The city mourns.

Queen. The very stones should grieve.

King. Shall a peasant rise against the Cross of Saint James? How could it be?

Queen. Woe to him if he does not hide well.

King. I swear before God that I shall punish him and make him an example at which the world shall tremble.

Enter a PAGE.

Page. Here is a peasant, my liege, who would speak with you.

King. Bid him approach.

The King *and* Queen *sit.*

Constable. He may bring information.

Enter Pedro *and* Casilda.

Pedro. I kneel, great lord, your humblest subject.
King. Rise and speak.
Pedro. My lord, how can I begin? To look upon your face has robbed me of all words. But since I must, inspired by knowledge of your justice, I will speak. I am Peribáñez.
  King. Who?
Pedro. Pedro Ibáñez, the peasant of Ocaña.
King. The murderer? Seize him, guards. Take him to his death!
Pedro. Since you condemn me, will you not hear me speak? My liege, you are known as Henry the Just.
Queen. He says well. Hear him, my lord.
King. Speak then.
Pedro. My lord, although I am a peasant, I am of pure Spanish blood untainted by any drop of Jew or Moor. I was held in high esteem among my equals; six times I held the wand of office in our Guild and always had the casting vote in any decision. I married this woman you see here, also of true Spanish blood, though a peasant. A woman of pure virtue, despite envy's assault on her good name. Don Fadrique, our overlord and Commander of Ocaña, fell in love with her. Pretending to do me honor, he regaled my house with gifts of rich tapestries, decorated with noble crests and mottoes. He gave me two good mules, but not so good that they could draw my honor from the slough of my disgrace. At last, one night when I was away from Ocaña, he attempted to seduce my wife, but was forced to leave, his proud hopes dashed. I returned and learned of his attempt. I took down the cloths which bore his arms, fearing they might prove the cape which attracts the bull. Then one morning he summoned me and told me he had letters from Your Majesty saying he must send arms and men to take part in your campaign. He made me captain of a hundred men, and with this gallant company I left Ocaña. When night had fallen, knowing my honor was threatened, I mounted my mare and rode like the wind, back to Ocaña. I reached my house by ten

o'clock to find the doors open and my wife, her hair disheveled, like a lamb between the jaws of a ravening wolf. She cried out and I ran forward, drawing my sword, that sword I wore in your service, my lord, I little thought for so sad an action. I ran him through the heart and like a shepherd I snatched my lamb from his jaws. I came with her to Toledo and found that a thousand ducats were offered for me, dead or alive. Therefore I begged my Casilda to deliver me to justice. I ask you, sir, to grant her this mercy, that since she must be widowed of me, she shall not lose the reward.

King. My Queen, what is your opinion of this story?

Queen. I weep to hear him. That is all I can reply, but I think it is enough to prove that his was an act of valor, not a crime.

King. It is strange that one so humble should hold his honor so high. I swear before God it would be unjust to punish him. I grant him his life. But why should I grant it? It is his right! I would not lose such a valiant man, I will keep him as captain of that same company from Ocaña. He shall lead them in my campaign. Give his wife the reward that my promise may be kept. And last, Peribáñez, I give you leave to carry arms as a gentleman, for the better guard of your person.

Pedro. How rightly have you been called King Henry the Just.

Queen. To you, Casilda, I give four of my dresses, so that you may be dressed as befits the wife of a captain.

Pedro. My lords, how happy is he who marries a faithful wife. Thus ends the tragicomedy of Peribáñez and the Commander of Ocaña.

FUENTEOVEJUNA

(Fuenteovejuna)

CHARACTERS

KING FERNANDO OF ARAGON
QUEEN ISABEL OF CASTILE
RODRIGO TÉLLEZ GIRÓN, MASTER *of the Order of Calatrava*
FERNANDO GÓMEZ DE GUZMÁN, *Chief* COMMANDER *of the Order*
DON MANRIQUE
A JUDGE
ORTUÑO }
FLORES } *servants to the* COMMANDER

ESTEBAN }
ALONSO } *joint mayors of* FUENTEOVEJUNA

LAURENCIA }
PASCUALA } *peasant girls*
JACINTA }

JUAN ROJO }
FRONDOSO }
MENGO } *peasants*
BARRILDO }
LEONELO, *a Bachelor of Arts*
CIMBRANOS, *a soldier*
A BOY

ALDERMEN, PEASANTS, SOLDIERS, MUSICIANS

The action takes place in and around FUENTEOVEJUNA, and in ALMAGRO, MEDINA DEL CAMPO, CIUDAD REAL, TORO, and TORDESILLAS, in 1476.

FUENTEOVEJUNA

ACT ONE

1

A room in the house of the MASTER *of the Order of Calatrava in* ALMAGRO

Enter the COMMANDER *and his servants,* FLORES *and* ORTUÑO.

COMMANDER. Does he know that I am here?

Flores. He is informed, sir.

Ortuño. He grows a little more serious as his years increase. Time may make him a gentleman.

Commander. Indeed? And is he also informed that I am Fernando Gómez de Guzmán?

Flores. He is only a boy, sir.

Commander. Or if my name is nothing to him, is my title also nothing—Chief Commander of the Order?

Ortuño. The fault will lie with flattering counselors who have told him that he has no need of common courtesy, now that he is Master of the Order of Calatrava.

Commander. He will earn little love if he continues so. Courtesy is the key to men's good will, discourtesy the surest way to enmity.

Ortuño. Indeed, if an arrogant man could see how he is hated, even by those who flatter him, he would rather die than continue in his insolence.

Flores. Arrogance is the worst form of insult, and makes for bitter feeling. Discourtesy is folly between equals, and sheer tyranny from a superior. But do not take it ill, my lord. He is but a boy and has not yet learned how much he needs the love of those whom he commands.

Commander. The sword of knighthood which he received when the cross of Calatrava first adorned his breast should have sufficed to teach him courtesy.

59

Flores. You will soon discover if any has been speaking ill of you.

Ortuño. If you have any cause to doubt him, wait no longer, my lord.

Commander. I wish to see what sort of youth he is.

Enter the MASTER *of Calatrava, accompanied.*

Master. Pardon me, I beg you, by my life, Fernando Gómez de Guzmán. Only now have I been told of your presence in the town.

Commander. I had good cause to blame you, since faith in your love and knowledge of your virtuous upbringing had led me to expect a fairer welcome, our ranks being as they are: you the Master of Calatrava, I your Commander —and your servant.

Master. I was ignorant, Fernando, of your most welcome arrival, but now I bid you welcome with great joy.

Commander. You do well to honor me, for on your behalf I have risked much, disputed much, before his Holiness the Pope was finally persuaded to overlook your age.

Master. It is true. And by the holy signs we two bear upon our breasts, I swear I will repay you with respect and honor you as a father.

Commander. I am content.

Master. What news of the war?

Commander. Attend closely, my lord, and you will learn soon enough where your duty lies.

Master. Proceed, and I will hear you.

Commander. Eight years ago, my lord, your noble father raised you to great estate, resigning into your young hands the Masterhood of our ancient Order. As a surety it was decreed by papal bull that your uncle, Don Juan Pacheco, Grand Master of Santiago, should act as your adviser, which decree was sworn to by kings and knights commander. Now that Don Juan Pacheco is dead, the responsibility is yours alone, and I have come to urge you to win fame and honor in this present quarrel between Portugal and the united strength of Aragon and Castile. You know well, Rodrigo, that since the death of Enrique IV your kindred have chosen to obey as vassals King Alfonso of Portugal, who, since his marriage to Juana, Enrique's daughter, lays rightful claim to her inheritance—the king-

dom of Castile. Fernando, Aragon's great King, makes a
similar claim through his wife, Isabel of Castile. But in the
eyes of your noble kindred, his claim is not so clear as that
of Alfonso, King of Portugal. Ties of blood, my lord, demand that you should aid Alfonso in this strife. And so I
have come to counsel you to gather together the knights
of Calatrava in Almagro, and to take by storm Ciudad
Real, which stands astride the frontier of Andalusia and
Castile and commands them both. Little force will be
needed, for there will only be a few knights and men from
the surrounding villages to uphold the cause of Isabel and
Fernando in Ciudad Real. Although you are only a child,
Rodrigo, you would do well to surprise those who say that
the cross you bear is too grave a weight for your weak
shoulders. Consider the Counts of Urueña from whom you
are descended and let the laurels they won urge you to
equal fame. Remember the lords of Villena, and all the
other noble captains, almost too numerous for the wings
of fame to bear them. Draw that white blade, which you
shall dye in battle as deep a crimson as the cross you wear.
Rightful Master of the Cross of Calatrava, both must be
the color of blood! And then, Rodrigo Téllez Girón, your
youth and valor will truly crown the fame of your immortal ancestors.

Master. Fernando Gómez, know at once that in this I
will uphold the cause of my family and Portugal, for I see
that so to do is right. And if my first step should be to
take Ciudad Real, then you shall see me strike its city
walls like a bolt from heaven. Let not my people think,
or those unknown to me, that because my uncle is dead,
my young spirit died with him. I will draw my white
sword and its brightness shall be bathed in blood till it is
the color of this cross. Where is your lodging? Have you
soldiers with you?

Commander. Few, but those my faithful servants. If you
will accept their services, my lord, they will fight like lions.
In Fuenteovejuna there are only humble folk, not trained,
though, for war, but skilled in labor in the fields.

Master. And that is where you live?

Commander. It is. I chose, from all my lands, a house
to suit me in these changing times. Call to your aid every
man you have, my lord, let not a vassal remain.

Master. This day you shall see me ride, Fernando, with my lance couched ready for action in the field.

✦

The square in FUENTEOVEJUNA

Enter PASCUALA *and* LAURENCIA.

LAURENCIA. I pray God he never comes back!

Pascuala. And yet I thought you looked just a little disappointed when I told you the news that he was gone.

Laurencia. I hope Fuenteovejuna never sets eyes on him again.

Pascuala. I have seen many girls just as proud, just as determined, as you, some even more so. But when it came to it—their hearts were as soft as butter.

Laurencia. I will no more budge than that holm oak.

Pascuala. How can you be so sure? Nobody can safely say "I will never do a certain thing."

Laurencia. Well, I do say it. And I mean it, Pascuala. Though you and the whole world contradict me! Say I were to fall in love with Fernando Gómez de Guzmán, what good would it do me? Would he marry me?

Pascuala. No.

Laurencia. Then there is your answer. I will have nothing to do with him. How many girls have I seen in this village put their trust in the Commander, only to find out how wrong and stupid they were!

Pascuala. I think it will be a miracle if you escape.

Laurencia. He has been following me for a month already, and not a glimmer of hope have I given him. And neither shall I. That Flores, his pander, and that other scoundrel, Ortuño, showed me a jacket, a sash, and a bonnet, and they brought me such messages from their master, Fernando, that I must say that at the time they scared me. But whatever those court caterpillars say will not change my mind.

Pascuala. Where did they talk to you?

Laurencia. Down by the stream, almost a week ago.

Pascuala. I am afraid they will deceive you in the end, Laurencia.

Laurencia. What, me?

Pascuala. Yes, you, Laurencia. Do you think I meant the priest?

Laurencia. The Commander may think I am just a spring chicken, but he will find me tough meat for his table. I do not want his so-called "love," Pascuala. I had rather have a sizzling rasher of bacon for breakfast, with a slice of my own baked bread, and a sly glass of wine from mother's jar. I would sooner watch a lump of veal bobbing about among the cabbage and bubbling its foamy midday music. Or arrange a tasty marriage between an onion and a slice of ham when I come home hungry. Or pass the time while supper cooks with a bunch of grapes from my own vineyard—may God keep the hail away! And when at last the supper is ready, it is a tasty fry of pork and peppers and spice all sizzling in olive oil. Then I go to bed content and say my prayers, and fall asleep when I reach "lead us not into temptation." For all their wiles and tricks, their so-called love serves no other purpose than to get us to bed with pleasure, to wake in the morning with disgust.

Pascuala. You are right, Laurencia. That is as long as their love lasts. They are no more grateful than the sparrows that flutter around your door in winter when all the fields are frozen, and twitter coaxingly "Sweety-heart, sweety-heart," and coyly accept the crumbs you give them. As soon as the cold weather is past and the flowers come out in the fields, and they see better food to be got elsewhere, they forget the "sweety-heart," and mock you from the roof with "Idiot, idiot!" Men are just the same. When they need us, we are their life, their being, their soul, their everything. But when their lust is spent, they behave worse than the sparrows and we are no longer "Sweety-hearts" or even "idiots," but drabs and whores!

Laurencia. You cannot trust one of them.

Pascuala. Not one, Laurencia.

Enter MENGO, BARRILDO, *and* FRONDOSO.

Frondoso. Barrildo! Why persist? You will not persuade him.

Barrildo. Ah, but here I see a judge who will settle the matter fairly.

Mengo. Agreed. But before she makes her judgment you must both promise to honor the wagers that you made, should she decide the matter in my favor.

Barrildo. Right. We agree. But if you lose, what will you give?

Mengo. I will give my fiddle. It is worth a lot of money, and I value it even higher than its worth.

Barrildo. Very well, I am satisfied.

Frondoso. Come then, let us approach them. God keep you, lovely ladies.

Laurencia. Did you call us ladies, Frondoso?

Frondoso. I was merely following the fashion. Nowadays the bachelor of arts is called professor, the blind man is said to be myopic, or, if you squint, you have a slight cast in one eye. A man with a wooden leg is a trifle lame, and a careless spendthrift a good chap. An ignorant ass is said to be the silent type, a braggart is known as soldierly. A large mouth is called generous, and a beady eye, shrewd. The quibbler is said to be punctilious, and the gossip, a wit. A chatterbox is called intelligent, and a loud-mouthed bully, brave. The coward is a quiet sort, the pusher, eccentric. A bore is companionable, and a madman easygoing. The grumbler is grave, a bald head is a noble brow, foolishness passes for wit, and large feet are firm foundations. One with the pox has a slight chill, an arrogant man is reserved, a wangler has a quick brain, and a hunchback is the learned type. I might go on forever, but I think I have said enough for you to see that I go no further than the fashion, when I address you as ladies.

Laurencia. That may be the courtesy used in the city, Frondoso, but I am more familiar with the sound of a less flattering vocabulary.

Frondoso. How does that go? Give us a sample of it.

Laurencia. It is quite the opposite of yours. For here a grave man is a bore, one who tells the truth is rude, a serious man, melancholy, and he who justly reprehends does so out of spite. Anyone who dares to give advice is a busybody, and if you are generous, you are an interfering nuisance. If you are just, you are called cruel, if merciful, then you are weak. One who is constant is called boorish, the polite man is a flatterer, one who gives alms, a hypocrite, and a true Christian is only doing it in order to get on. Hard-won happiness is called luck, truth is wild speaking; patience, cowardice; misfortune, proof of evil-doing. A virtuous woman is a fool, and a beautiful one is a whore,

however chaste she may be. And an honorable woman . . .
But that is enough. I have answered you.

Mengo. You are the very devil.

Laurencia. There, what did I tell you!

Mengo. I'll bet when you were christened, the priest
used something stronger than water.

Laurencia. I thought I heard you arguing. What was the
dispute?

Frondoso. Oh, yes, Laurencia, hear it, please.

Laurencia. Tell me then.

Frondoso. I trust your understanding completely.

Laurencia. I hope I can repay your trust. What was the
argument?

Frondoso. Barrildo and I were against Mengo.

Laurencia. And what does Mengo say?

Barrildo. He denies a known fact, which is certain and
undeniable.

Mengo. I deny it because I know I am right.

Laurencia. But what does he deny?

Barrildo. That there is such a thing as love.

Laurencia. I should have said that we could not do
without it.

Barrildo. We could not do without it. Exactly. The
world could not go on.

Mengo. I do not know how to philosophize. As for reading, I only wish I could. But if, as I hear, the elements
live eternally by discord, and if our bodies receive from
them all the sustenance by which they live: choler, melancholy, phlegm and blood, then there you are. That proves
it.

Barrildo. The world both here and yonder is all harmony, Mengo, not discord. And harmony is pure love, for
love is concord.

Mengo. I do not deny that there is such a thing as self-
love. I know the value of that. It governs and balances all
things we see, besides seeking to preserve them. I have
never denied that. . . . It defends things as they are—
the status quo. My hand will defend my face from the
blow that comes toward it, or my feet will protect my
body by running away from any danger that threatens it.
My eyelids will close at once to guard my eyes. But that is
only natural love—self-love.

Pascuala. Then what is the argument?

Mengo. That no one has any love other than for his
own person.

Pascuala. Forgive me, Mengo, but you lie. Can you deny
the power which makes a man love a woman, or an animal
its mate?

Mengo. That is still only self-love, I say. What is this
love you talk about?

Laurencia. It is a desire for what is beautiful.

Mengo. And what does it desire the beautiful for?

Laurencia. To enjoy it.

Mengo. There you are. Just as I thought: is not the enjoyment simply selfish?

Laurencia. It is.

Mengo. Then does not love seek the thing which will
give it pleasure out of sheer self-interest?

Laurencia. That is true.

Mengo. That proves my argument. There is no love
other than that which says: "I want a thing, and I want
it for myself alone, to give me pleasure."

Barrildo. I remember the priest once saying in a sermon
something about a man called Plato. He was supposed to
know all about love, and he only loved the soul and the
virtue in things.

Pascuala. Now you are talking right above our heads.
That is what the learned professors in schools and acad-
emies spend their hours boiling down and sorting out.

Laurencia. Pascuala is right. There is nothing for us in
this debate but frayed nerves and ragged tempers, so stop
arguing and give thanks to Heaven, Mengo, that it has
made you free from love.

Mengo. Do you love, Laurencia?

Laurencia. Yes—my honor.

Frondoso. May your hard heart be punished with the
pangs of jealousy.

Barrildo. Who is the winner of our argument?

Pascuala. You must take your problem elsewhere. Let
the sacristan or the priest resolve it for you. Laurencia says
she is not in love, and I have too little experience to tell
either way. So how can we give a judgment?

Frondoso. Well. That has put us in our place.

Enter FLORES.

Flores. God be with you.

Frondoso. Here comes one of the Commander's servants.

Laurencia. His bird of prey. Where do you come from, my friend?

Flores. From battle. Can you not see from my dress?

Laurencia. Has Don Fernando returned as well?

Flores. The battle is over, though not without costing us both lives and blood.

Frondoso. What happened up there?

Flores. Who can tell you better than I, whose eyes were witness to it all? To storm the city of Ciudad Real, our gallant Master of Calatrava, young Rodrigo, called to arms two thousand proud yeomen from among his vassals, besides three hundred mounted knights, both secular and clerical—for the red cross of Calatrava obliges all who bear it to respond to the call to arms, even though they be of holy orders—but only to war against the impious Moors, you understand. The gallant youth rode out, a figure of dazzling elegance and pride. The green surcoat he wore was bordered with golden ciphers and at the elbow, where the sleeve parted, the silver bracelets of his armor shone, linked with frogs cunningly wrought in gold. A dapple-gray charger bore him, a noble creature, born and bred on the banks of the Guadalquivir, that had drunk its clear waters and cropped its fertile pastures. Tooled leather strips bound his tail, his mane was adorned with bows of white ribbon which glittered in the sun like snowflakes, as if reflecting the brightness of those upon his dappled skin, where they seemed banked to greater depth in smooth, gleaming drifts on flank and shoulder. Your own Commander, Fernando Gómez, rode beside him, his mount a stallion the color of rich honey, shading to black, with a splash of brilliant white upon its nose. Over a coat of mail in the Turkish style he wore a brilliant breastplate and backplate, both edged with a bright orange border, trimmed with pearls set in gold. The helm, crowned with white plumes, seemed as a ripe orange that had spilled forth a spray of snowy blossoms. About his arm was a red and white garter couching a lance that seemed a whole ash tree, such that the fear of him might reach into Granada itself, and strike terror into every Moor that breathes there. The city rose to arms as they approached the walls and their spokesman declared boldly that they would never desert the royal crown of Fernando and Isabel, and

that they were ready to defend their city and their royal
masters. Battle was joined, but at length, after mighty
resistance, the Master forced his way in—as victor. He
ordered all rebels and any who had dared to insult his
honor to be beheaded, while those of vulgar blood were
to be publicly whipped with gags in their mouths. Now
he is so feared and so admired in Ciudad Real that all who
witnessed the youth perform such deeds in fighting, win-
ning, and chastising believe that when he grows to ma-
turity he will be the scourge of the African race, and ex-
tinguish every blue crescent moon that shines before his
scarlet cross. What is more, he showed such liberality to
the Commander, and to all who aided him in this enterprise, that the sack of the city looked like the sack of his
own fortune, such generous gifts did he give. But I hear
music! They are coming! Receive them joyfully, for no
victor's laurel is so welcome to the returning hero as the
good will of those he left at home.

Enter the COMMANDER, ORTUÑO, MUSICIANS, JUAN ROJO,
ESTEBAN, *and* ALONSO.

Musicians [*singing*].
Welcome the Commander,
Returned from conquering lands and killing men.
Welcome the Commander!
In him great Alexander lives again.
In Ciudad Real, he conquered and showed his might,
But now he returns in peace, a gentle, courteous knight.
He comes to Fuenteovejuna, his banners flying.
Long live our brave Commander,
May his fame be undying.
Commander. Fuenteovejuna, I give you thanks for the
loving welcome you have given me.
Alonso. Sir, we can only show the meanest tithe of what
we feel, for however great our love and loyalty, yet you
merit more.
Esteban. Fuenteovejuna and its municipal councilors,
whom you honor today, sir, with your presence, beg you to
accept this small token of loyalty. We offer it to you not
without some shame, sir, for these carts are loaded more
with our good will than with rich gifts. First there are two
baskets of our potters' best earthenware crocks, then in this

cart a flock of geese, all sticking out their heads to praise
your martial valor. Ten whole salted hogs, fine prime
beasts every one, not to mention other various trifles, such
as these sides of hung beef. But best among them, or so
we think, are the hides of these ten hogs, which to us are
of more worth than amber-scented gloves. One hundred
pairs of capons and hens, which have left their widowed
cocks in all the villages you can see around. We bring no
arms or horses, or trappings adorned with gold—unless
you consider the love of your vassals golden—but there is
one further thing, which in truth seems to me worthy of
mention: twelve skins of wine, such that if it should
reinforce your men, they would hold a wall for you even
in January weather and feel safer than with arms of steel,
and think it better than armor. For wine, they say, makes
swords flash brighter and more valiantly. I will not trouble
you to tell of the cheeses and other trifles, but let these
gifts speak to you in their own voices of the good will
which your vassals have for you, and may they bring good
cheer to you and to your household.

Commander. I am most grateful to the people and
councilors of Fuenteovejuna. May you go in peace.

Alonso. And may you, sir, have good rest, knowing that
you are most welcome back to us, and I would the cattail
and the sedge around your threshold were laden with orient
pearls, for so would they be if it lay within our power to
grant you the impossible.

Commander. I do believe you, good people. May God
go with you.

Esteban. Now singers! Give us the chorus once again!

Musicians [*singing*].

   Welcome the Commander,

    Returned from conquering lands and killing men.

          [*The* PEASANTS *and* MUSICIANS *go*

Commander. You there! Stay!

Laurencia. Is he speaking to you, Pascuala?

Pascuala. To me? Not likely. You know whom he means,
as well as I do.

Laurencia. Do you address me, my lord?

Commander. You, proud virgin, and the other girl: are
you not my vassals?

Pascuala. Yes, sir. Yours to command.

Laurencia. Within reason.

Commander. Come, do not be afraid to pass my gates. You will not be alone, my men are there.

Laurencia. If the councilors go in—and one of them is my father—then we will enter. If not . . .

Commander. Flores . . .

Flores. Sir . . .

Commander. You observe how they refuse to obey my will?

Flores. Go in.

Laurencia. Let go of us.

Flores. Go in.

Pascuala. Just so that you may lock the door on us?

Flores. Go in. He desires only to show you the spoils he has brought from the wars.

Commander. When they enter, Flores, see that the gates are closed.   [*Exit the* COMMANDER

Laurencia. Flores, let us go.

Ortuño. Are these presents, like all the other stuff?

Pascuala. How dare you! Get out of our way. . . .

Flores. Mind what you say! You are plucky little chicks. . . .

Laurencia. Has not your master received enough flesh for one day?

Ortuño. But yours is the kind he wants.

Laurencia. May it choke him.

The two girls break clear and run away.

Flores. Now what are we to do? He will hardly be pleased to hear that they escaped. There will be trouble for us.

Ortuño. You must expect that when you enter a great man's service. If you wish to prosper, you have to learn to bear his displeasure with patience. If it irks you, then my advice is, leave his service quickly.   [*They go*

A room in the palace of FERNANDO *and* ISABEL
in MEDINA DEL CAMPO

Enter the KING, QUEEN, DON MANRIQUE, *and* COURTIERS.

ISABEL. My opinion, sir, is that we should proceed swiftly and diligently, for Alfonso is known to be preparing his army even now, and holds a strong position. If we do not act at once, it may be too late.

King. We can rely on help from Navarre and from Aragon, and, given time, I hope to have the Castilian forces fully reorganized, so that together we may rout the Portuguese.

Isabel. Indeed, concerted action is the key to this.

Manrique. Sir, there are two aldermen from Ciudad Real without. They await your pleasure. Shall they be admitted?

King. Let them come in.

First Alderman. Most Catholic King Fernando, sent from Aragon by Heaven to be the strength and the protector of Castile: we present ourselves humbly in the name of Ciudad Real to crave your royal protection. We hold ourselves most fortunate in being your subjects, but adverse fate has now conspired to snatch that honor from us. Don Rodrigo Téllez Girón, the Master of Calatrava, is now, despite his youth, a knight renowned throughout the land for his reckless courage in battle. He, with intent to increase his noble estate, laid siege to our city. The citizens rose to arms and offered such a brave resistance that soon our streets flowed with streams of blood from the dead and wounded. Finally he gained possession of the town. And yet he would not have done so, had not Fernando Gómez assisted, advised, and controlled the young man's actions. Now he commands our city, and we, your rightful vassals, must become his, unless immediate aid is given us.

King. Where is Fernando Gómez now?

First Alderman. In Fuenteovejuna, I believe, sir, where he enjoys the title of overlord. He has a house and estates there. It is rumored that he keeps the citizens of that place far from contented with his tyranny.

King. Is there a captain among you?

Second Alderman. None, sir. Not a single nobleman escaped. All were captured, wounded, or killed.

Isabel. Ciudad Real must be retaken without delay, or the bold attacker will grow in strength and pride. Besides, sir, Portugal may see this as his chance to enter our kingdom without check or hindrance, using this new breach in Extremadura as the means to invade us.

King. Don Manrique, take two companies at once. Give the youth no respite until he has paid for his foolhardy venture. With you we shall send the Count of Cabra,

who has a world-wide reputation as a soldier. That is the
most I can spare you at this time.

Manrique. I shall obey your wise command with willing
heart. I will put an end to this boy's bold excesses if
my life is spared to me.

Isabel. With you, Manrique, leading our undertaking,
we are already sure of victory.   [*They go*

1

The countryside near FUENTEOVEJUNA

FRONDOSO *and* LAURENCIA *enter.*

LAURENCIA. Frondoso! Now do you see what lengths you
drive me to? I have had to leave the washing only half
wrung out down by the stream simply because the way
you were looking at me down there was enough to set
the whole village gossiping—not that they aren't already.
Oh, I admit I look at you too! Everybody has noticed
how smartly you dress—they all say you are quite the
most handsome, lively, and amusing boy in the village,
and as far as Fuenteovejuna is concerned, we are as good
as married already. So no wonder I had to leave the washing. You should be ashamed. . . . They are counting the
days till Juan Chamorro, the sacristan, will stop playing
his bassoon for a few minutes to write our marriage lines
in the vestry. They would be occupying their time more
usefully filling their barns with shining grain and their
jars with must. Why cannot they stop gossiping? But let
them do as they will. Nothing they say can worry me or
make me lose my sleep, since I know that it is quite
untrue.

Frondoso. My lovely Laurencia; why are you so cold
toward me? Every time I try to see you or to hear you
speak I feel as if I am taking my life in my hands. You
never reward me with one word of hope, and yet you
know that my desire and my intention is to be your
husband.

Laurencia. What should I do?

Frondoso. Laurencia, how can you see me in such agony,
not eating, not drinking, not sleeping, for thinking of
you, and still have no pity on me? How can your angel's
face be so harsh toward me? I mean it, Laurencia, my love
will drive me mad.

Laurencia. Then you had best try the apothecary. He might give you a remedy for madness.

Frondoso. You are the only apothecary that can cure me, and the remedy would be the two of us cooing happily together. . . .

Laurencia. Beak to beak?

Frondoso. After the Church has given us its blessing. . . .

Laurencia. Then tell my uncle, Juan Rojo. For though I do not say I am in love with you, yet who knows, I might. . . .

Frondoso. You might . . . ! Someone is coming.

Laurencia. It is the Commander. Hide there in those bushes.

Frondoso. Hide?

Laurencia. Yes, over there!

Enter the COMMANDER.

Commander. A happy stroke of fortune! I was hunting deer, but did not think to find such dear game as this!

Laurencia. I was resting here a moment, but with your leave, sir, I must now return to the stream and finish wringing out the clothes.

Commander. Sweet Laurencia, such rude behavior mingles strangely with the fair graces that Heaven has bestowed on you. Your actions should suit your looks, otherwise you will seem a monster of nature. But, Laurencia, if on other occasions you have fled from my gentle wooing, this time there is no need, for the countryside is a discreet and silent friend that will not carry tales. Why should you alone be so proud and haughty? Who are you that you can afford to scorn your master? Sebastiana Redondo was not so prim, and she was a married woman, neither was Martín del Pozo's wife, after only two days of marriage.

Laurencia. That may be, sir, but if they did give way to you, it was only because many other men had enjoyed their favors first. God be with you, sir, and may you catch your quarry, the deer which you were hunting. But for the cross you wear on your breast, I should take you for the Devil, dogging my footsteps.

Commander. Your manner of speech offends me, but I need no bow to bring this quarry down. I will overcome your peasant prudery barehanded. [*He puts down his cross-bow.*]

Laurencia. Have you lost your mind?

FRONDOSO *enters and takes up the* COMMANDER's *bow*

Frondoso. I have his bow! Oh, God, let me not have cause to use it.

Commander. Why resist? No one can hear your cries.

Laurencia. Oh, Heaven help me.

Commander. We are alone.

Frondoso. Noble Commander, leave the girl, or by my faith, your breast shall be the target for the arrows of my offended anger, though I confess I fear the cross you wear.

Commander. Peasant dog!

Frondoso. A peasant, but I see no dog. Now, Laurencia, run.

Laurencia. Frondoso, take care!

Frondoso. Run, quickly! [*She goes*

Commander. My sword! What madness to be parted from one's sword! Yet I left it behind for fear that it might frighten her.

Frondoso. Now, sir, I have only to release this trigger and you die.

Commander. She has gone now. Put down that bow, traitor.

Frondoso. So that you can kill me with it? Love is deaf and hears no reason. Love brooks no overlord.

Commander. What, shall a knight of Calatrava turn his back before a peasant? Shoot, peasant, shoot, and then beware, for I break the laws of knighthood to dally with you.

Frondoso. No. I will not shoot. A peasant cannot kill his overlord. But for the sake of my own life I will keep the bow.

Commander. This peasant shall pay dearly for insulting me. By Heaven, I will have vengeance!

ACT TWO

✦

The village square in FUENTEOVEJUNA

Enter ESTEBAN *and another* ALDERMAN.

ESTEBAN. I consider it wisest that we should draw no more on the stocks in the public granary. It looks like being a bad harvest. We should reserve what we have, even if it proves an unpopular measure.

Alderman. You are in the right. Caution has always been my watchword throughout many years of local government.

Esteban. Let us make an appeal to Fernando Gómez. We do not want any of those astrologers who know nothing of the future or anything else coming here, making their long speeches about things that are nobody's business but God's. They will discourse for hours about the theological implications concerning what has happened and what will happen, but if you ask any of them a straightforward question about what is happening now, then they do not know the first thing about it. You would think they keep the weather locked up in their top attics to let it out as they think fit. How do they know what goes on in heaven? And who gives them the right to scare us telling us about it? They tell us when and how to sow, where to put the wheat, where the cucumbers, and where the mustard. They foretell that a cow is going to die, and when it doesn't they tell you it happened in Transylvania. Or they tell you that wine will be short, but that there will be a glut of beer in certain parts of Germany. The cherry crop will be frozen in Gascony, and there will be a lot of tigers in Hircania. All of which is no help at all, and whatever we do, the year still ends in December.

Enter BARRILDO *and* LEONELO, *a bachelor of arts.*

Leonelo. Ah, we are not the first comers; I see the gossip's corner is already occupied.

Barrildo. How did you enjoy your time in Salamanca?

Leonelo. Oh, that is a long story.

Barrildo. You must be a real Bártolo.

Leonelo. No, I am not even the barber. But my faculty has afforded me many moments of amusement.

Barrildo. You must have studied very hard.

Leonelo. I managed to learn one or two of the more important notions.

Barrildo. Now they are printing so many books, everyone you meet imagines himself a sage.

Leonelo. And yet I should say that there is more ignorance in the world than ever before. For already an excess of printed matter has come from the presses, which, contrary to the original intentions of spreading knowledge, has only led to confusion, and those who read most become most befuddled with this mass of print. I do not deny that the invention of printing has brought to light the works of many writers whose works might otherwise have gone unnoticed save by a discerning minority, nor do I deny that it has great uses as a means of preserving works for posterity. It was invented, as I am sure you are aware, by a famous German from Mainz, called Gutenberg, whose name will long be remembered for this service. And yet many who passed for sages before have quickly lost their reputations now that their works have appeared in print. Besides, there are those who publish their own inanities under the name of some respected author and so damage his reputation in order to fill their own pockets, or else to make him they envy appear foolish in the eyes of the world.

Barrildo. I do not agree, Leonelo.

Leonelo. It has often been said that the ignoramus resents the man of knowledge.

Barrildo. But printing is important. It is a great step forward.

Leonelo. The writers of the past managed for centuries without it. Can you name one man of genius, a Saint Jerome or Saint Augustine, whom printing has given to the world?

Barrildo. Come, there is no need to get overheated about it. Let us sit down.

Enter JUAN ROJO *and another peasant.*

Juan Rojo. These days you need four farms to make up a dowry, and still they grumble and say it is not enough.

That is how the fashion goes, and a ridiculous fashion it is too. I say——

Peasant. What news of the Commander? If one dare ask that question.

Juan Rojo. What, after the way he treated Laurencia! . . .

Peasant. I'd be glad to see him hanged for a whoremaster and a tyrant. Hanged from that tree, I say.

Enter the COMMANDER, ORTUÑO, *and* FLORES.

Commander. God keep you all, my good people.

Alderman. Sir!

Commander. Remain seated, all of you.

Esteban. Sir, pray you be seated, we are well content to stand.

Commander. I say be seated.

Esteban. It becomes honorable men to give honor where it is due. And only those who have honor can give it.

Commander. Sit down. I wish to talk with you.

Esteban. Did you see the greyhound we sent, sir?

Commander. Yes, Alderman, my servants were delighted with its speed.

Esteban. It is a fine animal. It could outpace a prisoner on the run or the confessions of a coward under torture.

Commander. However, at the moment I am more interested in a certain young rabbit which I have pursued many times in vain. That would be an even more welcome gift.

Esteban. Where is it to be found, sir?

Commander. I think you know better than I where your daughter is to be found.

Esteban. My daughter!

Commander. Your daughter.

Esteban. Sir, is her rank such that she is worthy to be wooed by you?

Commander. She has been troubling me of late. I could name a woman—what is more, a woman of good standing, the wife of one present in this square—who was not above meeting me. She obeyed my wishes at once.

Esteban. Then she did wrong, and you, sir, do not do well to speak of it so freely.

Commander. What an eloquent peasant we have here.

Flores, see that he is presented with a copy of Aristotle. The *Politics* would amuse him, I think.

Esteban. Sir, we of this village would live honorably under your rule. There are people of worth among us, though of peasant blood.

Leonelo. Did you ever hear such brazen speech!

Commander. What, have I said something to offend you, Alderman?

Alderman. You have spoken unjustly, sir. It is not right that you should deprive us of our honor by speaking in such terms.

Commander. A peasant rebukes me, Flores. In the name of honor too. You will soon aspire to join the brotherhood of Calatrava, no doubt?

Alderman. There may be some that proudly boast the cross of knighthood, whose blood is not so pure.

Commander. Whose blood do I sully by joining mine with yours?

Alderman. Evil desires make any blood unclean.

Commander. I honor your wives by giving a thought to them.

Esteban. Your speech dishonors us and you, sir. We cannot believe you mean it.

Commander. Oh, this tedious peasant logic! Give me the city life where no one seeks to hinder the pleasures of a man of quality! There husbands are flattered when their wives receive attentive visitors.

Esteban. There is still God's justice, even in cities, my lord, and, so I understand, an earthly one too, which does not wait on Heaven before it takes revenge. You will not thus persuade us to live without honor or respect.

Commander. Go! Leave this place.

Esteban. Do you wish me to repeat what has passed between us?

Commander. Go, I say! Leave the square empty. Not one of you remain.

Esteban. We go.

Commander. Peasant insolence!

Flores. Sir, take care what you do.

Commander. These peasants have grown truculent in my absence! They will soon be forming factions.

Ortuño. Have a little patience, sir.

Commander. I marvel I have shown so much! Now,

each of you, off to your own home directly. I will have
none forming groups on the way, do you hear me?

Leonelo. Just Heaven, will you let this pass?

Esteban. I shall take my way home, my friends.

[*The peasants go*

Commander. Ortuño, what say you to these peasant
manners?

Ortuño. Sir, your own thoughts are clear, you have no
wish to hear our opinion any more than theirs.

Commander. Do they seek to make themselves my
equals?

Flores. That is not their intention, sir, I am certain.

Commander. And is the peasant that stole the bow to
go unpunished? A free man?

Flores. Last night I saw him outside Laurencia's door.
At least, I thought that it was he. I laid him out with a
blow behind the ear, only to find it was someone else
who looked like him.

Commander. And where is this Frondoso now?

Flores. They say he is about the village still.

Commander. What, does the man who threatened me
with death still dare to walk my lands?

Flores. Yes, like an unwary bird that does not heed the
snare, or an innocent fish swimming after the baited hook.

Commander. Córdoba and Granada tremble at the sight
of my sword, and now a village lout aims my own bow at
my heart! I think the world is coming to an end, Flores.

Flores. Such is the power of love.

Ortuño. You owe him a little gratitude, sir. He did not
kill you.

Commander. Ortuño, I have disguised my feeling beyond
all bearing. Had I given my anger its head, I tell you that
within two hours this whole village would have felt the
edge of my sword. Yet let it be. My revenge shall wait
until its time is ripe. What news of Pascuala?

Flores. She replies that she is already betrothed.

Commander. And desires credit until then? . . .

Flores. Never fear, sir, she will give you payment in
full.

Commander. And what of Olalla?

Ortuño. She sent back a witty answer, sir.

Commander. She is a lively girl. What did she say?

Ortuño. That her husband is very jealous of your attentions, but says that once his back is turned, you may enter as before.

Commander. Good news indeed. But her husband is too watchful.

Ortuño. Watchful, sir, and quick to anger.

Commander. And Inés?

Flores. Which Inés?

Commander. Inés de Antón.

Flores. She is ready when you are. I spoke to her in her back yard. You may enter there when you will.

Commander. Oh, these easy women. I love them well and pay them ill. If only they valued themselves at their real worth, Flores!

Flores. When a man is never put in doubt, the delight he gains means nothing to him. A quick surrender denies the exquisite anticipation of pleasure. But has not the philosopher said that there are also those women who as naturally desire a man as form desires its matter? And that it should be so is not surprising, for——

Commander. A man crazed with love is ever delighted to be easily and instantly rewarded, but then as easily and instantly he forgets the object of his desire. Even the most generous man is quick to forget that which cost him little.

Enter CIMBRANOS, *a soldier.*

Cimbranos. Is the Commander here?

Ortuño. Can you not see you are in his presence?

Cimbranos. Oh, gallant Fernando Gómez! Exchange, I beg you, that green cap for a helmet of shining silver, your soft coat for glistening armor. Don Rodrigo calls for aid! He is besieged in Ciudad Real by the armies of Queen Isabel, led by the Master of Santiago and the Count of Cabra. That which was bought with so much blood may soon be lost to us. The light from the beacons on the high battlements of the city reveals the troops of Castile and of León massed together against us, strong as castles, fierce as lions, and reinforced by solid ranks of sturdy Aragonese. And though the King of Portugal should heap every kind of honor and title upon young Rodrigo, yet we, sir, should be thankful beyond all present hope if he returns alive to Almagro. To horse, sir, for the very sight of you will suffice to put the enemy to flight.

Commander. Say no more. Ortuño, have a trumpet

sounded in the square immediately. What forces have I here?

Ortuño. You have fifty men at your command, sir.

Commander. Bid them all mount at once.

Cimbranos. If you do not make haste, Ciudad Real falls to Fernando and Isabel.

Commander. Have no fear. I come at once.   [*They go*

✓

A *field near* FUENTEOVEJUNA

Enter MENGO, LAURENCIA, *and* PASCUALA, *running.*

PASCUALA. Do not leave us, Mengo.

Mengo. Why, what are you afraid of?

Laurencia. These days we find it safer, Mengo, not to go out alone. We keep together as much as we can for fear of meeting him.

Mengo. We live in Hell fearing that pitiless devil.

Laurencia. He plagues us day and night.

Mengo. I would Heaven would send a thunderbolt to strike the madman.

Laurencia. And now he lusts for blood as well as flesh. He is a poisonous plague upon our lives.

Mengo. I hear Frondoso aimed an arrow at his heart and threatened to kill him to protect you, Laurencia, down by the stream.

Laurencia. I cared for no man, Mengo. But I have changed my mind since then. Frondoso was brave. But I am afraid that it may cost him his life.

Mengo. He would do best to leave the village if he values his skin.

Laurencia. I told him to, despite my love for him, or rather because of it. But he scorned my warning, even though the Commander has sworn that he will hang him by one foot.

Pascuala. May he be strangled!

Mengo. No, stoned, I say, and I would like the stoning of him. All I ask is one shot from my sling, the sling I take when I go to the sheepfold. I would show him with one shot to the head. Old Sabalus or whatever he was called, that Roman, was a saint compared to him.

Laurencia. You mean Heliogabalus, the tyrant. An inhuman beast they called him, too.

Mengo. Yes, that is right, Healy of Gabulous. I never could remember history. An inhuman beast? Is that what they said? Well, his memory will smell sweeter by comparison with this Fernando Gómez. Can there be another man in the world to match him for brutality?

Laurencia. No. Nature gave him the savagery of a tiger.

Enter JACINTA.

Jacinta. Help me, for the love of God, help me! For friendship's sake, or what you will, only help me.

Laurencia. What is it, Jacinta, what is it?

Pascuala. We will both stand by you.

Jacinta. The Commander's servants—they are setting out for Ciudad Real—armed rather with their own vicious natures than with sharp steel—and they intend to take me with them.

Laurencia. Then, Jacinta, may God help you. I cannot. If he will ill-treat you, he will do a thousand times worse to me. I must escape.   [LAURENCIA *goes*

Pascuala. Jacinta, I cannot protect you from them. I am not a man, I have no arms.   [*She goes*

Mengo. Well, that leaves me. Come, Jacinta.

Jacinta. Have you weapons?

Mengo. The first and best in the world!

Jacinta. I would you had.

Mengo. Stones, Jacinta, stones. Here, come on.

Enter FLORES and ORTUÑO with soldiers.

Flores. Did you think that you could run away from us?

Jacinta. Mengo, I am dead.

Mengo. Sirs, have pity on——

Ortuño. Do you defend the lady?

Mengo. As her close relation, I plead on her behalf. I would——

Flores. Kill the swine.

Mengo. Now, I warn you, do not push me too far. I will loose my sling at you, then you will buy her dearly.

Enter the COMMANDER and CIMBRANOS.

Commander. What is happening here? Must I dismount to deal with petty matters of this kind?

Flores. The people of this vile village are making trouble again, my lord. You would be wise to destroy it entirely, since nothing of Fuenteovejuna is pleasing to you. They defy our authority, sir.

Mengo. Sir, if pity can move you, then punish these soldiers for their cruelty. In your name they tried to seize this innocent girl, snatching her from her husband and her family. Give me leave, I beseech you, to take her home.

Commander. I give them leave to chastise your insolence. Put down that sling.

Mengo. Sir . . . !

Commander. Flores, Ortuño, Cimbranos, tie his hands with it.

Mengo. Is this your way to protect her honor?

Commander. What do they say of me in Fuenteovejuna?

Mengo. What have I done, sir, to offend you or the law?

Flores. Is he to die?

Commander. No! Do not soil your swords. They will be put to more honorable use soon enough.

Ortuño. What is your command?

Commander. Beat him. Take him and tie him to that oak. Strip him and beat him with your belts. . . .

Mengo. Pity, sir, pity, as you are a nobleman!

Commander. Beat him until the buckles come loose from their stitches.

Mengo. Dear God in Heaven, shall such ugly deeds go unpunished? [*They go*

Commander. You, girl, why do you flee from me? Is a laborer to be preferred to a man of my birth and valor?

Jacinta. Sir, is this all you will do to protect my honor?

Commander. They robbed you of your honor by trying to take you with them?

Jacinta. Yes, for I have an honored father, who, if he does not equal you in high birth, yet is a man worthy of respect and one who betters you in manners.

Commander. Such foolhardy speech will do little to cool my anger. Come.

Jacinta. Where to?

Commander. Where I take you.

Jacinta. Sir, think what you do.

Commander. I have thought, and it will be the worse for you. I will have none of you. You shall be the army's baggage and go with them, their common property.

Jacinta. No power on earth can force me to such a fate while I yet live.

Commander. Get along there!

Jacinta. Have pity, sir!

Commander. Enough of pity!

Jacinta. Is there justice in Heaven? Oh God, have mercy!
[*She is dragged off.*]

ESTEBAN'S *house*

Enter LAURENCIA *and* FRONDOSO.

LAURENCIA. You are risking death to come here, Frondoso.

Frondoso. Then the more is my love for you proved,
Laurencia. From the hilltop, I saw the Commander ride
out with his soldiers, and then I thought of you and all
my fear flooded away, and I came straight down to the
village. God grant he rides to a dishonorable death.

Laurencia. No, do not curse him. Those who are cursed
most, live longest.

Frondoso. Then may he live a thousand years, all happy
ones. That should settle his future for him! Laurencia, I
came here to discover if my loyalty has opened a door to
your affections. Tell me you love me! You yourself said
the whole village looks upon us as almost married already,
and marvels that we hesitate so long. Come, now, answer
me yes or no.

Laurencia. Very well, I answer both the village and you,
yes, we shall be!

Frondoso. Oh, Laurencia, I thank you, I kiss your hands,
I cannot speak for joy. . . . Laurencia——

Laurencia. Since we are decided, Frondoso, let us waste
no time in compliments. You must go and tell my father
at once. But here he comes, talking with my uncle. Have
no doubt, Frondoso, we shall be married. May good
fortune attend you.

Frondoso. I shall put my trust in God.

[LAURENCIA *hides*

Enter ESTEBAN *and the* ALDERMAN.

Esteban. The man is mad! For a moment I thought
there would be a riot in the square, he behaved so abomi-
nably. But Jacinta has suffered most at his hands, poor
girl.

Alderman. Spain will soon be under the laws of Fernando and Isabel—the Catholic Monarchs as they call them—then we can hope for better things. Even now I hear that the Master of Santiago has been appointed Captain General and has laid siege to Rodrigo Girón in Ciudad Real. But still, my heart bleeds for Jacinta. She was a good girl.

Esteban. And then to flog young Mengo for trying to defend her.

Alderman. I saw him. His back was like a bundle of red flannel and black mourning cloth.

Esteban. I cannot bear to talk about it. Only to think of the way he abuses us makes me burn with anger. Am I mayor of this village for nothing? Is this staff of office worthless?

Alderman. It is no fault of yours, Esteban. You cannot blame yourself for what his servants do.

Esteban. You may not have heard, but they told me that the day he raped Pedro Redondo's wife in the valley he flung her to his servants, once his own foul lust was satisfied.

Alderman. There is someone here! Who is it?

Frondoso. It is I. I was waiting to speak to you.

Esteban. Frondoso, you have no need to stand on ceremony in my house. I brought you up and you know I love you as a son.

Frondoso. Then sir, trusting in the love you bear me, I wish to ask of you a favor. You know me well and my father too——

Esteban. What is it, boy, have you also been offended by Fernando Gómez?

Frondoso. Not a little.

Esteban. I knew it in my heart.

Frondoso. But sir, I want to ask, as one more token of your goodness to me, if you will give me permission to marry Laurencia, whom I dearly love. Forgive me if you think this is an impertinence, for I know that some might say that I was forward in asking.

Esteban. My heart rejoices at your words, Frondoso. My son, I give thanks to God that you have come to protect Laurencia's honor with your pure and loving zeal. You have relieved me of my greatest fear. But we must not run before we walk. Have you your own father's consent? I happily give mine provided he agrees to the match. If so, then I count myself a fortunate man indeed.

Alderman. You should get the girl's opinion first, before making any promises, Esteban.

Esteban. Why, do you think they will not have got it all settled before coming to me? Now, about the dowry: I have a little put aside that will give you a start.

Frondoso. I need no dowry, sir. I beg you, do not trouble yourself about one.

Alderman. He will take her as God made her!

Esteban. I will call her and see what she says.

Frondoso. Oh, yes, sir, do. Her wishes must be considered.

Esteban. Laurencia! Daughter!

Laurencia. You called, Father?

Esteban. There, what did I tell you? You see how soon she answered! Laurencia, my dear, come here a moment. We have been asked our opinion as to whether your friend Gila would make a good wife for Frondoso. What do you think, is he worthy of her?

Laurencia. Is Gila getting married?

Esteban. I should say they will make an ideal match, wouldn't you?

Laurencia. Yes, Father, I agree.

Esteban. Yes, but on second thought, she is not as pretty as you, Laurencia. I should have thought a handsome boy like Frondoso would have set his cap for you. But apparently not. . . .

Laurencia. Father, your jokes are almost as old as you!

Esteban. Do you love him?

Laurencia. I have always been very fond of him, but of course, now he is going to marry Gila. . . .

Esteban. No more nonsense. Shall I tell him you will have him?

Laurencia. Yes, Father, tell him.

Esteban. Very well, the keys are in my hands. It shall be done. We will go and seek your father in the square, Frondoso.

Alderman. Come.

Esteban. Now, son, about the dowry, what shall we say? I can give you four thousand maravedis.

Frondoso. I told you, I do not ask for a dowry, sir.

Esteban. Come, Frondoso, you have too many scruples.

A little help when first married never hurt anyone. Refuse now and you may live to regret it.

> [*They go, leaving* FRONDOSO *and* LAURENCIA

Laurencia. Well, Frondoso, are you happy?

Frondoso. Oh, so happy! My heart is brimming over with joy. I am almost mad with happiness, Laurencia, to see you as my own sweet possession.

*

The countryside near CIUDAD REAL

Enter the MASTER, *the* COMMANDER, FLORES *and* ORTUÑO.

COMMANDER. Fly, my lord, fly! There is no other remedy.

Master. The weakness of the wall was to blame—and the strength of the enemy.

Commander. It cost them blood enough. They must have lost half their army.

Master. They can never boast that they took our standard of Calatrava. That is one honor they cannot add to their spoils.

Commander. Your hopes are at an end, Rodrigo, even so.

Master. A man can do little to turn back blind Fortune's wheel. Yesterday I rode on high, today she casts me down.

Voices [*off*]. Victory! Victory to Isabel and Fernando! Castile wins the day!

Master. Already they crown the battlements with the fires of victory, and deck the windows of the high towers with their flags.

Commander. They would do better to paint them with the blood that they have lost, for this day is more a tragedy than a feast, for victor and vanquished alike.

Master. I will return to Calatrava, Fernando Gómez.

Commander. And I to Fuenteovejuna. I will await your orders there, sir, while you decide whether you will continue on your kinsmen's side or make your peace with the Catholic Monarchs.

Master. I will write to tell you what I intend to do.

Commander. Time will teach you the best path.

Master. Perhaps, but I fear my youth is yet an easy victim for the deceits of time.

*

The countryside near Fuenteovejuna

Enter wedding guests, Musicians, Mengo, Frondoso, Laurencia, Pascuala, Barrildo, Esteban, Alderman, *and* Juan Rojo.

Musicians [*singing*].

Long live the bride and bridegroom!
Long may they live!

Mengo. I'll bet you did not spend much time composing the words to that song.

Barrildo. And the one you have written? Will it be any better?

Frondoso. I reckon you had all the music knocked out of you the other day, Mengo. Am I right?

Mengo. Some of you would not look so handsome yourselves if the Commander had——

Barrildo. Not now, Mengo. Let us not cast a shadow over the celebrations by naming him.

Mengo. A hundred to one, those were the odds against me, I tell you. . . . And there was I, armed with nothing but my sling. Oh, they administered a leathery, brass-buckled enema to a certain honorable man—whose name I need not mention. You needn't laugh, I did not find it funny.

Barrildo. No, I am sure you did not.

Mengo. The kind of enema my arse received was no joke. I know they say it is good for you and clears the system but it nearly killed me.

Frondoso. Come, Mengo, let us hear the verses you have written, provided they are fit for the ears of this present company.

Mengo.   Long live the happy pair,
                  That is my hope.
                  May no envy or jealousy
                  Make them worry or mope.
                  May their joys be long-lasting,
                  Their quarrels ephemeral,
                  And when they get tired of living,
                  May they have a happy funeral.

Frondoso. Thank you, Mengo, I hope so too. But Heaven did not intend you to be a poet, I fear.

Barrildo. Remember how quickly he wrote it.

Mengo. Well, if you want my opinion on poetry, it is

like a baker making doughnuts. He takes the lumps of
dough and throws them into the boiling oil until he has
a pan full. They start off all the same, but turn out different. Some puff up, light and fluffy, some go flat and
squashy. A few turn out perfectly round, while many of
them stick together in a soggy mess. Some get burnt to a
cinder, others are brown and crisp. That is how I see a
poet making up his verses. His subject matter is like the
dough; he makes lumps of it in the form of lines of
poetry, and then throws it down onto the paper which is
his pan, hoping that the dollop of honey in the middle
will make them acceptable. More often than not they are
too rich for anybody's palate but his own, and so he has
to eat them all himself. That is the tragedy of being a
baker.

Barrildo. Hush, Mengo, eat your doughnuts and be
quiet, we are here to give our respects and good wishes
to the bride and bridegroom.

Laurencia. We both kiss your hands in gratitude.

Juan Rojo. Mine, child? I have done nothing. Here is
your father; it is he that you should thank. Both you
and Frondoso have reason to be grateful to him.

Esteban. No, all I want is to see you happy, with
Heaven's blessing upon you.

Frondoso. But still we thank you, Father.

Juan Rojo. Come, musicians, let us have a song, now that
we seem to have them safely married at last.

Musicians [singing].
The maiden walks in the valley,
Her dark hair floats in the breeze.
The knight of Calatrava follows.
She hides, startled, among the trees.
    Why do you hide from me, sweet girl?
    For my desires, lynx-eyed, can see through walls.

She draws the boughs across her face
And shrinks deeper into the leafy shade.
If she could, she would weave an iron lattice
To defend her from the approaching lord.
    Why do you hide from me, sweet girl?
    For my desires, lynx-eyed, can see through walls.

Love leaps over mountains and oceans,
Love creeps between the branches of trees.

The knight's shadow falls where the maiden cowers.
She cannot avoid the searching eyes.
   Why do you hide from me, sweet girl?
For my desires, lynx-eyed, can see through walls.

Enter the COMMANDER, FLORES, ORTUÑO, *and* CIMBRANOS.

Commander. Pray do not interrupt the festivities on my account.

Juan Rojo. On the contrary, sir, we would honor you. Will you be seated? We must give you a conqueror's welcome, now you have returned from the wars.

Frondoso. This is my death! Heaven help me!

Laurencia. Quickly, Frondoso, run, this way.

Commander. Arrest that man.

Juan Rojo. Obey, my son.

Frondoso. What, would you have them kill me, Father?

Juan Rojo. No, they have no cause to kill you.

Commander. I do not kill a man without cause. But for me, these soldiers here would have run him through ere now. Take him to the prison where his own father shall try, and punish, his offense.

Pascuala. But, sir, it is his wedding day.

Commander. The cause of justice heeds not wedding days. I am sure there are others waiting and willing to take his place.

Pascuala. If he offended you, sir, forgive him, as you are a nobleman.

Commander. This matter does not concern me alone, Pascuala. It was Téllez Girón, the Master of the Order of Calatrava, who suffered insult indirectly at his hands. He who insults the honor of the Order must, I fear, be punished as an example. If he goes free others may be tempted to question its authority. For, lest any here are yet ignorant of this man's crime, know that he aimed a bow at the heart of the High Commander of the Order.

Esteban. I believe, sir, that it may not be out of place for a father-in-law to speak a word in his defense. Is it surprising, sir, that a young man in love should be moved to disloyal anger when you attempted to rob him of his wife? Is it surprising that he should seek to defend her?

Commander. Mayor, you are a bumbling fool.

Esteban. But a well-intentioned one, sir.

Commander. I made no attempt to rob him of his wife —he had none.

Esteban. My lord, you did. Let us hear no more. For there are a king and queen in Castile, who will create new orders of knighthood that shall put down the old disorders that have oppressed us. And when their wars are over, they will not tolerate proud, powerful men creating havoc in their towns and villages, bearing great crosses on their breasts. Let the king alone wear such emblems, since he alone is worthy of them.

Commander. Remove that staff from this old fool's hand.

Esteban. Take it, sir, I have no more use for it.

Commander. Let him be beaten with it for a disobedient ass.

Esteban. You are still my master, sir. Do as you will.

Pascuala. Do you beat an old man?

Laurencia. If this is your revenge upon me, how do you profit by it?

Commander. Take that girl, and let ten men guard her with their lives.   [*The* COMMANDER *and his men go*

Esteban. May justice descend from Heaven.   [*He goes*

Pascuala. The wedding has turned to mourning.

Barrildo. Is there no man here that will speak out?

Mengo. I have already been flogged till I had enough purple about me to fill the Vatican. Let somebody else try crossing him.

Juan Rojo. We must make a stand together.

Mengo. All keep quiet together, you mean. Unless you want a staff broken across your backs.

ACT THREE

1

Council room in FUENTEOVEJUNA

Enter ESTEBAN, ALONSO, *and* BARRILDO.

ESTEBAN. Are they not coming to the meeting?

Barrildo. As yet they have not come.

Esteban. Every minute our danger grows greater. . . .

Barrildo. They will come, have no fear. They all know about the meeting.

Esteban. Frondoso a captive in his tower, and my daughter taken too! If heavenly mercy does not intercede, then——

Enter JUAN ROJO *and the* ALDERMAN.

Juan Rojo. Esteban, why are you shouting? For all our sakes this meeting must be secret.

Esteban. The greatest wonder is that I am not shouting any louder.

Enter MENGO.

Mengo. I thought I would come after all.

Esteban. My honorable friends, a man whose gray beard is bathed in grief asks you what obsequies are to be said over the corpse of our lost honor. Is there any man among us who still can say he has not suffered some indignity at the hands of this barbarian, Fernando Gómez? Answer me. Can none reply? Then since every one of us feels degraded and dishonored, can we not act together? We are all equally affronted and yet we hesitate to take a just revenge. Could any misery be greater?

Juan Rojo. None. But already it is published abroad and known for truth that the rightful king and queen hold Castile in peaceful rule, therefore, I say, let two councilors be sent to Córdoba, where they are soon to hold court, and cast themselves at their feet and beg them to redress our wrongs.

Barrildo. King Fernando will never spare the time to deal with our problem. He will be too busy establishing his rule after his recent conquests.

Alderman. Friends, hear me a moment. I vote we evacuate the whole village, man, woman and child.

Juan Rojo. That would take too much time.

Mengo. Speak lower! If we are overheard, I fear this council will lose a few lives among its members.

Alderman. Now the mast of patience is broken and fear blows the ship wildly from its course. The daughter is violently stolen from a virtuous man who governs this town in which you live, and his staff of office is unjustly broken about his head. If we were slaves we could not be more harshly treated.

Juan Rojo. What would you have the people do?

Alderman. Die, or bring death to the tyrants, for we are many, they are few.

Barrildo. What, rise in arms against our master?

Esteban. Only the King is master under heaven, not Fernando Gómez. If God is with us in our zeal for justice, then how can we go wrong?

Mengo. Listen, sirs, we should tread carefully upon such shifting ground. I represent the laborers upon this council, and they are always the ones to get the heavier end of the stick, so I can best put forward their fears——

Juan Rojo. This misfortune is shared equally, Mengo. By all, whether laborer or farmer. Why do we hesitate to risk our lives? They burn our homes and our vineyards. They are tyrants. Let us have vengeance, I say.

Enter LAURENCIA, *disheveled.*

Laurencia. Let me come in. A woman has a right, if not to vote in this council of men, yet to have a voice. Do you know me?

Esteban. Great heaven! My daughter!

Juan Rojo. Laurencia!

Laurencia. Well may you doubt that it is I, seeing me as I am.

Esteban. My daughter!

Laurencia. Call me not daughter.

Esteban. Why Laurencia? Why not?

Laurencia. Why? I will tell you why! Because you allow tyrants to kidnap me and do not avenge me, traitors to snatch me, and do not rescue me. Oh, do not say it was Frondoso's duty as my husband, and not yours, for until the wedding night a bride is still her father's charge, and the night was not yet come. As when a jewel is bought, so the man who sells must guard it until it is handed over to the buyer. Fernando Gómez carried me off while you looked on. Like coward shepherds, you let the wolf make off with the lamb. You let me be threatened with knives, insulted with their foul language, and brutally maltreated in their attempts to avenge their lewd appetites upon my chastity! Look how my hair has been dragged and torn out! See the cuts and bruises where they tortured me! Do you call yourselves men? Do you? My father? Or you, Uncle? Are your hearts unmoved to see me so full of

woe? Well may this village be called Fuenteovejuna—
Sheepwell! for its people are nothing but sheep. A flock
of bleating sheep who run from curs. Give me a sword!
Let me have arms! Oh, you are stone, bronze, jasper!
Tigers without—— No! Not tigers, for tigers hunt and
slay any that steal their young before they have had time
to lock their gates in their faces. Meek rabbits were you
born, not noble Spaniards. Hens! You stand by and cluck
while other men enjoy your wives! Why do you wear
swords at your belts?—put distaffs there! By God, I swear,
only the women here shall have the glory of shedding the
blood of this tyrant, and when it is done we shall throw
stones at you, for the effeminate pimps and cowards
that you are. From tomorrow, go dressed in wimples and
petticoats and paint your faces with rouge. Even now the
Commander may be ordering Frondoso to be hanged, un-
tried, for so he has sworn to do. And he will do the same
to all of you. And I shall laugh to see it and be glad that
this village has been emptied of you, its old women, and
the days of the Amazons shall return in Fuenteovejuna,
to be the wonder of the earth!

Esteban. Daughter, I will not deserve the names you
give us. I will go alone, though all the world should stand
against me.

Juan Rojo. I too, though fearing the greatness of your
enemy.

Alderman. Let us all challenge death together.

Barrildo. Find a cloth and fix it to a pole. We will raise
our banner to the winds, and death to these monsters!

Juan Rojo. What shall be our order?

Mengo. Kill him! Never mind about order! We all agree,
the whole village knows what must be done. Down with
tyrants!

Esteban. Take any arms you can find!—swords, lances,
bows, pikes, sticks of wood.

Mengo. Long live the King and Queen!

All. Long live the King and Queen!

Mengo. And down with traitors and tyrants! Let Fernando Gómez bleed!

All. Death to the tyrant!   [*They all go*

Laurencia. May heaven hear your cry! Rise up, women
of Fuenteovejuna! Come out and win back your honor.

Enter PASCUALA, JACINTA, *and other women.*

Pascuala. What is it, Laurencia? What is happening?

Laurencia. Look there! They go to kill Fernando Gómez. Every man in the village, and young boys too, all running furiously with one intent—death! Shall we let them alone reap the honor of this deed? Shall we stay at home when we were the greatest sufferers from his wrongs?

Jacinta. What must we do? Tell us.

Laurencia. We shall march in order upon his house, and there take our revenge. Our vengeance shall strike fear into the hearts of men everywhere. Jacinta, you suffered most, you shall be corporal of this band of women.

Jacinta. You suffered no less.

Laurencia. Pascuala, you shall be our standard-bearer.

Pascuala. Give me a banner. I will fix it to a pole. I shall be a fine standard-bearer.

Laurencia. There is no time. We must strike now, our only standards must be the shawls we wear.

Pascuala. We must name the captain.

Laurencia. No. No captain.

Pascuala. Why not?

Laurencia. I for one can show my valor without any title of captain or general.   [*They go*

A room in the COMMANDER's *house*

Enter FRONDOSO *with his hands tied,* FLORES, ORTUÑO, CIMBRANOS, *and the* COMMANDER.

COMMANDER. Hang him up by the rope which binds his hands, he will suffer longer.

Frondoso. Your lofty titles, sir, conceal the truer names that men might call you.

Commander. Hang him from the nearest tower.

Frondoso. When I had the chance to kill you, I spared your life.

Flores. What is that noise?

Commander. What noise?

Flores. Now they would interrupt your justice, my lord!

Ortuño. They are breaking the doors down.

Commander. The doors of my house! The official residence of our great Order!

Flores. The entire village is coming.

Juan Rojo [off]. Smash, crush, cast down, burn, and kill!

Ortuño. A mass uprising!

Commander. The populace against me!

Ortuño. We shall never stop this mob.

Flores. They are advancing wildly. They have smashed the doors down.

Commander. Untie him. Frondoso, go out and pacify them. Show them you are unharmed.

Frondoso. I go. But remember it is love that drives them, sir.   [*He goes*

Mengo [off]. Long live Fernando and Isabel, and death to the Commander!

Flores. Sir, for God's sake, do not let them find you here.

Commander. They will not come this far. They dare not. Besides, this room is strong and well defended.

Flores. When outraged people rise, my lord, there is no quelling them until they have taken their full revenge.

Commander. Come, we will defend that door. Our swords shall be the portcullis to keep them out.

Frondoso [off]. Long live Fuenteovejuna!

Commander. What a captain! Let us attack these peasant curs, the sharp edge of our swords shall cure their madness.

Flores. They will cure yours, I fear.

Esteban [off]. There they are! There is the tyrant and his servants. Fuenteovejuna! Death to them all!

All the peasants rush in.

Commander. My people, wait!

All. Insults cannot wait. Revenge cannot wait!

Commander. What insults? What wrongs do you complain of? You shall have full redress.

All. Fuenteovejuna! Long live King Fernando! Death to the Commander! Death to the traitor! Death to the hypocrite. Kill the foul lecher.

Commander. Hear me. I speak. I am your lord——

All. Our lords are the Catholic Monarchs.

Commander. Wait——

All. Fuenteovejuna! And death to Fernando Gómez!

The peasants go off following the COMMANDER.
The women enter armed.

Laurencia. Stop. Here is the place where our honor shall

be avenged. Remember, show yourselves not as women in this deed, but as soldiers without pity.

Pascuala. Those we called women before have caught him already. They are letting his blood. Let us not wait longer.

Jacinta. We will impale his body on our spears.

Pascuala. We are all agreed. We will go together.

Esteban [off]. Die, treacherous Commander!

Commander. I die. Pity, oh Lord. I trust in your mercy!

Barrildo [off]. Here is Flores.

Mengo [off]. Let me get at the swine. He was the one that beat the hide off me.

Frondoso [off]. I shall not be avenged till I have the soul out of his body.

Laurencia. We must go in.

Pascuala. Be careful! We must guard the door.

Barrildo [off]. Plead with me? Now it is your turn to weep!

Laurencia. Pascuala, I go in there. My sword shall not remain imprisoned in its sheath.   [*She goes*

Barrildo [off]. Here is Ortuño.

Frondoso [off]. Slash his face.

Enter FLORES *pursued by* MENGO.

Flores. Pity, Mengo. I am not to blame!

Mengo. You were his go-between. I felt your belt on my back.

Pascuala. Leave him to us, Mengo. Stop! Leave him to us!

Mengo. There you are, he is yours. I have finished with him.

Pascuala. I will avenge your beating, Mengo.

Mengo. Do, Pascuala!

Jacinta. Death to the pander.

Flores. Among women!

Jacinta. A fitting death for such as you!

Pascuala. And do you weep now?

Jacinta. Die, you cringing pimp!

Laurencia [off]. Death to the traitor!

Flores. Pity, ladies!

Enter ORTUÑO *fleeing from* LAURENCIA.

Ortuño. Listen, I beg you, I am not the one——

Enter LAURENCIA.

Laurencia. I know who you are. Go in there, all of you. You will find employment for your conquering arms in there!

Pascuala. I will die killing.

All. God for Fuenteovejuna and King Fernando!

[*They go*

1

The palace of FERNANDO *and* ISABEL *in* TORO

Enter KING *and* QUEEN *and* DON MANRIQUE.

MANRIQUE. And so, sir, our timely action achieved the result that you desired, with few losses on our side. Little resistance was shown, and even if there had been more, I think it would have carried little weight against our forces. Cabra is now occupying the town lest by any chance the bold adversary should dare to attack again.

King. You have both done wisely. But he must be assisted further. Let forces be sent to fortify his position. Thus may we best guard ourselves against Alfonso, who is still gathering men in Portugal. I am well pleased to know that the Count of Cabra is holding Ciudad Real. He is a captain who has proved his skill and courage many times in battle. We can rely on him to be a watchful sentry against those who wish our kingdom harm.

Enter FLORES, *wounded.*

Flores. Catholic King, Great Fernando, to whom Heaven has granted the crown of Castile, as a worthy tribute to the greatest knight: hear now a tale of cruel rebellion, the worst ever known in any land between the rising and setting of the sun.

King. Speak.

Flores. Great King: my wounds do not permit me to dally in telling my sad story, for death will soon overtake me. I come from Fuenteovejuna, where, with remorseless hatred, the people have conspired together and have killed their rightful master. Fernando Gómez is dead, murdered by his own vassals, a mob inflamed with little cause to senseless fury. They all took up the cry, and, driven to frenzy by their own ever-increasing chant of "Traitor, traitor," they swept through his house, burning and destroying all that stood in their way. They took no heed of his noble promise that all their wrongs should be set right and all debts paid. Not only would they not listen to him, but, in their madness, they hacked his breast and the cross it wore with a thousand cruel strokes. They flung his body from the high windows to the ground where the women of the village impaled it on pikes and swords. Then they took his corpse to a house in the village where they fought among themselves to tear out his hair and beard in handfuls and slash his face. Their lust for blood grew to such a pitch that even when they had torn him into pieces, they were still unsatisfied. They hacked away his coat of arms above the door with their pikes, exclaiming as they did it that they would hang your royal arms there in place of his that had offended them. They sacked his house as if it had been the house of an enemy, and with delight divided his goods among themselves. I saw all this with my own eyes from where I was hiding, for, alas, unkind fate left me living amid the chaos. I lay hidden all day until nightfall when I could escape unseen to tell you of the deed. Sir, since you are known to be a just king, I beg you to revenge my master's noble blood, shed without reason by his barbarous vassals.

King. You may rest assured that they shall not go unpunished. I confess myself amazed at this tale of horror. We shall send a judge at once to confirm the truth of the matter, and to chastise the guilty as an example to all Spain. A captain shall go with the judge to protect him. Such bold treason shall receive fitting punishment. See that this soldier's wounds are attended to.   [*They go*

The village square in FUENTEOVEJUNA

Enter the peasants of FUENTEOVEJUNA *with the head of* FERNANDO GÓMEZ *on a lance.*

MUSICIANS [*singing*]. Long live Fernando and Isabel,
                    And death to tyrants.

Barrildo. Give us your verse, Frondoso.

Frondoso. Very well, here it is, and if the odd foot is missing here and there, then anyone more skilled in verses than I is welcome to improve it:

Long live Isabel the Queen,
And King Fernando too.
Long together may they reign,
And be the happiest couple in Spain
Till Heaven receive the two.
Long live our Catholic King and Queen,
And death to tyrants.

Laurencia. Let us hear yours, Barrildo.

Barrildo. Listen carefully. It took me hours to write it.

Pascuala. Be sure you give it a proper rendering and do it justice, then.

Barrildo. Long live our famous King and Queen,
May they be happy and serene.
God keep them free from woes,
And shield them from their foes,
Whether dwarves or giants.
And death to tyrants!

Musicians [*singing*]. Long live Fernando and Isabel,
And death to tyrants.

Laurencia. Now for Mengo's verse!

Frondoso. Yes, come along, Mengo.

Mengo. As you all know, I am a very gifted poet.

Pascuala. We all know you are a gifted whipping post.

Mengo. I've got the laugh on the Commander.
He played a tune on my backside:
Now the Commander is asunder,
But I am still inside my hide.
Long live our Catholic King and Queen,
And down with tyrants!

Musicians [*singing*]. Long live Fernando and Isabel,
And death to tyrants.

Esteban. Take down that head, good people.

Mengo. Yes, he does not look very happy up there, does he?

JUAN ROJO *brings on a shield with the royal arms.*

Alderman. Here is the new coat of arms.

Esteban. Hold it up, Juan, so that we can all see it.

Juan. Where is it to be placed?

Alderman. Here, on the front of the town hall.

Esteban. It is a fine shield.

Barrildo. Just what we wanted.

Frondoso. It is the sun that rises. Our day begins to dawn.

Esteban. Long live León, Castile, and Aragon, and death to tyranny! Now, my friends, will you hear an old man's advice? The King and Queen will order an inquiry into the death of the Commander, and they will be the more interested since their own route brings them to these parts. So let us be prepared and agree on what we shall say.

Frondoso. What would you advise?

Esteban. When we are questioned, we shall name no names, but say only: "Fuenteovejuna did it." Even if we die for it, we will say no more than that.

Frondoso. Yes, that is what we must do. Fuenteovejuna did it.

Esteban. Do you all agree to say that?

All. We do.

Esteban. Very well, we will have a rehearsal. I will be the judge. Now, Mengo, you are the one to be questioned.

Mengo. Could you not find someone weaker than me? Someone more likely to break down?

Esteban. We are only pretending, Mengo.

Mengo. Come along then, ask me.

Esteban. Who killed the Commander?

Mengo. Fuenteovejuna did it.

Esteban. Dog! I will put you on the rack!

Mengo. Nay! Kill me, sir.

Esteban. Confess, scoundrel.

Mengo. Very well, I confess.

Esteban. Who was it?

Mengo. Fuenteovejuna.

Esteban. Give the rack another turn.

Mengo. Give it twenty turns, I care not!

Esteban. That is the way we will treat them at the trial.

Enter the ALDERMAN.

Alderman. What in the world are you doing here?

Frondoso. What has happened, Cuadrado?

Alderman. The judge has arrived.

Esteban. Now scatter, all of you, to your homes.

Alderman. A captain has come with him.

Esteban. Let the devil come with him. You know what your answer is to be.

Alderman. They are already arresting everyone they see. Not a soul will be left out.

Esteban. Have no fear. Who killed the Commander, Mengo?

Mengo. Fuenteovejuna.   [*They go*

✦

In the MASTER OF CALATRAVA'*s house in* ALMAGRO

Enter the MASTER *and a* SOLDIER.

MASTER. What an unlooked-for misfortune! To murder the Commander of our Order! I have a mind to kill you for the news you bring.

Soldier. Sir, I am only a messenger. I have no wish to offend you.

Master. To think that a whole village should have dared to rise up and commit so terrible a crime. I will swoop down upon them with five hundred men and raze the village to the ground. Not so much as a memory of their names shall be left.

Soldier. Sir, stay your anger, for they have gone over to King Fernando. You were best not to incur his displeasure any further.

Master. How can they have gone over to the King? Their village belongs to my Order. It is part of my estates!

Soldier. The King himself can best answer that.

Master. No lawyer would support my claim if the King now rules in Fuenteovejuna. Whether I will or no, I must recognize him as my sovereign. Therefore do I stay my anger. My best course now is to crave audience of His Majesty. For though I have been guilty of offending him, my youth may excuse me in his eyes and incline him to pardon me. I go to him with shame, and yet I must, if I am to protect my honor, as my father bade me. [*They go*

✦

The square at FUENTEOVEJUNA

Enter LAURENCIA, *alone.*

LAURENCIA. Unhappy Laurencia, what will you do if unkind Fate snatches Frondoso from you? Fear is the rack on which my love is tormented. My mind, which I thought so steadfast, now quails in horror to think of our present plight. Oh, you Heavens, guard my husband from danger, for Laurencia becomes as nothing if she loses him. Oh, Frondoso, Frondoso, when you are here, I am terrified for your safety, and when you are gone, I can scarce live without you.

Enter FRONDOSO.

Frondoso. Laurencia!

Laurencia. Dear husband! How can you dare to show yourself here?

Frondoso. Laurencia; is this all the thanks you give me for my love in coming to you?

Laurencia. Frondoso, my love, take care. Think of the danger. . . .

Frondoso. Laurencia. Heaven would never be so cruel as to hurt you in anything.

Laurencia. But you see how ruthlessly the others are being treated, and they are not so deeply involved as you, Frondoso. If the judge is harsh with them, what will he not do to you? Save your life. Flee, my love. Do not wait here for evil to overwhelm you.

Frondoso. How can I, Laurencia? How can you ask? I could not leave the others in danger. And you, could I leave you when I cannot bear to be out of your sight? Do not tell me to flee. I will not leave Fuenteovejuna in agony to save my own skin. [*Voices off.*] Hark! It sounds as if the judge is using the rack! Listen. Perhaps we can hear what they say.

Judge [*off*]. Now tell the truth, old man.

Frondoso. Laurencia! They are torturing an old man.

Laurencia. They will stop at nothing.

Esteban [*off*]. Let loose a little.

Judge [*off*]. Let it go. Now tell me. Who killed the Commander?

Esteban [*off*]. Fuenteovejuna did it.

Laurencia. Father, may you live forever.

Frondoso. He kept his word.

Judge [*off*]. That boy! We will take him next. You know who did it, child. Come, tell me. What, will you be silent, dog? Turn the wheel, you drunken oaf.

Boy [*off*]. Fuenteovejuna, sir.

Judge [*off*]. Now, by the King's life, do you want me to

hang you all with my own hands? Who killed the Commander?

Frondoso. It is beyond belief. That they could torture a child, and he answer like that.

Laurencia. The village is showing great courage.

Frondoso. Courage and determination.

Judge [*off*]. Now stretch that woman on the rack. Good. Give it another turn.

Laurencia. He is growing wild with rage.

Judge [*off*]. Believe me, I will kill every one of you on this rack. I will find out the truth. Who killed the Commander?

Pascuala [*off*]. Fuenteovejuna, my lord.

Judge [*off*]. Go on. Tighter.

Frondoso. It is no good.

Laurencia. Pascuala is not giving in.

Frondoso. When the children will not confess, how could the rest?

Judge [*off*]. It seems they enjoy it. Give it another turn!

Pascuala [*off*]. Merciful heaven!

Judge [*off*]. Another turn, you fool, are you deaf?

Pascuala [*off*]. Fuenteovejuna killed him.

Judge [*off*]. Bring me that fat fellow, the one with the paunch and no shirt on.

Laurencia. Poor Mengo.

Frondoso. I am afraid Mengo will confess.

Mengo [*off*]. Oh! Oh!

Judge [*off*]. Now, begin.

Mengo [*off*]. Oh!

Judge [*off*]. Do you need help?

Mengo [*off*]. Oh! Oh!

Judge [*off*]. Now, slave, who killed your Master?

Mengo [*off*]. Oh, I will tell you, sir!

Judge [*off*]. Let loose a little.

Frondoso. He is giving way.

Judge [*off*]. No answer? Right, put your back into it.

Mengo [*off*]. No, no, I will confess.

Judge [*off*]. Who killed him?

Mengo [*off*]. Little old Fuenteovejuna did it.

Judge [*off*]. Was there ever seen such stubborn knavery as this? They mock at pain; even those in whom I placed most hope say nothing. Let them go. I am weary.

Frondoso. Oh, Mengo, Heaven bless you. You have banished all my fears.

The other peasants come out.

Barrildo. Bravo, Mengo!

Alderman. You did splendidly.

Barrildo. Mengo, well done.

Frondoso. Well done indeed.

Barrildo. Here, my friend, here is a drink for you. Have some of this too.

Mengo. Oh! Oh! What is it?

Barrildo. Candied fruit.

Mengo. Mm! Oh! Oh!

Frondoso. Give him another drink.

Barrildo. Here, Mengo.

Laurencia. Have another fruit.

Mengo. Oh! Oh!

Barrildo. Here, drink this, Mengo, it is on me.

Laurencia. Come, Mengo, there is no need to look so serious about it.

Frondoso. If he can mock at the rack, he has a right to take his drinking seriously.

Alderman. Have another, Mengo.

Mengo. Oh. Oh! Yes.

Frondoso. You drink your fill, Mengo, you have earned it.

Laurencia. Give him a chance, he is downing them as fast as he can already.

Frondoso. Put something round him. He is freezing.

Barrildo. Would you like any more, Mengo?

Mengo. Any amount. Oh, oh!

Frondoso. Is there any more wine?

Barrildo. Yes, drink as much as you can, Mengo. What is the matter?

Mengo. I think I have a cold coming on.

Barrildo. What you need is a drink.

Mengo. I think this is a little rough to the palate.

Frondoso. Have some of this. It is better. Who killed the Commander, Mengo?

Mengo. Little old Fuenteovejuna!

They go. FRONDOSO *and* LAURENCIA *are left.*

Frondoso. Mengo deserves all the honors they can give him. But tell me, my love, who killed the Commander?

Laurencia. Fuenteovejuna, my dear.

Frondoso. Who killed him?

Laurencia. Oh, you terrify me. Fuenteovejuna did it.
Frondoso. And how did I kill you?
Laurencia. How? By making me love you so much.

[*They go*

✦

In the royal palace at Tordesillas
Enter the King and Queen.

Isabel. Sir, I count myself most fortunate to meet you
here thus unexpectedly.

King. I am overjoyed to look upon you again, my queen.
Of necessity I had to halt here before resuming the expe-
dition against Portugal.

Isabel. Perhaps Your Majesty turned a little out of your
way because you wished to come here, as now you turn
your words to tell me it was "of necessity."

King. In what state did you leave Castile?

Isabel. Content and at peace.

King. How could it be otherwise, when it is you that
keeps it so?

Enter Don Manrique.

Manrique. Your Majesties, the Master of Calatrava has
just arrived. He begs that you may grant him audience.

Isabel. He arrives at a good time. I wished to speak
with him.

Manrique. Madam, I would urge you to do so, for, despite his youth, he is a valiant soldier.

Manrique goes, and returns with the Master.

Master. Rodrigo Téllez Girón, Master of Calatrava, who
never ceases to praise Your Majesties, humbly craves your
pardon and forgiveness. I confess that I was deceived, and
that I far exceeded the bounds of what was just and pleasing to you. I was misled by Fernando Gómez's advice and
my own desire for personal glory. I was faithful to the
wrong cause, and now I beg for pardon. And should I be
worthy of such mercy at your hands, then from this moment I offer myself as your faithful knight and will prove
to you the valor of my sword in your campaign against the
Moors of Granada. There shall you see me spread dismay
among the heathen, when I raise my red crosses upon their
highest towers. Furthermore, I will bring with me five

hundred soldiers to serve under your command, and give you my word as a true knight never in my life to offend you more.

King. Rise up, Master, from the ground. Now you have come to us, you shall evermore be welcome.

Master. Your Majesties, my heart finds consolation to hear you pardon me.

Isabel. We find you a perfect knight, and of rare valor.

Master. Most fair Esther, and divine Xerxes.

Enter MANRIQUE.

Manrique. Sir, the judge has returned from Fuenteovejuna, and would present himself before Your Majesty.

King. Be judge of these aggressors, Lady.

Master. Sir, if I had not seen your clemency, have no doubt that I would teach them to kill a Commander of our Order.

King. The matter no longer concerns you, Master.

Queen. I confess, I would prefer to leave this judgment to you alone, my lord.

Enter the JUDGE.

Judge. Your Majesties, I went to Fuenteovejuna as you commanded, and conducted the inquiry with particular care and diligence. But not one page of evidence was forthcoming with regard to the crime in question, for they all, as one man, and, I must confess, most courageously, replied when questioned: "Fuenteovejuna did it." Three hundred were rigorously questioned upon the rack, and yet, sir, I could extract no further information. All, from children of ten years of age upwards, were tried, but neither coaxing, nor threatening, nor the most cunning questioning would avail. Since I have had no success in revealing any proof of guilt, I submit to Your Majesties, that either you must pardon them or execute the entire population. They are all present here, ready to be brought before you if you wish for more information from them.

King. Let them come in.

Enter the ALDERMAN, FRONDOSO, ESTEBAN, MENGO, LAURENCIA, *and other villagers of* FUENTEOVEJUNA.

Laurencia. Are those the King and Queen?

Frondoso. Yes, the rulers of all Castile.

Laurencia. My word, how beautiful they are! May Saint Anthony bless them.

Isabel. Are these the murderers?

Esteban. Madam, Fuenteovejuna presents itself in all humbleness before Your Majesties, ready to serve you. The cruel tyranny of the late Commander, and the thousand insults which he heaped upon us, were the cause of the trouble. He robbed us of our property, raped our wives and daughters, and was a stranger to all pity.

Frondoso. Indeed, Your Majesties, even on our wedding day, he stole this girl whom Heaven blessed me with, and for whom I count myself the luckiest man alive. . . . On our wedding night, I say, he took her to his house as if she had been his own. If this virtuous girl had not shown the spirit she did in the defense of her honor, then the outcome could have been much worse.

Mengo. Now it is my turn to speak. If you will give me leave, then I will make you marvel at the way he abused me. Because I tried to protect a girl whom his men, with bestial arrogance, had tried to rape, that brutal Nero treated me in such a manner that the reverse side of my person was the color of smoked salmon. Three men flogged me and I can show Your Majesties, if you wish, the scars which I carry with me to this day. But suffice it to say that I have spent more than my land is worth in myrtle powders and liniments to heal the skin. . . .

Esteban. Sir, we would be your vassals. You are our rightful king, and therefore have we already presumed to set up your royal arms on our town hall. We hope for your clemency, and that you will accept the pledge of our innocence that we offer you.

King. Since there is no written evidence forthcoming, although the crime is great, it must be pardoned. And since its people have shown such loyalty to me, this village shall come under my direct jurisdiction. So it shall remain until such time as a Commander worthy of its charge shall emerge to inherit it.

Frondoso. Your Majesty has spoken the words that most delight our hearts. And so this tale of Fuenteovejuna ends in happiness.

THE DOG IN THE MANGER

(El Perro del Hortelano)

CHARACTERS

DIANA, *Countess of Belflor*
TEODORO, *her secretary*
COUNT FEDERICO
LEONIDO
MARQUIS RICARDO
COUNT LUDOVICO
OCTAVIO, DIANA's *major-domo*
FABIO, DIANA's *squire*
TRISTÁN, *servant to* TEODORO
ANTONELO
LIRANO
FURIO
CELIO
CAMILO
MARCELA ⎫
DOROTEA ⎬ *maids to* DIANA
ANARDA ⎭

The action takes place in the city of NAPLES.

THE DOG IN THE MANGER

ACT ONE

1

A room in the Countess' *palace*

Enter Teodoro *and* Tristán, *fleeing.*

Teodoro. This way, Tristán, this way!
  Tristán. What damned ill luck!
  Teodoro. Did she recognize us?
  Tristán. I know not, sir. I fear she did. May fortune——
  Teodoro. Tristán, come!

They go. Enter Diana.

Diana. Stay, sir! Stay! Hear me! Sir! Must I endure this insult? Come back! Stay! Listen! Where are my servants? Octavio! Fabio! That was no shadow that I saw, nor was it a dream that mocked my senses. What, are you all asleep?
  Fabio. Did you call, madam?
  Diana. Make haste, old fool, if it is within your power, and see what man it was who even now fled from this room! Hurry, Fabio! Oh, merciful Heaven, your aged dullness ill suits my present fears.
  Fabio. In this room, you say, madam?
  Diana. Answer me no more! Go after him.
  Fabio. Madam, I will.
  Diana. And find out who he is! There is some treachery here.

Fabio *goes. Enter* Octavio.

Octavio. I heard you call, madam, and yet my ears could not believe it was your voice, considering the lateness of the hour.
  Diana. Strange men enter my house in the middle of the

night, break into my own bedroom, and when I call, Octavio, all you can say, after they have gone, is that you could not believe your ears! Are you a man or a will-o'-the-wisp, that you are never where you are wanted? And when you do come, you crawl in so slowly and phlegmatically and stand there like a post, asleep on your feet. Is this how you will avenge my honor?

Octavio. I heard you call, madam, and yet my ears could not believe it was your voice, considering the lateness of the hour.

Diana. Go, before your ears tingle with the news of my displeasure. Go back to bed.

Octavio. Madam——

Enter FABIO.

Fabio. Never have I seen a man move so fast. He has flown with the speed of a hawk.

Diana. Did you recognize anything about him?

Fabio. What sort of thing?

Diana. Was there not a gold crest on his cloak?

Fabio. As he went down the stairs, he threw his hat at the lamp and put it out. So he fled through the courtyards in darkness, madam, and disappeared through the main gate brandishing his sword.

Diana. Cluck, cluck, cluck, what an old hen you are.

Fabio. Why, madam, what would you have had me do?

Diana. Why, close with him and kill him.

Octavio. If he was a nobleman and not a thief, then to expel him noisily and forcefully from your door, would, I fear, cast out your honor with him.

Diana. I did not say he was a nobleman, why should he be?

Octavio. Are there not many men in Naples blind with love of you, who are forever beseeching you to marry them? Might not one of these do all in his power to see you? And, madam, since you thought you saw gold on his cloak, and since he extinguished the lamp for fear of being recognized by Fabio, is it not most likely that he was a man of fame and position, in short, a nobleman?

Diana. No doubt you speak truly. It must have been some lovelorn knight who bribed my servants to give him entry. For you know, Octavio, how incorruptible my servants are. But I will find out who it was. There were long feathers in his hat, and it must be on the stairs. [*To* FABIO.] Go and fetch it.

Fabio. You want me to fetch it?

Diana. Go, fool. It must still be there. For he would scarcely have paused to pick it up as he fled.

Fabio. Very well. I will take a light.   [*He goes*

Diana. If my suspicions be true, then whoever is guilty shall not remain an instant longer in my service.

Octavio. You will do well, madam, and yet, if I might be permitted to mention a subject which I know is displeasing to you, perhaps the fact that you so adamantly refuse to marry may, to some small extent, be the reason for, or, I should say, a contributory cause of, so insolent an intrusion as took place tonight, on the part of one of your less scrupulous suitors, who might seek to compromise you, and place you in a position which would force you to accept his suit.

Diana. Do you know who it was?

Octavio. I? Know? . . . Madam, I only know that you are as determined as you are beautiful, and that since you are the heir to the Counts of Belflor, many nobles here aspire to your hand.

Enter FABIO.

Fabio. I found the hat.

Diana. Show me it. What is this?

Fabio. This is the hat the gentleman left. It smells, madam.

Diana. Are you sure this was the one?

Fabio. Why should I tell a lie? That was the only one I could find.

Octavio. These are fine feathers!

Fabio. It must have been a thief.

Octavio. A housebreaker.

Diana. Oh, I shall lose my wits between the two of you. . . .

Fabio. Well, this was his hat.

Diana. But the feathers I saw . . . why the hat was loaded with plumes, how can they have shriveled to this?

Fabio. They must have got burned when he threw it at the lamp, madam. Feathers would go up like chaff, you may be sure. Why, did not the very same thing happen to Icarus? As soon as he flew too near the sun, his feathers caught fire, and down he fell into the foaming sea. That is what must have happened. The lamp was the sun, the hat was Icarus, its feathers were consumed by fire, and it fell on the stairs—where I found it.

Diana. I am in no mood for jesting, Fabio. We must find out who the intruder was.

Octavio. There will be time enough for that, madam.

Diana. Time, Octavio? When?

Octavio. Let us sleep, now, madam; tomorrow you may find out all you wish.

Diana. No, I will not sleep until I have discovered who it was. Call my women to me.   [FABIO *goes*

Octavio. This is a wearisome way to spend the night, madam.

Diana. Do you expect me to sleep after an alarm like this, Octavio?

Octavio. Would it not be wiser to postpone the inquiry, madam, and then order a secret investigation of this outrage?

Diana. Doubtless you are wise, Octavio, but to sleep on an undiscovered secret is beyond all human discretion.

Enter FABIO *with* MARCELA, DOROTEA, *and* ANARDA.

Fabio. I have brought the more important of your ladies, madam. The others are fast asleep in their own quarters, and will be ignorant of the matter on which you would question them. Only the ladies of your bedchamber were awake.

Octavio. Shall we leave you, madam?

Diana. Yes, you may go, both of you.

Fabio [*aside to* OCTAVIO]. We shall have an inquisition!

Octavio. She is mad with anger.

Fabio. I am sure she thinks I know something about it.
                                                      [*They go*

Diana. Dorotea.

Dorotea. What would you, madam?

Diana. I wish to know the names of the men that pass regularly up and down the street outside this house.

Dorotea. Madam, there is the Marquis Ricardo, and sometimes the Count of Paris.

Diana. If you would not earn my wrath, answer truthfully.

Dorotea. I have no guilty secrets, madam.

Diana. With whom have you seen these gentlemen converse?

Dorotea. Though I should be burned in flames of fire, I could find no other answer than that I have seen them solely in your company, madam.

Diana. Have they never entrusted you with any letters? Has no page of theirs ever entered here?

Dorotea. Never.

Diana. Very well. [DOROTEA *joins the other ladies.*]

Marcela [*aside to* ANARDA]. A veritable catechism!

Anarda. Her ladyship looks determined.

Diana. Anarda.

Anarda. Madam?

Diana. Who was that man that was here just now?

Anarda. A man!

Diana. He passed through this room. Do not dissemble. I know what your intrigues are. Which of you has dealings with him? Who tried to bring him to my chamber?

Anarda. Oh, madam! None of your women would dare admit a man to you against your will. I assure you, madam——

Diana. Anarda, come here. I see it now. That man did not come to visit me at all, but one of my women. Am I right?

Anarda. Madam, I see you are angry, and since I know that your anger is just, I cannot lie to you, although I betray my friendship with Marcela. She loves a man, and he loves her, though who he is, I know not.

Diana. Anarda, you have confessed the greater part. There is no virtue in denying the rest.

Anarda. Madam, you know how difficult it is for a woman to keep another's secret. Do not force me to tell you, let it suffice that you know it was Marcela he came to see. Take the matter no further, madam, I beg you. After all, they only talk together, and their meetings only began a few days ago.

Diana. This behavior is shameless. Would these people rob me and my house of our reputation, besmirch the memory of the Count, my father——

Anarda. Madam, let me explain a little further. The man who talks with Marcela is no intruder, so none will see him entering or leaving the house to cause a scandal.

Diana. Is it one of my servants then?

Anarda. It is.

Diana. Who is it?

Anarda. Teodoro.

Diana. My secretary?

Anarda. I only know they speak together.

Diana. Very well, Anarda. That is all.

Anarda. Madam, you are most understanding.

Diana [*aside*]. I feel somewhat calmer to know at least that the intruder did not seek to visit me. Marcela . . .

Marcela. Madam . . .

Diana. I wish to speak to you.

Marcela. What would you, madam?

Diana. Marcela, have I not always trusted you?

Marcela. Why, has someone slandered me, that you should ask? I have always been loyal to you, madam.

Diana. Are you sure, Marcela?

Marcela. What have I done to offend you?

Diana. Have you not offended me by holding secret concourse with a man in my house, even in my private apartments?

Marcela. Forgive me, madam. Teodoro is young and thoughtless. He cannot resist speaking a hundred loving words to me whenever we meet, though it be sometimes in your chamber.

Diana. A hundred? This must be a record year for love if loving words come by the hundredweight!

Marcela. I mean simply that no sooner does a thought strike him than it is translated immediately into words and needs must come flowing out at his mouth.

Diana. Translated into words? What words? What does he say to you?

Marcela. I cannot remember them now, madam.

Diana. I think you can.

Marcela. Sometimes he says: My soul is dying with love of you, Marcela. Another time he will say: My soul lives for you alone. Or: All night I have not slept for longing for your beauty. And then sometimes he will ask me for a hair from my head to bind up his restless thoughts and give him peace of mind. But why do you ask? It is only childish nonsense.

Diana. And yet you seem to enjoy it.

Marcela. I have no cause to complain. For I know that

Teodoro is an honest man, and that his love is honorable, in that he wants to marry me.

Diana. Marriage is indeed an honorable estate. Do you wish me to arrange the marriage between you?

Marcela. There is nothing that could delight me more. And, madam, since I find such kindness in your displeasure, I dare assure you that I adore him, for he is not only intelligent, wise, and prudent, but also the most loving, yet most discreet, young man to be found in all Naples.

Diana. I know his qualities, Marcela. I too have seen them in his service to me.

Marcela. But madam, the writing of a letter is not so sweet as murmuring softly side by side. "Dear madam" and "Your faithful servant" cannot compare with whispered terms of love.

Diana. Marcela, although I am resolved that you should marry—after a fitting time has elapsed, during which the necessary arrangements shall be made—yet I must respect my position, as the head of a distinguished family, and must not appear to harbor an affair which might damage the honor and reputation of my house. [*Aside.*] I must control my feelings and not be too harsh with her. [*To* Marcela.] But since all of my household know of your love already, I will only ask you to take more care in the future, and I will help you. Teodoro was brought up in my house, and I know him to be a sensible young man. Not only have you served me well, but also ties of blood decree that I should help you in this matter.

Marcela. Madam, I am your most grateful and devoted servant.

Diana. You may go now, Marcela.

Marcela. I kiss your hands.

Diana. Leave me, Marcela.

Anarda [*aside to* Marcela]. What did she say to you?

Marcela. Her displeasure turned to my good.

Dorotea. Does she know about Teodoro?

Marcela. She does, and has given us her blessing.

Marcela, Dorotea, *and* Anarda *curtsy to the* Countess *and go*

Diana. I too have often noted Teodoro's handsome looks, his wit, his charm, and if my rank did not forbid it, I should hold him in the most dear esteem. Love is the common tongue that everyone understands. And yet, what can I do? For I hold the honor of my family above the promptings of my heart. I fear that envy may soon take root in me, if it be true that the good fortune of others sows the seed. For I have much cause to complain, and wish that Teodoro's position were greater, that it should equal mine, or mine were less, that it might equal his.

She goes. Enter TEODORO *and* TRISTÁN.

Teodoro. I cannot rest, Tristán.

Tristán. I am not surprised, sir. If we were recognized, then that is the end of your career as her ladyship's perfect secretary. I told you you should have left her to go to bed in peace, but no, there you are, you would not listen.

Teodoro. Love never listens to advice, Tristán.

Tristán. But sir, you are too reckless. You take no precautions.

Teodoro. With skill none is needed.

Tristán. If you are as clever as you say, why are we in this dilemma now?

Teodoro. The question is: Did she recognize me?

Tristán. She did not recognize you, but she saw enough to make her suspicious.

Teodoro. When Fabio followed us downstairs, it was a wonder I did not kill him.

Tristán. That was a neat shot, when I threw my hat at the lamp.

Teodoro. Had he come farther I would have struck him down as he ran. So your hat did him a good turn, Tristán.

Tristán. It was the only thing to do: I said to that lamp: "Tell them we are not of the house!" It replied: "You lie!" So I took off my hat and hurled it at it. Thus did I avenge the insult to my honor.

Teodoro. Tristán, I await the death sentence.

Tristán. You lovers always say that, with cause or without.

Teodoro. Tristán, you will admit my position is dangerous. What can I do?

Tristán. You could fall out of love with Marcela, for if the Countess finds out about that, then nothing you can do will save you from being thrown out of this house.

Teodoro. Is there no other way than to forget her?

Tristán. Come, sir, I will give you lessons in the passing of love. Remember, anything can be achieved with skill and application. Now listen, and you will see how simple it is. First, you must resolve to forget Marcela, and give no thought to all that nonsense about loving forever. For if you start thinking in that way, and clinging even to the faintest hope of returning to her, then you have lost before you start. For, what do you suppose it is that prevents a man's forgetting a woman? Simply that he is entertained by the thought of a passionate reconciliation. You must control your imagination so that it never begins to move in that direction. Have you never seen a clock without its mainspring, how all its wheels are still, deprived of movement? So is hope to love. Banish hope and all love's power is dead.

Teodoro. But does not memory then come running with a thousand tricks to keep such thoughts alive, recalling all the joys of love, none of its miseries?

Tristán. Ah, yes, the lover's chiefest enemy is a fertile memory, as the poet said. But, even so, there is one sure way of defeating the imagination.

Teodoro. And what is that?

Tristán. To think of her defects and not her assets. This is the method a wise man uses to bore himself with the thought of his beloved. A philosopher once said that the best part of beauty is a good tailor. So, do not imagine her leaning over her balcony looking so slim and elegant in all her finery, with a golden girdle about her waist, and high-heeled shoes. All that is nothing but so much architecture. No. When you think of her, imagine her as a sinner in a penitent's robe. She will not look so enticing without her embroidered skirts and trimmings. In short, remember all her faults and you will soon find there is no better cure for love. Just think how, if you witness a repulsive and nauseating spectacle, it may put you off your food for a month. So, every time you think of her, think of something repellent about her, and there is your cure.

Teodoro. What a vulgar, rustic remedy, and a crude surgeon! Your panaceas are such as I should have expected from your rough hand. You are a quack, Tristán, you know nothing of the art. I could never imagine any woman that way. I can only see them all as pure, beautiful, and clear as crystal.

Tristán. All their promises are as easily broken, that is

the only likeness I can see. But it is quite clear, sir, that you are determined not to use my remedy and not to forget her. I was in love once myself, I swear it, an old bag of lies she was too, and fifty if she was a day. Now, among some two thousand or so defects she had, the most apparent was the size of her belly. It could have held all the heaps of paper and rubbish piled upon any five hundred desks in the country, and still leave room for a few small architectural constructions here and there—bridges, parapets, palisades, and that sort of thing. Or if you prefer a classical turn of phrase, it could have held as many Greeks as the Trojan horse. Did you never hear of that famous walnut tree, in some village or other, which was so big that a poor clerk and his wife and family lived comfortably in its hollow trunk without being squeezed? Well, a weaver and his wife and family and loom could have lived in comfort inside that stomach of hers. Now, it so happened that I wanted to forget her—you can well understand that I might—so, instead of letting my imagination run away with me, and thinking of her in terms of lilies, jasmine, and orange blossom, of ivory, silver, and snow all veiled by that fair curtain—her skirt—I kept a short rein on myself and thought of her in more suitable terms. I envisaged baskets full of moldy pumpkins, old battered hampers, dirty linen chests, postmen's pouches loaded with letters, sacks full of old mattresses, bedding, and bundles of old rags. Well, after a few such exercises of the imagination, all my love and hope turned to hatred and disdain. I forgot her, belly and all, for ever and ever, amen. And that was no small task, I assure you, for you could have packed four pestles into the folds of her flesh. But enough. I have made my point.

Teodoro. Marcela has no faults. I fear I shall not forget her.

Tristán. I see you will persist in your folly, sir. You are determined on your own destruction.

Teodoro. She is all delights. What can I do?

Tristán. Think of Marcela, and look for a new employer.

Enter DIANA.

Diana. Teodoro . . .
Teodoro [*aside*]. Here she is.
Diana. Teodoro.

Teodoro. What is my lady's will?

Tristán. If she asks him about last night, that is the end of him and me and Marcela too.

Diana. A friend of mine, a diffident creature, has asked me to write this letter for her. I could not, out of friendship, refuse her, and yet I know naught of love, Teodoro. I should like you to read what I have written and improve upon it. Take it, and read it, Teodoro.

Teodoro. Madam, if your hand wrote this, then any attempt on my part to equal it would be vain and gross conceit. I need not read it to know that it is perfect. Send it to your friend, my lady, and have no doubts.

Diana. Read it.

Teodoro. I shall learn a new style here, for, like you, I have never had experience in matters of love.

Diana. Never, Teodoro?

Teodoro. I never loved. I am too conscious of my own defects. I too am diffident.

Diana. Ah, that must be why you go in disguise.

Teodoro. I, madam? When? How?

Diana. Last night, for instance, I heard that you went out in disguise. My major-domo saw you.

Teodoro. That must have been when I was playing a trick on Fabio. We often jest together, do we not, Tristán?

Tristán. You do indeed, sir.

Diana. Read the letter, Teodoro.

Teodoro. I fear that someone must be jealous of me to tell such tales.

Diana. I do not doubt that soon some will be jealous of you. Read it, Teodoro.

Teodoro [*reads*].

"Jealousy comes oft to loving heart,
  And yet my heart loved not.
  Then why, in heart and mind that never loved,
  Did jealous thoughts take root?

"Why was I jealous if I did not love?
  For my cold heart loved not.
  Then I must think it was from jealousy
  That loving thoughts took root.

"Or did those kindred passions both conspire
  My stubborn heart to move

To envy that it never coveted
And love the object of another's love?"

Diana. What do you think?

Teodoro. That if this truly represents the feelings of the sender, then I have never seen a more wondrous piece of writing. But I confess I do not understand how love can be born of jealousy, nor yet come together with it in one instant, for it is always said to be the father of jealousy.

Diana. Because this lady, so I imagine, had always taken pleasure in the sight and company of the gallant, but had never felt any loving desire for him. But when she saw him love another, the jealousy she felt awoke her love for him, and so the two were born in her together. Is that possible?

Teodoro. I will concede it may be, madam. And yet, that jealousy she felt must itself have sprung from some cause, and that was undoubtedly love. She must have loved before, but did not know it.

Diana. I know not, Teodoro. I only know what my friend told me—that never before had she felt more than liking for the gentleman, but once she knew he loved another a thousand strong desires swept her from the strait path of her honor and banished forever from her mind the tranquil and honest thoughts she imagined hers.

Teodoro. Then your lines have spoken truly. I dare not attempt to write an equal to them.

Diana. Go in and try, Teodoro.

Teodoro. Madam, I dare not.

Diana. I beseech you, by my life.

Teodoro. You would have me prove my unlettered ignorance.

Diana. I will wait here. Return when you have written it.

Teodoro. As you will, madam.   [*He goes*

Diana. Tristán.

Tristán. Madam, I tremble to come before you in these old breeches. But you understand, your secretary, my master, has of late been a little absent-minded. For it ill becomes a gentleman to allow his servant to appear badly dressed, since the servant is the mirror and the façade by which observers judge the master. A wise man once said: when the master is on horseback, the servant walking, then it is the servant that is noticed first because the eye travels by way of the servant's body up to the master's face, as it were. I know not, but that we do our best——

Diana. Does he gamble?

Tristán. I wish to heaven he did! A gambler is never short of money, one way or another. In olden times kings always learned a profession so that if they lost their realm they would always have a means to earn their living. Those who had been gamblers usually did better after they were deposed than before. Gaming, madam, is a noble skill by which a living may be gained with a minimum of exertion. Take a great artist, for example, he will spend months chasing, engraving, and polishing a work of art until it reaches perfection, and then, if fools should say it is only worth melting down, what can he do about it? Nothing. But when a gambler puts his money on the right number, there it is, one hundred per cent profit and no argument.

Diana. He does not gamble, then?

Tristán. The more is the pity.

Diana. From what I hear, he has many love affairs.

Tristán. On the contrary, madam, he is like a block of ice in that respect.

Diana. I mean of an honest kind, do not misunderstand me, Tristán. Why, a good-looking, intelligent young man such as he, must have.

Tristán. I look after his horse and his personal comforts, madam. I know nothing of any finer dealings he may have. And yet I know that he is fully employed all day as Your Ladyship's secretary. I think he has time for little else.

Diana. But at night, Tristán? Does he never go out at night?

Tristán. I never go with him. I have a broken hip.

Diana. A broken hip! How did that happen, Tristán?

Tristán. I fell downstairs, as the wives of jealous husbands say when you ask who blacked their eye.

Diana. You fell downstairs?

Tristán. Yes, full length. I counted every step with my ribs.

Diana. But then, Tristán, what could you expect, when you had thrown your hat at the light?

Tristán [*aside*]. Oh, God, she knows the whole story!

Diana. Why do you not answer, Tristán?

Tristán. I was just trying to recall what occasion you were referring to, madam. Ah, yes, I remember now. Last night there was a great flight of black bats swooping around the house—you must have noticed them—well, one of them went for the light, I took a swipe at it with my hat, caught the lamp by mistake, the lamp went out, my legs slipped from under me, and there I was, sprawling full length down the stairs.

Diana. It is a good story, Tristán, and I am glad you have warned me of the bats. I will find a remedy. I will no longer harbor such disturbances in my house.

Tristán [aside]. Heaven help me, I think I shall end up as chief bat-catcher in the galleys.   [*Exit* TRISTÁN

Diana. Oh, how confused are my thoughts.

Enter FABIO.

Fabio. Madam, the Marquis Ricardo is here.
Diana. Set out the chairs.

Enter RICARDO *and* CELIO. FABIO *and* TRISTÁN *set out the chairs and go.*

Ricardo. Diana, I come, full of that gentle care and sweet longing that will make smooth all paths that lead me to my goal. Love it is that drives me to persevere in my suit though many say my ambition is in vain. Yet do not think that though I show less confidence than others, I bear you less love. It is not so. I will not ask if you are well, for I have only to look at you, and see your radiance and your beauty to know that you are, for what better sign of health is there in a woman than . . . er . . . radiant beauty? Therefore, I know that you are well, and will not ask. Yet for myself, my condition is more uncertain, for it depends on you to grant me health or woe. . . .

Diana. Sir, your delicate tongue and subtle thought give the name of beauty to a trait more often known as gaiety. And yet I think I lack the power to decide whether you are ill or well.

Ricardo. Madam, my very being depends upon your word. The honest intention of my love and desire is known throughout this city, and my family and yours are alike in hopes that you will speak with me of marriage. Only your word is lacking; that is most needful, without which all my hopes and plans are nothing. If those lands which I have inherited were increased one hundredfold, and stretched from the farthest southern shores known to the scorching sun, to Aurora's distant bedside in the east . . . If all the gold desired by men, all the pearls, the congealed tears of heaven, all the diamonds for which men ever toiled to open paths across unfriendly seas, were mine, then I would offer them as willingly. And do not doubt, lady, that I would venture beyond the realms where the sun has ever shone, if by so doing I should do you service. Or travel over worlds of water, continents of salt, in a small wooden bark to the most distant shores of the antipodes to serve you.

Diana. Sir, I know how steadfast is your love, and how great your virtue. Fear not, but I will presently arrange that your hopes may have their reward. Yet I hope Count Federico will not be too much offended.

Ricardo. The Count is wily, and envies me already. But I trust that the good you see in me will turn the darts of his malice.

Enter TEODORO.

Teodoro. Madam, I have written as you bade me.

Ricardo. My lady, I see you are busy. I will not steal another moment of your time.

Diana. There is no haste. It is a letter to Rome.

Ricardo. Nothing is more tiresome than long visits when one is dealing with one's correspondence.

Diana. You are most understanding, sir.

Ricardo. I would do your pleasure in all things. [*Aside.*] Celio, what think you?

Celio. Your love is certain of its reward.

[RICARDO *and* CELIO *go*

Diana. You have written, Teodoro?

Teodoro. Madam, I have, but with no confidence in my ability. I had no choice. I did as you commanded.

Diana. Show it to me.

Teodoro. Read it, madam.

Diana [*reading*].

"Love may lie long concealed within the heart
    Until another covets that it loves.
  Then will it rise and show its sovereign power.
  Thus envy rouses love, and love's strength proves.

"So do the kindred passions both conspire
   To move the stubborn heart
But where there is no sleeping love to rouse,
   Envy alone cannot true love impart.

"Thus do I know that there was love before,
   But more I must not seem to understand
Lest I presume to rate myself too high,
   And so invite love's vengeance at your hand."
Your lines are most correct and in exquisite taste.

Teodoro. Madam, you mock me.

Diana. No, I do not jest. I would I did.

Teodoro. What is your opinion, madam?

Diana. That your verses surpass mine, Teodoro.

Teodoro. Then I am sorry. For a servant to appear more accomplished than his master is a sure way to earn hatred. A king once asked one of his ministers to prepare a second draft of a document written in the king's own hand, and as soon as he knew that the king preferred the rival version, the minister said to the eldest of his three sons: "Come, we must all make haste and leave the kingdom, for the king realizes that I am wiser than he." I fear that I am in the same position.

Diana. No, Teodoro, for although I praise your letter and say it is more polished than mine, that is because it follows my theme so well. And though I admire the work of your pen, I shall not therefore lose confidence or cease the use of mine. Besides, I am a woman, and prone to errors, though I never thought till now, to indiscretion. Do not fear to offend, for you write of love, and there can be no offense in love.

Teodoro. You reason well. And yet Icarus, and Phaëton too, plunged down to their destruction, the one with his wax wings destroyed by the furnace of the sun, and the other the golden horses cast headlong upon a rocky mountain, because they aimed too high.

Diana. But the sun is not a woman. If you should ever love a highborn woman, serve her and have no fear. Love is but a matter of persistence, and women are not stones. I will keep your verses and read them at leisure.

Teodoro. Madam, you will find a thousand errors there.

Diana. I see none.

Teodoro. I wish you were right. I have your verses still, lady. Here they are.

Diana. Keep them. . . . No, tear up the paper.

Teodoro. Tear it up?

Diana. It is of no matter, when greater things than a
few verses might be lost.   [*She goes*

Teodoro. It cannot be! And yet . . . No, the Countess
is too modest, too conscious of her honor, to declare her
love so openly, so soon. And yet, she has never spoken so
before. No. I flatter myself in this. She is too wise, too
noble. But what meant she when she said she feared to
lose something greater than a few verses—did she mean
the friend she spoke of? No, there can be no doubt she
meant herself—Diana—she who is courted by noble princes
who would not think me worthy even to be their slave.
I fear I am in great danger. She knows that I have courted
Marcela, she saw through my deceit and mocked me for
it, only a few moments ago. But it was not all mockery,
for when has joking ever brought forth such an ebb and
flow of blushes, such hesitancy, such nervousness? When
she looked on me, her lips parted in a smile like a rose
opening its crimson petals to greet the gentle rain of a
summer morning. And when she blushed, her pale cheek
was as an apple ripened by the autumn sun. Can there be
truth in what I thought I saw—and heard? If not, then I
am mad. Yet stay, my thoughts. For she is great beyond
your scope—and beautiful beyond the scope of any human
thought or dream.

Enter MARCELA.

Marcela. Teodoro, I would speak with you.

Teodoro. As you will, Marcela. Have I not said I would
die for you? To speak with you is a greater pleasure still.

Marcela. I have counted every minute of the night like
a lonely sparrow, until I could speak with you. And when
at last I saw the first reflection of Apollo's brightness in
the farthest east, I said, "Soon I shall see my own Apollo,
Teodoro." Oh, such things have happened. . . . The
Countess would not go to bed until she had discovered
the whole of the story. My friends, who envy me my happiness with you, have told the Countess. Oh, never believe
that there is friendship between those who serve together,
though it should seem so. All is false. But, to tell it briefly,
the Countess knows all about our meetings. Well do they
call the moon that spies on lovers Diana, for the Countess

came too soon from behind her clouds and saw us together.
But, Teodoro, do not fear, for the greatest good fortune
is to come from this mishap. I told her how honest were
your intentions and that you hoped to marry me. I even
told her how much I adore you. I praised all your virtues
to her, your manners, your noble and gentle nature. And,
in return, she showed her greatness and generosity to me!
She said she was happy that I should love you, and that
she would see that we were married soon! I feared she
would be angry, that the whole house would be set in an
uproar, you and I dismissed, the others punished. But I
misjudged her. She was so magnanimous, so understanding. She recognized your worth and has been just and
merciful. Oh, what a blessing it is to serve such a mistress.

Teodoro. She said she would allow me to marry you?

Marcela. Never fear, she will not break her word.

Teodoro [*aside*]. My own foolishness deceived me. Oh,
what a simpleton I was to think that the Countess could
love me. She would never stoop to one as base as I.

Marcela. What are you muttering, Teodoro?

Teodoro. The Countess spoke to me, too, Marcela, but
gave me no hint that she knew that it was I who left her
apartments in disguise.

Marcela. She is discreet. By pretending not to know,
she is not obliged to punish us. Instead her reward is that
we may marry—with her blessing.

Teodoro. You are right. She is the soul of discretion,
and marriage is the most honorable reward she could have
granted us.

Marcela. Are you not happy, Teodoro?

Teodoro. I am most fortunate.

Marcela. Then show it, Teodoro.

Teodoro. My arms shall show you I am willing, and
seal you to me in love's truest bond.

Enter DIANA.

Marcela. Madam!

Diana. I rejoice to see you both so happy.

Teodoro. I was just telling Marcela how troubled I was
last night, lest you should think I had brought your name
into disrepute, and she in her turn assured me that you
had shown your mercy to us by agreeing to our marriage,
wherefore I took her in my arms as a seal to that agree-

ment. I could have lied to you, madam, and found a dozen excuses for our being here together, but I know I need not fear to tell the truth to you.

Diana. Teodoro, you deserve to be punished for the disloyalty you have shown to me and my house, and my lenience to you both last night is no excuse for your behavior now. Love is always kindly looked on while it observes the bounds of propriety, but once it exceeds those bounds its privilege is lost and it is no longer exempt from blame or punishment. Therefore, I think that it is best that you and Marcela should be separated until you are married, lest you prove a bad example to my other servants. Dorotea! Dorotea!

Enter DOROTEA.

Dorotea. Madam?

Diana. Take this key, and shut Marcela in my room. Do not say that this is done in anger; there is much sewing she has to do there.

Dorotea [*aside*]. What is this, Marcela?

Marcela. The cruel will of greatness. I am to be kept from Teodoro.

Diana. Do not fear any imprisonment or treachery here. Love holds the master key. [*They go.*] And so, you wish to marry, Teodoro?

Teodoro. I only wish to do your pleasure, madam, and, believe me, I have not offended so gravely as the scorpion tongues of envy have reported to you. Had Ovid known what it is to serve a great lord or lady, then he would have set the seat of envy among those who serve together, not in the barren mountains.

Diana. Then is it not true that you love Marcela?

Teodoro. I could live without Marcela.

Diana. But I was told that you were almost out of your wits with love for her.

Teodoro. My wits being but small, that would be no great thing. But I speak truly when I say I have not paid so many attentions to Marcela as have been reported to you. No doubt she deserves them, but she has not received them from me.

Diana. But have you not spoken of love to her so often and so ardently that a woman of greater worth than she might have been deceived?

Teodoro. Words cost but little, madam.

Diana. But what did you say to her, Teodoro? What do men say when they court women?

Teodoro. They speak as one that loves and one that begs, decking one small truth, if indeed there be one, in a thousand lies.

Diana. But what are the words they speak?

Teodoro. Madam, you press me too far. . . . "Those lovely eyes," I might say, "are the sun and the moon by which I see." Or: "The coral and the pearl of that heavenly mouth . . ."

Diana. Heavenly?

Teodoro. Such phrases are the common jargon and etiquette of love, lady.

Diana. Teodoro, I begin to lose faith in your judgment, for I well know that in Marcela there are more faults than graces. The more closely I look, the more I see them. Apart from that, I have found while she has been in my service that she is not so fastidious in her habits as might be thought desirable. . . . But there, you love her, I would not disillusion you for the world, but I could tell you . . . But let it be. Her graces, or disgraces, are nothing to me. I am well pleased that you should love her. We must arrange your marriage with all speed. But since you are well versed in the ways of love, pray, Teodoro, give me some advice for that friend of mine who is so troubled with love for a man of humble estate. Does she not offend against her own position of authority? And yet, when she tries to renounce her love, she is almost out of her mind with jealousy. The man suspects nothing of her love. He is always distant, reticent, and far too discreet.

Teodoro. I have told you, madam, I know naught of love.

Diana. Have you not said you love Marcela? Have you not whispered a thousand loving words to her? Oh, if these doors could speak, they would tell——

Teodoro. There is nothing these doors could tell.

Diana. There, you are blushing. Your own face contradicts you, even as you speak.

Teodoro. What has she told you, madam? It is true that I once took her hand, and held it for less than one second——

Diana. Yet long enough to kiss it, perhaps?

Teodoro. Very well, lady, I confess, I cooled my lips upon the hand she offered me, looking as it did like snow and lilies blended.

Diana. Snow and lilies blended! Is that a remedy to cool a loving heart? Well, Teodoro, what is your advice?

Teodoro. If the man she loved is so far beneath her that for her to desire him would prejudice her honor, then she should come to him in disguise, so that she may enjoy his company and he not recognize who she is.

Diana. There would still be the danger that she might be found out. Should she not kill him, rather, and thus put temptation out of her sight?

Teodoro. They say that Marcus Aurelius gave his wife, Faustina, the blood of a fencer to cure her of a similar passion. But that was a pagan remedy, ill-suited to our times.

Diana. You say true. And yet there were such true and noble people as Lucretia, Torquatus, and Virginius in those days—people whose like we do not see today. Although, it is true, that age had Messalinas and Poppeas too. Write me some verses upon this subject, Teodoro. Now God be with you. Oh, heavens! I slipped. Come, Teodoro, help me. Give me your hand.

Teodoro. Madam, it was respect prevented me.

Diana. What courteous discourtesy! Why do you offer me your hand covered with your cloak?

Teodoro. Fabio does so when he accompanies you to church.

Diana. But his is a hand I never asked for; besides it has been a hand for seventy years, and might have been dead for as many, it is so cold. But to stand and stare when someone falls is like going for armor when you see a friend attacked. Besides it is mere prudery, not courtesy, to imagine that an honorable hand should ever be covered.

Teodoro. I fear to appear presumptuous lest I should seem insensible of the honor of serving you.

Diana. Were you a squire, then it would be fitting for your hand to remain beneath your cloak, but you are my secretary. Keep my fall secret, Teodoro, if you wish yourself to rise.   [*She goes*

Teodoro. Can I believe what I have heard? Yes, for Diana is a most beautiful woman, in whom all things are

possible. She asked for my hand, and her face was pale
with fear. Then, as I gave it, a soft blush drove out the
paleness of her fear. I felt her tremble. What should I
think? What can I do? Pursue this happy chance and
banish fear? If I do, then I must abandon Marcela forever, who pines for me. I do not wish to cause her sorrow.
But women themselves are fickle. She would desert me if
some new object of delight caught her fancy. Therefore,
if men are to suffer the pangs of unrequited love, women
too must learn to take the consequences.

ACT TWO

1

The street outside a church

Enter COUNT FEDERICO *and* LEONIDO.

FEDERICO. Have you seen her?

Leonido. Yes, I saw her go in. I swear that as she passed
over that carpet in the doorway, the embroidered flowers
there glowed as though they grew in a meadow and dawn's
first light shone on them at that instant. The service will
not be long. I know the priest, and he can hurry through
the Mass faster than any priest in Naples.

Federico. Oh, if only I might speak to her.

Leonido. But you are her cousin, surely no one would
deny that you have a right to speak to her.

Federico. Unfortunately, Leonido, since I wish to marry
her I am barred from the easy familiarity of a cousin.
Before I loved her, I was never diffident when speaking to
her. Now I love her, etiquette forbids me her presence,
and when I do see her, emotion binds my tongue. My
condition is such that I almost wish I did not love the
Countess, having lost the carefree happiness of her sight
and converse.

Enter RICARDO *and* CELIO.

Celio. She came on foot, accompanied by a few of her
household.

Ricardo. This street is honored indeed to contain the
church where Diana comes to worship.

Celio. Have you never seen a fair May morning break,

when the sun shines in the sign of the bull—the white
bull, the poets call him—that grazes among the ruddy
clouds of dawn? So came she forth, and yet more perfect,
for Diana, the Countess of Belflor, shines with two suns,
while the heavens boast only one.

Ricardo. My love has turned you painter, Celio! You
do well to depict so fair a landscape and to portray Diana
as the sun, for so she is, and as the sun passes through
each sign of the zodiac in turn, so her eyes pass over her
suitors, resting on none. See, there is Federico, waiting
for his share of the golden beams.

Celio. Which of you will prove the bull this morning?
Upon whom will her spring light fall?

Ricardo. Federico was here before me, and so wins the
sign of Taurus, but I will be the Lion, and hope her
warmer gaze shall shine on me.

Federico. Is that Ricardo?

Leonido. It is.

Federico. It would have been a marvel had he not been
here.

Leonido. He is looking gallant this morning.

Federico. Leonido, that is no way to speak to a jealous
lover.

Leonido. Are you jealous?

Federico. Have I not cause? And now you make matters
worse by praising him to me.

Leonido. But why should you be jealous? Diana does
not favor him. She loves no one.

Federico. But she might one day. She is a woman.

Leonido. No, she is too proud, too vain, too cold in
nature.

Federico. Great beauty has reason to be proud; if it
were not, then it would not be great.

Leonido. Ingratitude is never beautiful.

Celio. Here she comes, my lord.

Ricardo. My day is dawning.

Celio. Will you speak to her?

Ricardo. If my rival is not there before me, I will.

Enter DIANA, OCTAVIO, FABIO, *followed by* MARCELA,
DOROTEA, *and* ANARDA.

Federico [*to* DIANA]. I have waited here, madam, in
expectation. Hoping for a glimpse of you.

Diana. I am happy to meet you here, Count Federico.

Ricardo. I, too, have waited, lady, in the hope of speaking with you and of serving you.

Diana. My lord, I am most fortunate to deserve such attentions.

Ricardo. And I more fortunate to be allowed to render them.

Federico [*to* LEONIDO]. You see how she favors him? I am excluded.

Leonido. Speak to her again.

Federico. Who can speak, Leonido, knowing he gives no pleasure to the hearer?   [*They go*

✦

A *room in the palace of the* COUNTESS

TEODORO. My imagination soars. My thoughts whirl on the winds beyond the farthest bounds of possibility, and I delight in watching their mad career, urging them ever onwards when I should curb my fancy. But when Diana is the prize, who would count the risk? Be still, wild hopes, while I again examine the source from which you spring. I love the one I serve. My eyes and all my senses tell me I have good cause for love, for she is fair beyond the bounds of praise. Yet I would not build towers of diamonds upon a heap of straw. Should I do so, my reason is to blame, that allows my hopes to soar too near the sun. Yet love it is that bears them to the height, and were I not so base, my love would not prove disproportionate. My hopes are the nobler part of me, let me follow where they lead. Be bold my thoughts, and if I fail, no man may scorn Teodoro for being a laggard coward in love, rather it will be said I followed the noble yearnings of my heart toward a nobler object. To fail in a great enterprise is a worthier fate than to fear the consequence and so never make the attempt.

Enter TRISTÁN.

Tristán. If I might intrude a moment, sir, I have here a letter from Marcela, full of love and woe at her imprisonment. I do not expect to be paid for its delivery, since nobody pays for a thing unless they are going to profit by it, just as no one wants to meet a man unless some advancement may come from it—as I soon learned

when I came to court. Oh, yes, I also know that chattering
visitors are a tedious bore to a man of exalted position,
as you would seem to be, sir, were I not so well acquainted
with you as to know otherwise. But when a man's fortune
fails him, not a soul will come near him. He will be
shunned as if he had the plague. Would you like me to
sterilize this letter in vinegar before you handle it?

Teodoro. To have been carried by your hands, Tristán,
will have served the same purpose. Come, give it me.
[*Reads.*] "To Teodoro, my husband . . ." Her husband?
How absurd.

Tristán. More than absurd. . . .

Teodoro. Foolish girl, fluttering butterfly. Am I a candle,
that she must ever fly around me and never leave me in
peace?

Tristán. Read it, for heaven's sake, however high and
rarefied you have now become. There are always flies
around wine, but that does not detract from its value.
Besides, I remember a time when this butterfly, as now
you term her, was a beautiful, elegant, soaring eagle.

Teodoro. Tristán, my thoughts now fly so high it is a
wonder they can see her at all.

Tristán. That is all very fine, sir, but what are we going
to do with the letter?

Teodoro. This.

Tristán. Do not tear it up, sir.

Teodoro. There, it is done.

Tristán. But why?

Teodoro. That is the shortest answer I can make.

Tristán. Sir, you are unnecessarily hard upon Marcela.

Teodoro. I have changed, Tristán.

Tristán. Changed, have you? You lovers are a sort of
love-apothecaries, scribbling your loving notes and verses
as they do their prescriptions. You are skilled in your
cures too. Potion for raging jealousy: water of blue violets.
Cure for a rare disdain: boracical syrupi (followed by a
liberal dose of alcohol) should temper the humors. Pre-
scription for absence of the beloved: a poultice on the
chest, to be worn preferably in the presence of congenial
company. Cure for the inclination to marriage: a diet of
alcohol and good living for ten days, followed by a purge
of antimony on the eleventh. Remedy for that heavenly
sign known as Capricorn, the horned goat: the patient

must either live with his complaint, or else carry out amnesia upon himself. Cure for an injured purse as a result of the removal of a jewel or gown from a shop: tablets of gold and silver must be applied to the wound until it is fully healed. So you go on, year in, year out, getting sick and then effecting cures as quickly. And no payment is required for the treatment. The paper—record of both the malady and cure—is soon destroyed, and it makes no difference whether the patient recovers or not. Thus is your account invalid with Marcela, and the cure, no longer needed, is destroyed without revealing its message.

Teodoro. Tristán, you have been drinking again.

Tristán. Oh, I thought you were going to faint. The height is too much for you, perhaps?

Teodoro. Tristán, all men must follow their own fortune, and fate decrees that I must either die in disgrace and misery or live to be the count of Belflor. So mock me not for aspiring beyond my rank, since you have never felt the force of that fatal power which drives me on.

Tristán. Cesare Borgia had for his motto the words: "Caesar or nothing," sir, and for his epitaph was written: "You would be Caesar or nothing, and you have all your wish, being both Caesar and nothing."

Teodoro. I have taken the first step, Tristán, and I will take the motto for my own, let Fortune do what she will.

Enter MARCELA *and* DOROTEA. *They do not notice* TEODORO *and* TRISTÁN.

Dorotea. Dear Marcela, if any among all of us who serve the Countess feels for your misfortunes, it is I.

Marcela. Since I have been locked up in her room, you have shown me such friendship that I never hope to value a friend more than I value you, Dorotea. Anarda thinks I do not know that she is in love with Fabio. It was she that told the Countess of my love for Teodoro.

Dorotea. There is Teodoro.

Marcela. Oh, my love, Teodoro! . . .

Teodoro. Marcela, stop.

Marcela. But my love, how shall I, when I adore you, and suddenly you are here before my eyes?

Teodoro. Have a care, Marcela, the very tapestries have ears. They have spoken too, and may again. Why else

do you suppose figures are portrayed upon them, but to
remind the observer that there may be someone behind
them? And those embroidered figures will speak as surely
as did that dumb prince they tell of who never spoke a
word until the day he saw his father killed, when he
cried out to alarm the palace.

Marcela. Did you read my letter?

Teodoro. No. There it is. All the love I spoke of to you
is destroyed with it, for I have learned wisdom and will
play at love no more.

Marcela. Are those the remains?

Teodoro. Yes, Marcela.

Marcela. My love lay there within it.

Teodoro. Marcela, no good can come of it, only trouble
and great danger. I beg you, if you can, to forget the letter
and your love for me. Speak of love no more.

Marcela. Teodoro, I do not understand you.

Teodoro. I have no wish to displease the Countess
further.

Marcela. I feared that it would come to this.

Teodoro. Marcela, may God go with you, and though
our love must end, let not our friendship.

Marcela. Teodoro, is it you that speaks?

Teodoro. Yes, it is I. I would keep the peace and
preserve propriety in this house that has made me what
I am, and given me my being.

Marcela. Listen, Teodoro——

Teodoro. Leave me, Marcela.

Marcela. Why do you treat me like this?

Teodoro. Marcela, I am weary of these games.   [*He goes*

Marcela. Oh, Tristán, Tristán!

Tristán. What is the matter?

Marcela. What has happened to Teodoro?

Tristán. My master has taken a leaf out of the women's
book: he has changed his mind.

Marcela. Not mine. What women?

Tristán. Oh, women made of honey, made of——

Marcela. Tristán, tell him——

Tristán. I cannot tell him anything. He is the sword,
I am merely the scabbard, the envelope to his letter, the
hatbox to his hat, the cloak to the traveler, nourishment
to his varied appetite, his comet's tail, his second string,
his shadow, the summer storm to make his sun seem

brighter. And finally I am the nail upon his finger, and may be trimmed at any moment.   [*He goes*

Marcela. Dorotea, what think you?

Dorotea. I dare not speak my thoughts.

Marcela. No? Then I will.

Dorotea. I cannot, Marcela.

Marcela. I can and will.

Dorotea. Remember the tapestries, Marcela.

Marcela. Love spurned fears no danger. If I did not know how proud and conscious of her position is the Countess, I would say that Teodoro hoped to win her. Surely it is not for nothing that he has been so required and favored lately.

Dorotea. Hush. You speak in anger.

Marcela. But I will be avenged. I am not such a fool that I lack the craft to make them sorry.

Enter FABIO.

Fabio. Is not her ladyship's secretary with you?

Marcela. Do you mock me?

Fabio. My dear young lady, I am looking for the secretary. My mistress desires him.

Marcela. Ask Dorotea. I cannot account for his movements. I doubt if he can himself. He is like a madman at large in the house.

Fabio. A madman? Her ladyship's secretary? . . . Ah, you cannot play tricks like that with me. Do you think I do not know about the two of you? You know where he is. It is a plot between you.

Marcela. A plot between us! Ha!

Fabio. You cannot deceive me, young lady.

Marcela. I confess, Fabio, there was a time when I listened to Teodoro's raving, but now I only have eyes for a somewhat older man.

Fabio. An older man?

Marcela. He looks a little like you, Fabio.

Fabio. Like me, Marcela?

Marcela. Fabio, I speak to you in the strictest confidence, and if I lie when I say I love you to distraction, then may I die of the world's most fatal malady—love unrequited. Your face, your form, are my greatest delight. Everything about you persuades my heart and soul that they are yours.

Fabio. This is an obvious deceit. Why should I believe it? If this is some plot or jest, I fail to see the purpose of it.

Dorotea. Take advantage of the occasion, Fabio. Marcela has no other course but to love you now.

Fabio. If I could believe it . . .

Dorotea. Teodoro flies high. He is beyond Marcela's reach.

Fabio. Ah, yes, yes, Teodoro. . . . I must go and find him. I see what a slight thing I am to you, Marcela. Your love is like a letter addressed to Teodoro, but in his absence to be delivered to Fabio. But I will forgive you the slight, although it offends my dignity. I will speak further with you some other time. I am ever your servant, madam.   [*He goes*

Dorotea. What means this, Marcela?

Marcela. I do not know. Does not Anarda love Fabio?

Dorotea. Yes, she does.

Marcela. Then I will be avenged on two at once. For love is the god of envy and of injury.

Enter DIANA *and* ANARDA.

Anarda. And now you know the cause, madam, perhaps you will forgive me.

Diana. The reason you give leaves me more confused than before.

Anarda. Look, there is Marcela, talking with Dorotea.

Diana. The sight of her here gives me little pleasure. Marcela, go to your room.

Marcela [*aside to* DOROTEA]. She fears to speak with me, Dorotea.   [MARCELA *and* DOROTEA *go*

Anarda. May I speak openly to you, madam?

Diana. You know you may.

Anarda. Your two suitors have just now departed in sorrow for the disdain you show them. They are mad with love, and yet you show yourself colder than Anaxarete towards them, chaster than Lucretia. To despise so many men——

Diana. I have heard enough, Anarda.

Anarda. Which of them do you think to marry? Does not the Marquis Ricardo equal, if not exceed, in generosity and good looks the richest, most powerful man in the land? And would the noblest of women consider herself too good for your cousin Federico? Why have you dismissed them with such scorn?

Diana. The one is a fool, the other a madman. And you are as foolish as they, Anarda, not to have understood me better. I do not love them because I love another, and hopelessly.

Anarda. You . . . ! Love . . . !

Diana. Why should I not? Am I not a woman?

Anarda. Yes, but one of ice and snow that even the sun may shine on and not melt.

Diana. And yet a man of humble circumstance has melted the ice and snow.

Anarda. Who is he?

Diana. Shame prevents me from telling you his name. Enough to say that it injures my honor to love such a man.

Anarda. If Pasiphaë loved a bull, Semiramis a horse, besides those others we hear tell of that loved monsters, what shame can there be in loving a man, whoever he be?

Diana. One who loves can, if he will, turn his love to hatred and hate as truly as he loved. So will I do.

Anarda. Is that possible?

Diana. I will do it. I loved because I wanted to. Now I wish it no more, I will love no longer. [*Music is heard off.*] Who is that singing?

Anarda. Fabio and Clara.

Diana. I would their music could solace me.

Anarda. Music and love agree well together. Listen.

Singers [*off*].

Oh, for the power to turn love's darts at will:
          Turn love to hate,
          And hate to love.
Oh, for the power to turn love's darts at will.

Anarda. Do you hear the song, madam? Does it not contradict what you were saying?

Diana. I hear it, but I best know my mind, and will change to hatred a love which so ill suits my state. I am determined.

Anarda. Such power is beyond human strength.

Enter TEODORO.

Teodoro. Madam, Fabio told me that you wanted me.

Diana. That was long ago.

Teodoro. I am here to obey your wishes. Forgive me if I have been slow to answer your call.

Diana. You have seen those two gentlemen . . . my two suitors, have you not?

Teodoro. Yes, madam.

Diana. They are both handsome men.

Teodoro. Very handsome.

Diana. I do not want to make a decision without your advice, Teodoro. Which of them should I marry?

Teodoro. Madam, how can I advise you on a matter that concerns your personal taste alone? Whichever of them you choose to give me for my master, I shall esteem the better.

Diana. You ill reward my faith in you as a good counselor in questions of importance.

Teodoro. Madam, are there not older, wiser men than I in this house who better understand these things? Octavio, your major-domo, has much experience. He is old and knows the world.

Diana. I want you to be pleased with the master you will have. Is the Marquis more handsome than my cousin, Federico?

Teodoro. Yes, madam.

Diana. Then I choose the Marquis. Go, and give him the happy news, Teodoro.   [DIANA *and* ANARDA *go*

Teodoro. What a misfortune is mine! How swiftly she has changed. Is this the end of all my hopes? Oh, sun, melt to nothing the waxen wings that bore me up so presumptuously to set myself beside an angel! Oh, what a fool I was to base so many hopes upon one word of love. Love can never be between those of unequal birth! And yet, is it surprising that I was deceived by those eyes that would have seduced Ulysses from his course? There is none to blame, only myself. Besides, I cannot say that I have lost her, since she was never mine. I must make believe it was some grave accident, and while it happened I suffered a delirium. No more. I must banish from my mind the thought that one day I might be the Count of Belflor, and pursue my former course. I will love Marcela, and let Marcela be enough. Great ladies seek great lords. Love is born between equals. And you, my thoughts, since you are born of air, return to air again,

for where merit is lacking, those who seek to rise will
ever fall.

Enter FABIO.

Fabio. Have you spoken to the Countess?

Teodoro. Yes, Fabio, even now, and I have happy news.
My mistress is resolved to marry. Each of her suitors
adores her, and she in her rare wisdom has chosen the
Marquis.

Fabio. She is most wise.

Teodoro. She asked me to bear the good news to him,
but since you have been such a good friend to me, Fabio,
I will give that pleasurable task to you. Go quickly, Fabio,
and tell him the joyful news.

Fabio. A joyful task indeed! I hope I may show you
similar generosity one day. I will fly like lightning with
the glad tidings, and then come back to you. I am delighted with the whole business. The Marquis is to be
congratulated. It was no mean feat to conquer the Countess.

He goes. Enter TRISTÁN.

Tristán. Ah, there you are. I have been looking for you.
Is it true? I have heard . . .

Teodoro. Yes. It is true, Tristán, if it is my disillusion-
ment that you have heard of.

Tristán. I heard that she had decided, but which of the
two old jackdaws is to take the prize, I know not.

Teodoro. That fickle sunflower, that weather vane, that
glass, that tidal river which casts its waters out and then
draws them back again, this Diana, this changing moon,
this woman, this piece of witchcraft, monster of a thousand shapes, she who took an easy victory over me only
to humiliate the vanquished. . . . She asked me to say
which of the two pleased me more, for she would not
think of marrying without my advice! I was as one struck
dumb, or dead. I felt I should run mad, and the mark of
my lunacy was that I said nothing! Finally she announced
that she preferred the Marquis, and that I should go and
give him the good news.

Tristán. So she has decided at last?

Teodoro. The Marquis Ricardo.

Tristán. If I were not so considerate of the state you

are in, and were prepared to add insult to injury, I might say "I told you so," and mock your high-flying thoughts of becoming a count.

Teodoro. Yes, I flew high, Tristán, but now I plumb the depths.

Tristán. You have only yourself to blame.

Teodoro. I do not deny it. I believed too readily what I read in a woman's eyes.

Tristán. I tell you, there is no poison so potent to a man's good senses as that in women's eyes.

Teodoro. I feel I can never raise my eyes again. It is over, Tristán. The only remedy is to bury this foolish episode and the memory of my love in forgetfulness.

Tristán. And so you return, sadder and wiser, to Marcela.

Teodoro. That is a broken friendship which can soon be mended.

Enter MARCELA.

Marcela [aside]. How hard it is to pretend to love when we feel it not. How hard to forget a love that is a year old. The more I try to cheat my thoughts of their desire, the more persistent are the memories that return. But if it is ordained so, and if it is within the limits fixed by honor, a remedy may be found in another's love. Yet how can I suppose it is possible to have two loves at once? Or that, by having them, one would have revenge? I rather fear the greatest revenge is likely to be against myself. It would be better to wait in patience than to risk my heart again in a pretended love which might prove as real as the love that it should cure.

Teodoro. Marcela . . .

Marcela. Who is it?

Teodoro. It is I. Have you forgotten me so soon?

Marcela. Forgotten you! Why, I have driven my very soul out of my body in order to forget you. For wherever my soul is, it brings with it thoughts of you. But can you bear to speak to me? Does it not offend your lips to utter my name?

Teodoro. Marcela, I only wished to test your faithfulness to me, and now I know how little you valued our love, for I hear that your distress was such that you instantly found another to replace me.

Marcela. Any wise man knows that the fragile glass of a

woman's faith should never be put to the test. I do not believe you, Teodoro; I know you too well. Ambition crazed your mind. How is it with you now? Has it not turned out as you imagined? Must you now pay for your foolish dreams? Is your good fortune not quite so divine as the charms of your mistress? You look troubled, Teodoro; what is the matter? The wind has changed, perhaps? And do you now return to seek your equal once more? Or is it that you want to wish me happiness?

Teodoro. If it is revenge you wanted, can there be any more cruel than this, Marcela? I beg you, remember that love is the child of noble parents. Do not be harsh with me, for vengeance is base and ignoble, not worthy of the conqueror. You have conquered. I return to you, Marcela. The thoughts I had before were madness. If you hold any love for me, forgive my rashness. Not because I found my hopes impossible fantasies, but because memories of you have brought me back. Let then my memories awaken yours, and let me confess you victorious.

Marcela. Heaven forbid that I should spoil your chance to advance yourself. Do not give up now, go on, serve her, pursue your aims, or else your mistress will call you coward. Follow your fortune, and I will follow mine. I do not betray you in my love for Fabio, for you left me first. I will not say that I have a better lover; let it be enough that I have evened the score. Now, God be with you. I am weary of talking with you, and besides, I should not like Fabio to find us here, for I am engaged to be married to him.

Teodoro. Stop her, Tristán, do not let her go.

Tristán. Madam, wait, madam. He loves you. That is to say, he never stopped loving you. If he insulted you, then his apology is his return to you. Come back, Marcela. Listen to me.

Marcela. No. I will not listen to you, Tristán.

Tristán. Wait one moment.

Enter DIANA and ANARDA.

Diana [*aside*]. Teodoro and Marcela are here!

Anarda [*aside to* DIANA]. Madam, you have turned pale.

Diana. Let us hide behind this curtain, Anarda. [*Aside.*] Jealousy begins to stir up love again. [DIANA *and* ANARDA *hide.*]

Marcela. Let me go, Tristán.

Anarda. Tristán is bringing them together. It seems they have quarreled.

Diana. Oh, that that pander of a servant can rob me of my senses so!

Tristán. He was bewitched by the shallow beauty of that foolish woman that adored him for no longer than a flash of lightning illumines the sky, and then it was past. Now he scorns her riches and holds as far more precious your charm and gentleness. That love was not a blazing sun, but merely a passing comet. Teodoro, come here.

Diana. See how that lackey sets himself up as his spokesman!

Teodoro. If Marcela says that she now loves Fabio, why do you call me, Tristán?

Tristán. Oh, now he is angry too!

Teodoro. Let them marry if they will. I care not.

Tristán. Now, master, you must not be difficult. You must co-operate. Now come here. Give me your hand first and let friendship be made afterwards.

Teodoro. Fool, do you think to sway me?

Tristán. Now, lady, just for my sake, I would like you to give him your hand, just this once.

Teodoro. When did I ever say to Marcela that I loved another, and now she tells me——

Tristán. She does not mean it. It was only to maintain her dignity when you left her.

Marcela. That is not the reason. I am going to marry Fabio.

Tristán. Hush, child. Come here. Oh, what a pair of fools!

Teodoro. I asked her back. She refused. Everything is over between us as far as I am concerned. I will go no further.

Marcela. I have no more to say. May I be struck dead if I speak to him again.

Tristán. Do not swear.

Marcela [*aside to* TRISTÁN]. I am only feigning anger.

Tristán. Clever girl. Keep it up.

Diana. That rogue of a servant is too wily.

Marcela. Let me go, Tristán, I have work to do.

Teodoro. Let her go, Tristán.

Tristán. Very well.

Teodoro. Stop her.

Marcela. Fabio! I come!

Tristán. Will you not go? I do not prevent you.

Marcela. I cannot go, Teodoro.

Teodoro. And I am as firmly rooted as a rock in the sea.

Marcela. Let me embrace you.

Teodoro. Come to my arms, Marcela.

Tristán. Have I been wasting my time?

Anarda. What think you, madam?

Diana. I see how little men and women may be trusted.

Teodoro. Oh, how many insults you heaped upon me.

Tristán. Ah, well, I am glad to see you in agreement. It is the greatest joy of a go-between to see a deal brought off, however it be done.

Marcela. I would sooner die than ever change you for Fabio or the whole world.

Teodoro. I too rediscovered my love today, Marcela. If ever I forget you, may heaven punish me with the sight of you in Fabio's arms.

Marcela. Will you make amends with me?

Teodoro. I will do anything with you or for you.

Marcela. Say that all other women are ugly.

Teodoro. Compared with you, they are. Is there anything more?

Marcela. There is still one thing. Now that we are friends again, I suppose I can mention it before Tristán . . .

Tristán. Speak freely, even if it concerns myself, which I doubt.

Marcela. Say that the Countess is ugly.

Teodoro. She is the devil himself.

Marcela. Is she not foolish?

Teodoro. Utterly.

Marcela. Is she not a gossip?

Teodoro. She is a bore.

Diana. I must stop them, or there will be no end to this. My jealous anger will drive me to madness.

Anarda. Take care what you do, madam.

Tristán. Now, if you would like to hear someone tear the Countess's reputation to pieces, just listen to me.

Diana. Am I to endure such shame?

Tristán. First——

Diana. I will not stay to hear his second.

DIANA *and* ANARDA *come out from behind the curtain.*

Marcela. Excuse me, Teodoro, I must go. [*She curtsies* to DIANA *and goes.*]

Tristán. The Countess!

Teodoro [*aside*]. The Countess!

Diana. Teodoro . . .

Teodoro. Madam . . .

Tristán. The thundercloud approaches. I will not wait to see the lightning.   [*He goes*

Diana. Anarda, bring a writing desk. Teodoro is to write me a letter. I will dictate it to him here.

Teodoro [*aside*]. My heart trembles. Did she hear what we were saying?

Diana [*aside*]. Each time jealousy reawakens love, it returns with more strength than before. To think that he loves Marcela, and should find me inferior to her! Oh, that the two of them should mock me!

Teodoro [*aside*]. She murmurs to herself, and seems troubled. Why could I not learn my own lesson, that in great houses tapestries have ears and tongues?

Anarda. Here is the desk and the inkwell, madam.

Diana. Come, Teodoro, take the pen.

Teodoro [*aside*]. She will either kill or exile me this day.

Diana. Write.

Teodoro. I am ready.

Diana. You are not comfortable like that, kneeling on the floor. Anarda, fetch Teodoro a cushion.

Teodoro. I am perfectly comfortable, madam.

Diana. Put it there, Anarda. Do not be so foolish.

Teodoro [*aside*]. She was angry, and now her favors frighten me. I fear she honors my knees but would cut off my head. I am ready, madam.

Diana. Write this . . .

Teodoro [*aside*]. Oh, I would cross myself a thousand times.

Diana. When a great lady has declared her love for a man of humble birth, then it is a most heinous crime for him to converse with other women. And he who does not value the good fortune that has blessed him can be held as nothing more than a fool.

Teodoro. Is that all?

Diana. Is there more to say? Seal the letter, Teodoro.

Anarda [aside to DIANA]. Madam, what is this you do?
Diana. It is foolishness, but love makes me act so.
Anarda. Love for whom, madam?
Diana. Will you pretend you do not know? I know that every stone of this house tells tales.
Teodoro. I have sealed the letter, madam. To whom shall I address it?
Diana. Write "Teodoro." And do not let Marcela read it. Perhaps when you have studied it, you may understand.

[DIANA *and* ANARDA *go*

Teodoro. What a rare confusion is this: this woman loves me in fits and starts, as though the blood throbbing in the very pulse of love ruled the rhythm of her impulses.

Enter MARCELA.

Marcela. What did the Countess say to you, my love? I stood trembling behind the curtain, but could not hear.
Teodoro. She told me that she wished to marry you to Fabio, and dictated this letter to me in which she asks her bankers to dispatch the money for the dowry.
Marcela. What are you saying?
Teodoro. I wish you well, and since you are to marry, then do not speak my name again, either in jest or earnest.
Marcela. Teodoro, listen.
Teodoro. It is too late.   [*He goes*
Marcela. No. I will not believe it. She has bestowed her favors once more in his direction and has turned him from me again. For Teodoro is like a bucket in a well which she draws up and down as she pleases. When she fills him with her favors, he is hers. When the bucket is dry he returns to me. But, alas, how soon am I forgotten. She has only to call once and he runs to do her bidding. Oh, Teodoro, when she wants you, you leave me. When she leaves you, you want me. Who could be treated so and still have patience?

Enter RICARDO *and* FABIO.

Ricardo. Oh, Fabio, I cannot wait one moment longer, but I must see her at once. I kiss your hands a thousand times for the tidings you have brought me.
Fabio. Marcela, tell my mistress that the Marquis is here.
Marcela. Oh, cruel tyrant, jealousy, what would you now? My thoughts are all awry; I know not what I do.

Fabio. Will you not go?

Marcela. I go.

Fabio. Tell her that our new master and her husband is here.   [MARCELA *goes*

Ricardo. Fabio, go to my lodging, and tomorrow I will give you a thousand escudos and a thoroughbred Neapolitan horse.

Fabio. Sir, I shall treasure your gift, though I fear I may not ride upon it.

Ricardo. This will only be a beginning, for you are not only Diana's servant and vassal, but also my dear friend.

Fabio. Sir, I kiss your hand.

Ricardo. You have served me well.

Enter DIANA.

Diana. My lord, I did not think to see you here.

Ricardo. How could I have stayed when you sent such a sweet message to me by Fabio? So you have chosen me for your husband and your slave? I kiss your hands. I think I shall go mad and doubly mad with the delight of this moment. I never thought to know such happiness, never thought to deserve you, or ever dreamed of knowing greater happiness than merely to desire you.

Diana. My lord, I would answer you, but know not how. I sent no message. Do you jest with me?

Ricardo. Fabio, what does this mean?

Fabio. I would not have fetched you, my lord, or brought you here if Teodoro had not told me——

Diana. I understand, Ricardo. Teodoro is to blame. He heard me praise you above Federico as a courteous, rich, and noble gentleman, and must have imagined that I intended to offer you my hand. I beg you to pardon my fools of servants, sir.

Ricardo. When such a fair image as you intercedes for him, what need has Fabio of my yea or nay for pardon? I thank you humbly for the favor you have shown me, and hope one day my love may melt your icy resolution.

[*He goes*

Diana. Now idiot, are you contented with the mischief you have done?

Fabio. Madam, why do you put the blame on me?

Diana. Call Teodoro here. [*Aside.*] How readily these other tedious suitors come, and I must call for Teodoro.

Fabio [*aside*]. A thousand golden escudos I have lost, and a horse, true-bred from Naples.   [*He goes*

Diana. Love, what do you want with me now? Had I not forgotten Teodoro? I can guess love's excuse even now. It will not be love that caused this confusion, but his ever-present shadow, jealousy. Oh, jealousy, will you stop at nothing? You are an evil counselor to women, who, if they listen to you will do such things as will destroy their honor in a moment. I love a man, and yet I know too well that I represent a mighty sea of honor, the culmination of many streams and rivers that have built up my family, and Teodoro is but a small ship upon this ocean. How, then, can the sea drown itself for the sake of one weak craft? My soul is tossed hither and thither. What danger am I in! I fear my heart will break from the strain that honor puts upon it.

Enter TEODORO *and* FABIO.

Fabio [*to* TEODORO]. The Marquis nearly killed me in his anger, but, to tell the truth, what most upset me was the thought of that thousand escudos.

Teodoro. Then I will give you a piece of advice, Fabio.

Fabio. What is that?

Teodoro. Count Federico was wild with fury to hear that she was to marry the Marquis. Go, tell him that the wedding is not to be. He will give you a thousand escudos for that piece of news.

Fabio. I will go at once.

Teodoro. Go then. Make haste. [FABIO *goes.*] You called me, madam?

Diana. That fool, Fabio, was wise to leave when he did.

Teodoro. Madam, I have perused your letter at length, and considered what you say. I find that my cowardice sprang from my great respect and diffidence towards you. But now you have shown me that I do wrong to remain so backward, I am resolved to tell you openly that I love you. . . .

Diana. And I believe you, Teodoro. Why should you not love me? I have always treated you well, and favored you above my other servants.

Teodoro. Madam, I do not understand this new style of speech.

Diana. There is nothing to understand, Teodoro. Do

not imagine hidden meanings where there are none. Curb your desires, Teodoro, and remember that from a woman of my position, the slightest favor to a man of your lowly rank should be sufficient honor to add more luster and more pleasure to your life. Do not ask for more.

Teodoro. Madam, forgive me if I speak presumptuously, but you have often shown many signs of excellent judgment. Why did you lead me on and load me with hopes until I was brought to such a pass that I am sick with love? Why do you, as soon as you see me cool toward you, burn with flames of fire to set me alight again, and when you see me consumed with love, why do you become as ice again? You could leave me in peace with Marcela, but no, you are like the dog in the manger. Your jealousy cannot bear to see me marry Marcela, and when you see that I do not love her, you turn away from me. Madam, you rob me of my senses. You will not leave me to sleep or wake in peace. Either eat or let another eat, for I will no longer cling to such doubtful hopes. If you will not have me, then from this moment I swear only to love where I am loved.

Diana. But not Marcela, Teodoro. I will not permit you to marry Marcela. Find some other woman. Not Marcela.

Teodoro. Why not Marcela? Why ask me to seek another? Why should I pretend to love another? I adore Marcela. She adores me, and our love is honorable.

Diana. You infamous slave! I will have you killed.

Teodoro. Madam, why do you beat me?

Diana. You foul-mouthed, gross and filthy rogue!

Enter FEDERICO *and* FABIO.

Fabio. Oh, will you wait a moment, sir?

Federico. You are right, Fabio, it would be wiser not to interrupt your mistress. No, on second thoughts, perhaps I will. . . . Madam, what is this?

Diana. It is nothing. A fleeting disagreement, such as are wont to occur between servants and their lords.

Federico. Is there anything I can do for you, madam?

Diana. Thank you, my lord, there is nothing.

Federico. Perhaps I may speak with you later, at your convenience.

Diana. I will speak with you. Go in, and you shall hear what I intend for the Marquis Ricardo.   [*She goes*

Federico. Fabio . . .

Fabio. Sir . . . ?

Federico. I suspect some hidden motive behind her anger.

Fabio. I swear I know not what to think. But I confess I am amazed to see her treat Teodoro so badly. Never before have I seen my lady, the Countess, behave so.

Federico. She has given him a bloody nose. Look at his handkerchief.   [FEDERICO *and* FABIO *go*

Teodoro. If this be not love, then what other name can there be for such willfulness? If this is the love of noble ladies, then they are furies, not women. If your greatness denies you the pleasure you would have, must you turn to cruelty and seek to kill the one you love? Oh, how I long to kiss that hand that has the power to kill me, in gratitude for the proof of love it has shown in this chastisement. I never imagined she had so fiery a temper, but if the only excuse she could find to touch me was to strike me, then Diana has acted without a precedent and derived some joy from jealousy.

Enter TRISTÁN.

Tristán. Like the cowardly swordsman, I only arrive when the excitement is over.

Teodoro. Oh, Tristán.

Tristán. Sir, what is this? There is blood on your handkerchief.

Teodoro. Love has signed its name there with the hand of jealousy.

Tristán. And used a sharp pen, from the look of it.

Teodoro. Never fear, Tristán. She is madly in love, but since she despises herself for loving me, she sought to destroy this face, the mirror in which she sees reflected her honor's death. This was her revenge upon it.

Tristán. Sir, if Jane or Lucy, or some such village wench in clogs and homemade stockings had gone for me like that, by way of breaking off our friendship, swearing I had done her wrong, and beating me about the face to prove it, it would be only as I should expect. But for a noble lady to forget herself so far as to start brawling, why, sir, it is inexcusable.

Teodoro. I know not, Tristán. But I do know that I am at my wits' end to see her adoring me one moment and hating me the next. She does not want me for herself, and yet she is determined Marcela shall not have me. If I cease to look at her, then she finds some ruse to speak with me. She is the dog in the manger, Tristán, neither in nor out. She will not eat nor let another eat.

Tristán. Sir, a wise professor had a housekeeper and a handyman who never ceased quarreling. They quarreled at breakfast, they brawled at supper, at night could not sleep for the noise they made arguing, and by day, he could not study for the clamor they made. Then one day, he returned home from a lecture suddenly and unexpectedly. He entered the house, and the first thing he saw was the housekeeper and the handyman in bed together making love. He said "Thank God for peace at last!" And left them to it. I think the story may apply to you.

Enter DIANA.

Diana. Teodoro . . .

Teodoro. Madam . . .

Tristán [*aside*]. Is the woman a sprite, that she is everywhere?

Diana. I came to ask you how you were.

Teodoro. You see me. What think you?

Diana. How do you feel?

Teodoro. As well as may be expected.

Diana. Is that all? Do you no longer say: "I am at your service?"

Teodoro. Am I expected still to be "at your service" when your servants are treated so?

Diana. How little you understand, Teodoro.

Teodoro. Indeed, I understand little of your words, but have no doubt about your actions. If I love you not, you are angered, and if I love you, you are roused to fury. If I forget you, you write me letters, and if I think of you, then I insult you. You want me to understand you, and if I show that I do, then I am called a fool. Kill me or let me live, but cease this tormenting vacillation.

Diana. Did I make your nose bleed?

Teodoro. Can you not see you did?

Diana. Show me your handkerchief.

Teodoro. Why?

Diana. Give me it.

Teodoro. Why do you want it?

Diana. I want it, Teodoro. Go and speak to Octavio.
I have ordered him to give you two thousand escudos.

Teodoro. For what?

Diana. You will need some new handkerchiefs. [*She goes*

Teodoro. Did you ever hear such madness?

Tristán. She must be bewitched.

Teodoro. She has given me two thousand escudos.

Tristán. At that price you could endure another four
good hidings.

Teodoro. She said it was to buy handkerchiefs, and then
she went away with my bloodstained one.

Tristán. Remember the housekeeper and the handyman!

Teodoro. I pray Heaven you prove right, Tristán.

ACT THREE

1

A *street in* NAPLES

Enter RICARDO, *and* FEDERICO, *followed by* CELIO.

RICARDO. I cannot believe it.

Federico. I swear it is true. I saw it with my own eyes.

Ricardo. She really struck him?

Federico. I admit that servants can be tedious, but there
are limits, Ricardo. And the fact that a woman of her
caliber has once attacked a man in that way—why it is all
too clear that she might do it again. And there is another
thing. Have you noticed how much his fortune has im-
proved of late?

Ricardo. But he is her servant.

Federico. He is asking for trouble. The moral philosopher tells a fable of two pots that looked alike, except that
one was made of clay, the other of metal—copper, or iron,
or some such—and they were both carried swirling down
a swift flowing river. The clay pot was wise enough to
avoid the metal pot, lest the torrent should throw them
together and the clay one break. It may be the same with
them, and unless Teodoro keeps his distance from Diana,
he may well find that he will be smashed to pieces.

Ricardo. We may yet see that day. But I am astonished

that Diana, with all her pride and watchful elegance, should endure such a situation. It cannot be for nothing that Teodoro now dresses so finely and has a retinue of servants, pages, and horses, which he never had before, and plenty of money to scatter abroad. He must have done something to earn such riches.

Federico. Yes, and what is more, this liaison will soon be the talk of all Naples. Before that happens and the honor of our noble family is dragged down into the mud, Teodoro must die.

Ricardo. You speak truly. He must die. Despite Diana.

Federico. Can it be done?

Ricardo. Easily. There are men in Naples who live by that very trade, and receive in gold what they return in blood. All we must do is find such a ruffian and it will be done.

Federico. It must be accomplished swiftly.

Ricardo. He shall pay for his presumption this very day.

Enter Tristán *in a new suit,* Furio, Antonelo, *and* Lirano.

Federico. Are these the kind of ruffians you would hire?

Ricardo. No doubt of it.

Federico. May offended heaven assist you in your just device.

Furio. You must pay for the wine, Tristán, to celebrate your new finery.

Antonelo. Of course he will. Tristán knows how to behave.

Tristán. Gentlemen, you are all my guests.

Lirano. Your suit is a marvel of fine tailoring, Tristán.

Tristán. All this is a mere nothing to the things I shall have. Why, if things keep on the way they are going, I shall soon be the secretary's secretary.

Lirano. The Countess shows your master many favors, Tristán.

Tristán. He is her favorite, her right-hand man, her very private secretary. He is the door through which you must pass to win her favor.

Antonelo. To hell with fortunes and favors. Come, let us drink.

Furio. They tell me there is an excellent Lachrymae

Christi and a rare old Malmsey to be found in this taber-
nacle which we see before us.

Tristán. No. We will drink Greek wine, for I have a
desire to speak Greek, and the wine should loosen the
tongue and make the language flow.

Ricardo. That fellow with the dark hair and pale face
looks the boldest ruffian, for see how the others speak to
him. They seem to respect him and treat him with courtesy. Celio . . .

Celio. Sir?

Ricardo. Call that pale-faced gentleman. Say I would
speak with him.

Celio. Ah! Sir! Before you enter this holy hermitage, my
master, the Marquis, would speak with you.

Tristán [*to his friends*]. Friends, you must excuse me
for a while. The prince wishes to speak with me, and I
cannot refuse him. Go in! Order a couple of gallons of
the best wine they have, and a bite of cheese or whatever
you fancy.

Antonelo. Do not be long then.

Tristán. I will be with you in a moment. [FURIO, ANTON-
ELO, *and* LIRANO *go.*] What is your wish, sir?

Ricardo. Seeing you amid such a show of bravery
prompted Count Federico and myself to discover if you
are a man that might, if required, kill another.

Tristán [*aside*]. By Heaven, they are my mistress's suitors.
They are plotting some mischief too. I will not undeceive
them.

Federico. Will you not answer?

Tristán. I wondered whether your lordship mocked me,
for by the creator of all brute force, I swear there is no
man in all Naples that does not tremble at the slightest
whisper of my name. Have you not heard of Hector? Well,
Hector is a mere pigmy to my mighty arm. Besides, he
was a Trojan. I am Italiano.

Federico. This is the man we seek, Ricardo. Upon my
life, we do not mock. But if your spirit is as great as your
renown, and if you will dispatch the man we name, we
will pay you any price you ask.

Tristán. Two hundred escudos will suffice, though it be
the devil himself.

Ricardo. I will give you three hundred, so it be done
this night.

Tristán. All I need is the name of the man and some of the money in advance.

Ricardo. Do you know Diana, Countess of Belflor?

Tristán. I have friends in her house, sir.

Ricardo. Will you kill a servant of hers?

Tristán. Menservants, maidservants, even her coach horses. It shall be done.

Ricardo. Then kill Teodoro.

Tristán. That, gentlemen, is not so easy, for I know that Teodoro does not go out at night. He fears that he has offended you, and so has asked me to serve him as his bodyguard, in the guise of a servant. Let me continue in his service, sir, and one night soon I will give him a couple of neat jabs with this dagger which will write R.I.P. on him for good and all, and no one will suspect that I have done it. How does that suit you?

Federico. We could not have found a surer executioner in all Naples. Serve him then, and one day shortly when he is unaware, seize your opportunity and kill him. Then come to us and you shall receive——

Tristán. I need one hundred escudos now.

Ricardo. Here are fifty in this purse. When I see you in Diana's house, I will give you the rest of the hundred. There will be many more hundreds to follow if you dispatch——

Tristán. I will be satisfied with my quoted price. And now, good day to you, gentlemen, my friends await me, Redhot, Wallbuster, Ironhand, Scarface, and Devilscarer, and I should not like them to be inquisitive about this business.

Ricardo. You are wise. God be with you.

Federico. What a piece of luck!

Ricardo. Teodoro is as good as dead.

Federico. That ruffian cuts a fine figure!

[FEDERICO, RICARDO *and* CELIO *go*

Tristán. I must warn Teodoro. The Greek wine and my friends must excuse me. I must return to Teodoro with all haste, and I have far to go. But here is my master now. [*Enter* TEODORO.] Master, where are you going?

Teodoro. I know not myself, Tristán, nor what drives me. You saw how Diana talked to me yesterday? And today she is so changed that you would swear she scarcely knew me. And Marcela watches and laughs to see my suffering.

Tristán. Go home, sir. The two of us must not be seen together.

Teodoro. Why not, Tristán?

Tristán. I will tell you on the way. There is a plot to kill you.

Teodoro. To kill me? Why?

Tristán. Keep your voice down, and listen to me. Ricardo and Federico spoke to me, sir. They are plotting against you.

Teodoro. They wish to murder me?

Tristán. They have guessed that Diana loves you. And thinking that I was one of those roaring lions that rove this city seeking such employment, they have engaged me to kill you for one hundred doublons, and have given me fifty escudos as a guarantee. I told them I had already been asked to serve you, and that from today I would be in your service. I also told them I would await my best opportunity to kill you. All this I said to protect you from that fate.

Teodoro. I wish you would kill me, so you might release me from this living death which now I suffer.

Tristán. Are you mad?

Teodoro. Tristán, how can I accept my present situation and still be calm? If Diana could find the smallest loophole, she would marry me tomorrow. But her honor prevents her, and forces her to show herself colder and colder toward me as her love grows warmer.

Tristán. If I were to provide a remedy, what would you say?

Teodoro. That your cunning surpassed that of Ulysses.

Tristán. If I were to bring to your door a noble father who would make you the equal of the Countess, would that not solve the problem, sir?

Teodoro. It would.

Tristán. Count Ludovico, an ancient gentleman, some twenty years ago, sent a son who bore your name to Malta, where his brother was the master of the Order of the Knights of Saint John. Moors from Bizerte captured the ship and the child was never heard of again, dead or alive. This Ludovico must become your father, sir, and you his son, and never fear but I will bring it about.

Teodoro. Tristán, such a stratagem may cost us both our lives and our honor. . . .   [*They go*

✱

A room in the palace

TRISTÁN. Now you are home again, I must leave you, sir. There is much to be done, for before midday tomorrow you will be Diana's husband.   [*He goes*

Teodoro. No. This affair must end another way. Distance is love's greatest enemy. Love is a feeble traveler, who hardly ever survives the journey that puts miles between the lover and the beloved. This way love is turned to dust beneath the traveler's feet as surely as if it were buried in earth. I will travel and so bury my love for dead.

Enter DIANA.

Diana. You were sad, Teodoro. Have you recovered?

Teodoro. When my sorrow springs from adoration of so fair an object, I should be churlish indeed to desire recovery from my sickness. Madam, only when I think I may recover do I become melancholy, for there are maladies so sweet that a man considers himself most fortunate to die of them. My regret is that my position is such that I am forced to remove my sorrow from its cause, its mistress.

Diana. Why must you go, Teodoro?

Teodoro. There is a plot to kill me.

Diana. You do not surprise me. You will have many enemies.

Teodoro. There are some that envy me my sorrow. Therefore I beg your permission to go to Spain.

Diana. In this resolve you show the true nobility of a generous spirit. By doing so, you will remove the cause of your trouble, and, though my eyes will weep, the honor of my house will be preserved. Since Federico saw me strike you, there have been many suspicious rumors in the city. So, Teodoro, I must not see you. Go to Spain. I will have six thousand escudos given you.

Teodoro. My absence will silence your detractors. I kiss your hand.

Diana. Go quickly, Teodoro. No more. Leave me. I am a woman.

Teodoro. She weeps, but what can I do?

Diana. And so you are going, Teodoro?

Teodoro. Yes, madam.

Diana. One moment. . . . Go then. . . . But stay a moment. . . .

Teodoro. What would you?

Diana. No. Nothing. Go.

Teodoro. I will.

Diana [*aside*]. I am troubled. Is there any torment like that of love? [*To* TEODORO.] Are you not gone yet?

Teodoro. Madam, I go now.   [*He goes*

Diana. It is done. Oh, honor, I curse your name. What a thoughtless invention you are, to cut so cruelly across our natural inclinations. Who invented you? And yet, it was a just invention, for your bridle curbs much evil. . . .

Enter TEODORO.

Teodoro. I have returned to ask your leave to go today.

Diana. I cannot say. You know not how it troubles me to see you. Why did you return, Teodoro?

Teodoro. Madam, I could not prevent myself. My soul remains here when I should part from you.

Diana. It is not in my power to return it to you. Go, Teodoro, for love fights with honor and you are a stumbling block to the nobler part. Do not ask for your soul, for you take mine in exchange.

Teodoro. God be with Your Ladyship.   [*He goes*

Diana. God curse my ladyship that tears me from him I love with all my being! What shall I do, now that the light of my eyes has gone from me? Eyes, you shall pay for looking so lovingly upon him, for nevermore shall you see clearly but be ever clouded with tears. For you are to blame. Yet do not weep, for tears temper the heart's sorrow. Eyes, what excuse have you for your folly? Is it that the sun may look on what it pleases, however base, and never suffer for it? Then do not weep, though you have gazed on Teodoro, for if you do you will weep away all memory of him.

Enter MARCELA.

Marcela. Madam, may I take advantage of my years of faithful service to ask most humbly for your favor? At the same time, you may use this opportunity to dismiss me, for since I have offended you it is best that you should see me no more.

Diana. What is it you want, Marcela? What is the opportunity?

Marcela. Teodoro leaves for Spain today, fearing certain dangers that threaten him. Will you not marry me to him and give me leave to go with him? Then you need see me no longer, since it seems I have offended you.

Diana. Does he wish it?

Marcela. Madam, I would not ask you, if I were not sure of that.

Diana. Have you spoken to him?

Marcela. I have, and he asked me to go with him.

Diana [*aside*]. How promptly this new misfortune follows upon the heels of the other.

Marcela. We have already discussed it and arranged the way it may most conveniently be done.

Diana [*aside*]. Oh, foolish honor, forgive me, for love presses me too hard.

Marcela. Will you not answer me, madam?

Diana. I cannot do without you, Marcela. I am displeased that you should ask to go. Not only do you offend me, but also Fabio, who I know adores you. Let me marry you to Fabio. Let Teodoro go.

Marcela. I hate Fabio. I love Teodoro.

Diana [*aside*]. Could she have found a crueler moment to declare it! I must be calm. [*To* MARCELA.] Fabio would suit you better.

Marcela. Madam——

Diana. Do not argue with me.   [*She goes*

Marcela. Why are my mind and senses all determined when so great a power as Diana opposes them? Her jealousy will dare anything. I must turn back, before my feet lead me to disaster. Who knows what madness jealousy may cause? Unlucky love is like a tree whose blossoms are withered by an untimely frost. Nothing can bring them back. My soul rejoiced in the bright colors of its love, but a greater power than I has changed them into black mourning. How often does one love freeze another! And what though the flowers were beautiful, if they died before the fruit appeared?   [*She goes*

A *room in* COUNT LUDOVICO'S *house*

CAMILO. It is the only remedy, sir, if you would have an heir.

Ludovico. Marriage? It is out of the question; I am too old. Too many years are worse than too many rivals, Camilo, when it comes to marriage. Besides, it is unwise to marry late in life even if you do want an heir. Why, you might marry and still have no issue, which, you must admit, is a worse calamity than to be unmarried with no issue. A wife to an old man is as ivy to an elm tree. Although she covers him with her embraces, he dries up and withers, while she blossoms and grows plump. Besides, when I think of marriage, Camilo, it brings back the sad past and renews my wretchedness. Even now, after twenty years, I still hope each day that I may see Teodoro again.

Enter a PAGE.

Page. There is a Greek merchant would speak with your lordship.

Ludovico. Let him come in.

The PAGE *brings in* TRISTÁN *and* FURIO *dressed as Greeks.*

Tristán. I kiss your hand, sir, and may mighty heaven, of its divine power, give you the greatest consolation you could hope for.

Ludovico. You are welcome. What has brought you so far from your land?

Tristán. I came from Constantinople to Cyprus, sir, and from thence to Venice with a ship laden with rich Persian stuffs. I had in mind an ancient tale I once heard, and, wishing to see this beautiful city of Naples, I left my servants there in Venice to sell the merchandise, and came here, where my eyes have been beguiled by the greatness and beauty of the city.

Ludovico. Naples is great and beautiful indeed.

Tristán. It is, truly. My father, noble sir, was a merchant in Greece. Among his many dealings, he profited most from the buying and selling of slaves. One day at the market of Azteclias, he bought a boy, the most beautiful ever known to eye of man, living proof of that power which Heaven has bestowed on Nature. Some Turks were selling the boy, together with some other upstanding captives, who had been taken off a Maltese galley, captured by the Turks off Chafalonia——

Ludovico. Camilo, my heart trembles with anticipation.

Tristán. My father took a liking to this lad, bought him, and took him to Armenia, where he brought him up with me and my sister.

Ludovico. My friend, pause for a moment. You pierce my entrails with your story.

Tristán [*aside*]. It is working beautifully.

Ludovico. Tell me, what was his name?

Tristán. Teodoro.

Ludovico. Oh, heaven! The truth you speak strikes me to the heart. Already my beard is wet with tears of joy.

Tristán. Serpalitonia, my sister, and this boy—would he had not been so fair—loved each other, as was natural since they were brought up together, but as they grew so their love increased until, at the age of sixteen, my father being away on business at the time, their love became a fact. So much so that it went on growing within her till it was plain to see. Teodoro fled in fear before the baby was born. Catiborratos, my father, was not so upset by the injury as by the loss of Teodoro. But one way and another he died of grief. We had the child baptized, for that part of Armenia has the same customs as yours, although our Church is different. We called the child Terimaconius, and he is at this moment in the city of Tepecas, a fine boy. As I walked around the city of Naples, looking at the sights, I took from my pocket a paper I had brought with me on which were written the details about Teodoro. On returning to my inn I asked a Greek slave there if he knew anything of him. He replied, "Can that be Count Ludovico's son?" A new light shone in my soul and I realized what I shall now relate to you. Some of the customers at the inn told me that there was a Teodoro of that description in the service of the Countess of Belflor, and so before coming to see you I went to her house and the first man I saw——

Ludovico. My soul trembles.

Tristán. Was Teodoro.

Ludovico. Teodoro!

Tristán. He would have liked to run away, but he could not. At first I was in some doubt whether it was he, for he has changed and has grown a beard. I followed him, and finally caught up with him and took him by the arm. He spoke with me, though with much shame, and begged that I should tell no one in the house who he was lest they should mistrust him when they knew that he had been a slave. I said to him: "But if I know that you are the heir to a title in this country, why should you be ashamed of having been a slave?" He laughed at me, and would not believe my story. So I have come to you to see if your history agrees with what I know of him, and if it does, and if this is indeed your son, then to give you some news of your grandson. And I beg you to allow my sister to bring him to Naples, not that she may marry Teodoro —although she is not lacking in nobility—but so that Terimaconius may see his illustrious grandfather.

Ludovico. Let me embrace you a thousand times, for I know within my soul that this tale of yours is true. The joy I feel assures me it is so. Oh, my son, that I have found you again after so many long years' absence! Camilo, what must I do?

Camilo. Why, sir, do you not know? Go, fly, and crown your years of sorrow with the joy of his embrace.

Ludovico. My friend, if you will go with me, I shall be the more certain to meet with good fortune. But if you prefer to rest, then you may wait here. My house and all I have is yours, for the good deed you have done me. I must go now. I can wait no longer.

Tristán. I left some diamonds with a merchant who lives close by, so I will set out with you and then go on my way. Come, Mercaponios.

Furio. Come, sir.

Tristán. This trickopulous works very wellocules.

Furio. Splendidiferous.

Tristán. Comealongocles.   [TRISTÁN *and* FURIO *go*
Camilo. It is a rare language!

Ludovico. Come, Camilo, follow me.   [*They go*

∮

A street, outside a house. The door is shut

TRISTÁN [*opening the door a little*]. Are they out of sight?

Furio. The old man just flew, without waiting for his coach or servants.

Tristán. What if it were true, and Teodoro really was his son?

Furio. You told so many lies, it is a fair chance that some of them are true.

Tristán. Hold some of this Greek garbage. I must get out of this costume quickly, before someone who knows me sees me.

Furio. Hurry then.

Tristán. To think how far a father's love can stretch!

Furio. Where shall I wait for you?

Tristán. At the sign of the Elm.

Furio. I will see you anon.   [*He goes*

Tristán. Oh, what rewards are owed to a lively imagination! [*He comes out of the porch into the street.*] Now I have the cloak folded back underneath. I had it on before as a short gown, so that in an emergency I could slip off my Armenian turban and my baggy Greek breeches quickly and deposit them in a doorway and be myself again.

Enter RICARDO *and* FEDERICO.

Federico. There he is. That is the bold killer who promised to put an end to Teodoro for us.

Ricardo. Now, sir, is this how men who profess themselves honorable, and seek to be held in esteem, perform those deeds they readily promised to accomplish?

Tristán. Sir——

Federico. Do you perchance think that we are your equals, that you——

Tristán. Do not condemn before you hear me. Even now I serve that wretched Teodoro, and by this mighty hand, he is soon to die. But I would do you a disservice by publicly staining this bright blade with blood. No. Prudence is a heavenly gift, and was justly celebrated by the ancients as a unique virtue. Know for certain, gentlemen, that you may count him among the dead. He is melancholy by day, and at night shuts himself away in his room. Some strange fantasy must be troubling his thoughts. Leave it to me, for one cold stab will silence his vital breath. Do not be hasty. Trust me, and I shall kill him at the right moment.

Federico. He speaks good sense, Marquis. Besides, he has already taken action by becoming his servant. Have no doubt. He will do it.

Ricardo. Yes, I believe it. Teodoro is dead.

Federico. Hush, speak softly.

Tristán. While his certain death creeps up upon him, have your lordships by any chance fifty escudos? For I would buy a horse to flee the instant that the deed is done.

Ricardo. Here, take it, and be assured that once this deed is accomplished the least we shall do for you is to pay you.

Tristán. I will venture my life in my profession, which is truly to serve good men. And now, farewell. I must not be seen in conversation with you.

Federico. You are prudent.

Tristán. Time will show what will result from my caution.

Federico. He is a bold man.

Ricardo. Astute and ingenious.

Federico. He will kill him beautifully!

Ricardo. Brilliantly!

Enter CELIO.

Celio. I never heard such a strange, fantastic story.

Federico. What is it, Celio? Where are you going? Wait.

Celio. A most amazing, and I fear, for you, unfortunate occurrence. . . . Have you seen the people flocking to Count Ludovico's house?

Ricardo. Why, is he dead?

Celio. Listen to me, I beg you. They are going to congratulate him on finding the son he thought he had lost forever.

Ricardo. But how can Ludovico's good fortune affect us, Celio?

Celio. Does it not affect your ambitions for Diana's hand when I tell you that Teodoro, her secretary, is the Count's new-found son?

Federico. You strike me to the soul.

Ricardo. What? The Count's son? How has it become known?

Celio. It is a long tale, and as many as relate it tell it differently, so that I have had neither time nor memory to recall it all.

Federico. Who ever knew such misery as this?

Ricardo. My hope of glory is turned to bitter sorrow.

Federico. I will go and find out the truth for myself.

Ricardo. I will come with you, Count.

Celio. You will soon see that what I say is true. [*They go*

✦

A room in the COUNTESS' *palace*

Enter TEODORO *dressed for travel, and* MARCELA.

MARCELA. You are determined to go, Teodoro?

Teodoro. You are the cause of my departure. No good ever comes from ill-matched opposites.

Marcela. Your excuse is as false as your betrayal. You are leaving because in hating me and loving Diana, your impudent desires have come to nothing. That is what you are trying to forget, not me.

Teodoro. Who told you I loved Diana?

Marcela. It is too late to deny it, Teodoro. Your high hopes drove you to be both overbold and cowardly. You were a coward in that you have kept your distance out of respect for her, and overbold because your baseness dared desire her great worth. Between love and honor there are many icy mountain peaks. I have my revenge upon you, and although I confess I still love you I shall soon forget you, being avenged. For love avenged is soon forgotten. If you should remember me, think how I have forgotten you, and then you will love me again, for I know how strong a man's love becomes when he knows he is despised.

Teodoro. How many chimeras crowd your mind to justify your marriage with Fabio.

Marcela. You have provoked them by disdaining me, and have brought about my marriage yourself.

Enter FABIO.

Fabio. Since Teodoro will be gone from here within the hour, I cannot deny you the pleasure of dallying with him.

Teodoro. You are right, Fabio. Do not be jealous of one who must shortly travel far away.

Fabio. You are really going?

Teodoro. You see I am ready for the journey.

Fabio. My mistress comes to speak with you.

Enter DIANA, DOROTEA, *and* ANARDA.

Diana. And so, Teodoro, you are ready to go?

Teodoro. I would I had wings on my feet, madam, though spurs might serve as well, that I might be gone the sooner.

Diana. Anarda, is everything prepared and properly packed?

Anarda. All is ready, madam.

Fabio [*aside to* MARCELA]. I believe he is really going.

Marcela. Are you still jealous?

Diana. Teodoro, I would speak with you apart.

Teodoro. I am at your service, madam.

Diana. Teodoro, you are going away. I love you with all my heart. . . .

Teodoro. It is for your sake that I am leaving.

Diana. I am what I am. What could I do?

Teodoro. You are weeping.

Diana. No. I have something in my eye.

Teodoro. Is it love, perhaps?

Diana. It may be. But it has been there a long time. Now it would come out.

Teodoro. Madam, I go, but my soul remains. It will ever be at your service, for such heavenly beauty as yours should be served only by the souls of men. What would you command me? All that I am is yours.

Diana. This is a sad day.

Teodoro. Farewell, madam. Farewell.

Diana. You are weeping?

Teodoro. No. I too have something in my eye.

Diana. Did I put it there?

Teodoro. I think so.

Diana. You will find a hundred silly baubles in a trunk which is with your luggage. Forgive me, it was all that I could do. If you open it, and look at them as you might on spoils after a victory, say: Diana put these here, and wept as she did so.

Anarda [*aside to* DOROTEA]. See how they are lost in each other.

Dorotea. How ill can love be hid.

Anarda. He should not go. See, he takes her hand. They are exchanging tokens.

Dorotea. Diana has become the dog in the manger.

Anarda. She takes his hand too late.

Dorotea. She should eat or let another eat.

Enter LUDOVICO *and* CAMILO.

Ludovico. Great Diana, boundless rejoicing licenses a man of my years to enter thus unannounced.

Diana. Count Ludovico, what brings you here?

Ludovico. Can you alone be ignorant of what all Naples knows? Why, in the very instant that the news arrived, the street outside my house was packed with people, so that I could scarcely make my way here to see my son.

Diana. What son is this? What is the cause of such rejoicing, sir?

Ludovico. Madam, have you never heard my story, how twenty years ago I sent a son to Malta with his uncle, and how Ali Baja's galleys captured him?

Diana. I have some slight remembrance of it.

Ludovico. Heaven has granted that I should see my son again, after the many adventures he has undergone.

Diana. I am grateful to you, Count, for bringing me the news of your good fortune.

Ludovico. In exchange, madam, you must give me my son. He is in your service, and little dreams that I am his father. Oh, if only his dear late mother were alive!

Diana. Your son is in my service?—Can it be Fabio?

Ludovico. No, madam, it is not Fabio. It is Teodoro.

Diana. Teodoro!

Ludovico. Yes, madam.

Teodoro. But how can this be?

Diana. Speak, Teodoro.

Ludovico. Is this then he?

Teodoro. But sir . . . I must tell Your Grace——

Ludovico. There is nothing to tell, my son, son of my heart. My happiness is fulfilled if I die in your arms.

Diana. This is most strange.

Anarda. Madam . . . Then Teodoro is a noble . . . a highborn gentleman.

Teodoro. Sir, I am confused. Am I in truth your son?

Ludovico. Were I not certain, I should know it just by looking at you. You are exactly as I was at your age.

Teodoro. Sir, I kiss your feet, and I beg you——

Ludovico. No, no, my son, do not speak, say nothing. I am beside myself! Oh, how handsome you are! God bless you. What a royal presence! How truly nature stamped your face with your nobility, Teodoro! Come,

Teodoro. Come home with me. Come and take possession of my house and my estate. Come and behold the portals, crowned with the noblest arms in all Naples.

Teodoro. Sir, I was about to leave for Spain, and I must——

Ludovico. To Spain? Nay, Spain shall not have you. Come to my arms, which would give the whole world for you.

Diana. Your Grace, I beg you, let Teodoro remain here until he is prepared, and then come to your house dressed as befits your son. Besides, I should not like him to leave my house while the mob still throngs the streets.

Ludovico. Madam, you speak wisely. Although I can hardly bear to leave him for a minute, I shall go alone, to prevent any greater uproar and disturbance, but I beg you, madam, let not the sun go down before my dear son returns to me.

Diana. I give you my word.

Ludovico. Farewell, my Teodoro.

Teodoro. Sir, I kiss your hands.

Ludovico. Camilo, I am ready for death now, whenever it comes.

Camilo. Teodoro is a fine youth.

Ludovico. I must be calm, else I shall go mad with joy and happiness.   [LUDOVICO *and* CAMILO *go*

Dorotea. Let us all kiss your hands.

Anarda. You are a great lord, Teodoro.

Dorotea. We are at your service.

Marcela. Your gracious nobility commands the respect and good will of all of us. We kiss your hands.

Diana. Let me have room. You will smother him with your prattling. Teodoro, sir, give me your hands.

Teodoro. Madam, I am, more than ever, your servant.

Diana. Leave us for a while.

Marcela [*to* FABIO]. What think you of this?

Fabio. I cannot believe it.

Dorotea [*to* ANARDA]. I know not what to say.

Anarda. I think my mistress will no longer be the dog in the manger.

Dorotea. Will she eat, or let another eat?

Anarda. What think you?

          [MARCELA, FABIO, DOROTEA, *and* ANARDA *go*

Diana. You will not go to Spain?

Teodoro. To Spain?

Diana. I thought your lordship might say: "I go, madam, but my soul remains."

Teodoro. Do you laugh to see how fortune favors me?

Diana. She has done excellently.

Teodoro. We are equals now. Nobles together.

Diana. You are changed, Teodoro.

Teodoro. I think you love me the less for it. You are sorry to see me your equal, though you loved me as your servant. It is love's custom to love best that which is inferior to it.

Diana. I love you not less. There shall be no more delay. I will marry you this night.

Teodoro. I have no more to say. Fortune, hold your wheel steady, and do not turn from this point of greatest happiness.

Diana. I think there is no woman on earth more fortunate than I. Go and dress as befits your station, Teodoro.

Teodoro. I will. And then I will go and see the inheritance I have gained this day, and the father I have found, I know not how nor where.

Diana. God be with you, Count.

Teodoro. And with you, Countess.

Diana. Teodoro . . .

Teodoro. What is it?

Diana. "What is it?" Is that a way for a servant to answer his mistress?

Teodoro. The game has changed. I am the master now.

Diana. Let Marcela no longer give me cause for any pangs of jealousy. I know this new turn of fortune will distress her.

Teodoro. Never fear. Nobles never stoop to love their servants.

Diana. You must watch your words, Count Teodoro.

Teodoro. And watch you do not offend my honor, Countess Diana.

Diana. Teodoro, who do you think I am?

Teodoro. My wife.   [*He goes*

Diana. There is no more to be desired. Hold firm now, fortune, as Teodoro asks. You have done all. Do not undo us now.

Enter FEDERICO *and* RICARDO.

Ricardo. Madam, are not your friends and kinsmen to be told what is the cause of the excitement and rejoicing that is heard in every street of this city?

Diana. I will tell you all you ask to know.

Federico. First, I should like to know how your servant has suddenly become great.

Diana. That is as suddenly answered: Count Teodoro is to be my husband.   [*She goes*

Ricardo. What think you of that?

Federico. I cannot believe my eyes and ears.

Ricardo. Oh, if only that idle rogue had killed him at once!

Federico. See, here he comes.

Enter TRISTÁN.

Tristán. Everything is as I planned it! Oh, it is marvelous to think that the wit of a lackey can put all Naples in an uproar.

Ricardo. Hey there, Tristán, or whatever you call yourself.

Tristán. I am known as "The Killer" to my friends.

Federico. We have seen how well you deserve that name.

Tristán. All would have been as you desired, but he is a Count now.

Ricardo. What difference does that make?

Tristán. Ah, when the agreement was made, I settled to do the job cheaply, for a mere three hundred, because it was only one Teodoro, a servant, that was to be removed, not a Count. But Teodoro the nobleman is a different matter, and will be naturally a little more expensive. It is much more difficult to kill one Count than four or even six servants, who are half dead before you start, from hunger, or ambition, or envy, or some other killer of that kind.

Federico. How much do you want? He must be killed tonight.

Tristán. A thousand escudos.

Ricardo. You shall have them.

Tristán. I shall need some token.

Ricardo. Take this chain.

Tristán. Count out your money. Have it ready.

Federico. It shall be done immediately.

Tristán. So shall the deed. But hear. . . .

Ricardo. What? Do you want more?

Tristán. Not a word of this, to anyone.

[RICARDO *and* FEDERICO *go*

Teodoro. I saw you talking to those two killers, Tristán.

Tristán. Sir, they are two of the biggest fools to be found for miles around. They gave me this chain, and promised me a thousand escudos to murder you today.

Teodoro. What have you been saying, Tristán? I tremble to think . . .

Tristán. If you could have seen me talking Greek, Teodoro, you would have given me more than those two fools have promised me. But, by heaven, it is the easiest thing on earth to Greekalize! After all, it is nothing but talk. The names I used—oh, you would have thought me the most learned scholar!—Azteclias, Catiborratos, Serpalitonia, Xipatos, Atecas, Filimoclia. . . . Who knows, it may even have been Greek! For it was Greek to them.

Teodoro. Tristán, if this deceit is discovered, I can expect no less than to have my head cut off.

Tristán. Is that all the thanks you have . . . ?

Teodoro. Tristán, you are the very devil, to——

Tristán. Let fate have its way, and wait and see what will happen.

Teodoro. Here comes the Countess.

Tristán. I will hide. She must not see me. [*He hides.*]

Enter DIANA.

Diana. Have you not gone to see your father, Teodoro?

Teodoro. A grave dilemma has prevented me, and finally I have decided to ask your permission to proceed with my plan to go to Spain.

Diana. If this is Marcela's doing . . .

Teodoro. Marcela? How could she influence me?

Diana. Then what is the matter?

Teodoro. My lips can scarce bring themselves to speak it.

Diana. Speak, Teodoro, though it be a thousand times against my honor.

Teodoro. Tristán—to whose honor deceit itself should build statues, industry write odes, and Crete surrender all its labyrinths as to its superior—seeing my love, and my eternal sorrow, and knowing that Ludovico had lost a son, decided that I should be that son. I, that am son only of the earth, that have never known any father other than my own wits, my reading and my pen! The Count believes the story, and although I might be your husband and own much happiness and great riches, my conscience will not allow me to deceive you, for I am by nature a man that professes the truth. And so, I have come to ask your leave to go to Spain. For I will not deceive your love, your blood, and your high qualities.

Diana. Teodoro, you show yourself both wise and foolish! Wise in that you have demonstrated your nobility in your declaration, foolish to think that I would not wish to marry you, when I have found in your humility that very quality I desire. For pleasure is not in greatness, but rather in the fitness of what is desired by the loving soul. I will marry you, and so that Tristán shall not reveal this secret, I will, when he is sleeping, have him cast down the deep well of the house.

Tristán [*coming out of hiding*]. Hey, what do you mean?

Diana. What is that?

Tristán. What?—Why, Tristán, popped up to complain justly against the greatest piece of feminine ingratitude ever known to man. After all I have done for you! And then you would throw me down the well for thanks.

Diana. What, were you listening?

Tristán. You will not catch me in your bucket.

Diana. Stay.

Tristán. Not I.

Diana. Stay, Tristán. You are a witty fellow, and I give you my word that you shall never find a truer friend in the world than me. But you must keep secret this invention, which, after all, is yours.

Tristán. Am I likely to let it out? I should have the worst of the bargain if I did.

Teodoro. Listen. What is that shouting?

Enter LUDOVICO, FEDERICO, RICARDO, CAMILO, FABIO, MARCELA, ANARDA, *and* DOROTEA.

Ricardo [*off*]. We will accompany your son.

Federico [*to* LUDOVICO]. Fair Naples waits at the door to see him.

Ludovico [*to* TEODORO]. With Diana's permission, a

carriage is waiting for you, Teodoro, and all the nobility of Naples is mounted and waiting to accompany you. Come, my son, to your own house. After so many years of absence, you shall see the place where you were born.

Diana. Before he goes, I would have you know, Count Ludovico, that I am to be his wife.

Ludovico. May Fortune's wheel stop even at this moment of her greatest good. Let it be fixed eternally with golden nails! I take two children from this house, when I came for only one.

Federico. Come, Ricardo, let us offer our felicitations.

Ricardo. I sincerely wish long life to Teodoro. Jealousy drove me to offer this coward here one thousand escudos, beside that chain he wears, to kill him. Let him be arrested, for he is a thief and a trickster!

Teodoro. He is no thief that defends his master.

Ricardo. No? Then what was he?

Teodoro. Tristán was ever my faithful servant. And as a reward to him for protecting me from death, not to mention certain other private debts I owe him, with Diana's permission, I will marry him to Dorotea, since Her Grace has already promised Marcela to Fabio.

Ricardo. I will give Marcela a handsome dowry.

Federico. And mine to Dorotea shall equal it.

Ludovico. My son is sufficient dowry for the Countess. I need no other.

Teodoro. And so, noble jury, ends the play of "The Dog in the Manger," and I beg you tell no man of Teodoro's secret.

THE KNIGHT FROM OLMEDO

(*El Caballero de Olmedo*)

CHARACTERS

Alonso
Rodrigo
Fernando
Don Pedro
King Juan II
Constable
Inés
Leonor
Ana
Fabia
Tello
A Peasant
A Figure
Servants, Lackeys, *etc*.

The action takes place in Olmedo, Medina del Campo, and on a road between the two towns.

THE KNIGHT FROM OLMEDO

ACT ONE

1

ALONSO. Let no man speak Love's name that has not felt his power. And yet none breathes who does not bear Love's emblem, since Nature ordained that by the power of Love should humankind increase. No sooner had I seen her than our eyes met and in that instant Hope and Love grew together. She looked on me, not proudly, but with a sweet changefulness that gives me cause to hope. Dare I believe that the blind god shot matching arrows? That in her breast burns a flame of the same color as this which consumes my heart?

Enter TELLO, ALONSO's *servant, and* FABIA.

Fabia [*to* TELLO]. You say your master has business with me?

Tello. He has.

Fabia. People must take me for a dog, that I should be at the beck and call of every stranger.

Tello. My master has great respect for you.

Fabia. Well, what is the matter with him? Is he sick?

Tello. He is.

Fabia. What is his trouble?

Tello. Love.

Fabia. Love? Who does he love?

Tello. There he is, Fabia, he can tell you better than I can.

Fabia [*to* ALONSO]. God be with you, gentle sir.

Alonso [*to* TELLO]. Is this the worthy woman?

Tello. The very same.

Alonso. Oh, Fabia! True model and breathing portrait of all wisdom nature ever bestowed upon mankind. Second Hippocrates, skilled in the ways of curing love! Let me kiss your hand, most reverend doctor.

179

Fabia. You make your sickness plain with every word you utter.

Alonso. A strong desire is master of my will.

Fabia. A lover's pulse can be seen in the face. Who has bewitched you?

Alonso. An angel.

Fabia. And then?

Alonso. The solutions are two; both are impossible, and between them I fear I shall lose my reason, Fabia. One is that she should love me, and the other that I should cease to love her.

Fabia. I saw you yesterday at the Feria; you had eyes only for a certain maiden who wore a peasant's costume to disguise her noble birth, though nothing could hide her grace and beauty, for surely Doña Inés is the flower of all Medina.

Alonso. Nothing escapes you, Fabia. That peasant girl is she who causes me to burn with love.

Fabia. You aim high.

Alonso. I only desire her honor.

Fabia. I am sure of that.

Alonso. For God's sake, I beg you, hear my story. That afternoon at the Feria her loveliness was such that it seemed as though the dawn were breaking anew. Her waving tresses spread a web for lovers, so cunningly masked by her ribbon that many were ensnared unknowingly. Her lively eyes glanced here and there over the crowd claiming a life wherever they chanced to rest, yet those whose lives she pardoned deemed themselves unfortunate beside those who had been stricken. As she talked, her graceful hands, encircled at the wrists by cuffs of driven snow, danced so nimbly and yet so much to the purpose that you would have thought them two foils used with grace and skill by expert swordsmen, and indeed each flicker of her finger inflicted a mortal wound. Her sweet mouth did the office of a bugle, for though no captain, she soon recruited all the men in the town, an army of adorers! She wore neither corals nor pearls, for with her lips and her teeth she needed none. Her petticoats were in the French style, and over them she wore a sea-green skirt such as Basque women wear, so that although her every movement proclaimed her grace, her clothes spoke in foreign tongues to keep her secrets. At every step, her

dainty slippers took with them, unawares, eyes glued to
their ribbons and souls clinging to their heels. An almond
tree in blossom never looked so lovely or so delicate, and
as she moved the natural fragrance about her was sweeter
than almond paste. Love ran beside her, invisible, laughing to see how the simple fish on every side were caught
by his lovely bait. Everywhere she went she was offered
ribbons, silken sashes, jewels for her ears, but she heeded
none. She passed on, cold as an asp—and what use is it
to offer earrings to an asp? Or pearls to a neck like hers?
Pearls are as nothing to her, she being made of pearl. I
stood in wonder, my only speech in my eyes. What could
I offer her? Nothing! Except my soul a thousand times,
in poor exchange for every hair of her head. Or my life
for her every step. She looked at me without speaking
and yet it seemed that her eyes were saying: "Do not
return to Olmedo, Alonso, stay here in Medina." I trusted
in my hope, Fabia, and I stayed. And, sure enough, my
hopes did not betray me; this morning she came out to
go to Mass, no longer in a peasant's guise, but in the
dress of a lady. Doubtless you have heard how the ivory
horn of a unicorn has power to sanctify water. So did
her crystal finger sanctify anew the holy water when she
touched it. And at the same time the venom of her
basilisk gaze was tempered; she looked at her sister and
as their eyes met they laughed together; her beauty as
she laughed increased my love and strengthened my determination. They went into a side chapel. I followed
them. Torn as I was between fear and ambition, my
mind could apprehend one image only—a wedding! Such
is the effect of love! I saw myself sentenced to death and
it seemed that love was saying to me: "Tomorrow you
die, for already you are in the chapel." I dropped my
glove! And then as I bent to pick it up, my rosary slipped
from my fingers. Small wonder, for my eyes strayed constantly to Inés, and, Fabia, she looked at me. And since
she did, I think she recognized my love and my nobility,
for who does not think, does not look, and to look without thinking, Fabia, is only found in fools, and would
imply an impossible contradiction if an angel, for such
she is, should fail in understanding. In this belief, that
what I most wish is true, I have written her this letter.
So if you would win favor and show courage enough to

convey it to her hands, and thus bring my love some way toward its goal, which is to marry her—for it is firm enough to desire that already—then your reward shall be myself as your devoted slave, together with this rich chain of gold.

Fabia. I have heard your tale.

Alonso. What do you think?

Fabia. I see for you . . .

Alonso. What?

Fabia. Great danger.

Tello. Don't try to reason with him, Fabia, unless you seek, like a skillful surgeon, to make his wound instantly fatal.

Fabia. Tello, I will use such skill as I have and place the letter in her hands, though it cost me my life. All this I shall do without hope of reward, for where the stakes are high, only I dare venture. Where is the letter? [*Aside.*] I must improve upon it a little first.

Alonso. How can I hope to repay you for my life, my very soul, which may yet be returned to me by those saintly hands of yours?

Tello. Saintly?

Alonso. Are they not, when they are to work miracles?

Tello. With the Devil's aid.

Fabia. I will try all ways humanly possible, for Fabia was never too proud to accept the encouragement of a gold chain. Besides, I was born a trusting soul.

Tello. So was I, till I met you.

Alonso. Come, Fabia, come reverend mother, I must show you where my lodging lies.

Fabia. Tello . . .

Tello. Fabia . . . ?

Fabia [*aside to* TELLO]. Guard your tongue, for I have a certain brunette, with an excellent face and figure.

Tello. I'd make do with you, if that chain were the reward for my labors!   [*They go*

✓

A *room in* DON PEDRO's *house*

INÉS *and* LEONOR.

INÉS. But I was always told, Leonor, that it was engendered by the stars.

Leonor. You mean that if there were no stars, no one in the world would fall in love?

Inés. Tell me this then: for two years now Rodrigo has been my suitor, and all his efforts, all his pleading, his appearance, and everything he says and does, is like an icy wind that freezes any feeling I might have for him. And yet, I had only to see that noble stranger for an instant when I felt my soul say within me: "I love him," and all my will could answer was "So be it." What power is it that causes for one man, love, for another, hate?

Leonor. They say love shoots blindly, often errs, and rarely scores a true hit. Besides, I cannot deny it—even though your despised Rodrigo is a friend of Fernando, for whose sake I should plead Rodrigo's case—your stranger is attractive.

Inés. It was his eyes that drew mine to them, for I think I saw in them the very same passion that at once took form in me; but what use is it to talk? He will be far away by now.

Leonor. I saw him too, and I think he will not live long before trying to see you again.

Enter ANA, *a servant.*

Ana. Madam, a woman is here who calls herself Fabia, or Fabiana.

Inés. Who is she?

Ana. She is one who peddles rouge for the cheeks and powder for the face.

Inés. Shall we call her in, Leonor?

Leonor. How dare she call at honorable houses? I know who she is. I know her reputation. But I wonder what she wants.

Inés. Ana, call the woman.

Ana [*goes to the door*]. Fabia, my mistress bids you enter.

She goes. FABIA *enters.*

Fabia [*aside*]. As if I did not know she would! Ah, ladies, may God give you the enjoyment of your grace, your beauty, and your charm; for whenever you happen to pass me in the street, so beautifully and elegantly dressed and walking so proudly, I pour a thousand blessings on your heads. And I remember as if it were yesterday

that noble lady, your mother, the very phoenix of Medina,
so perfect she was in every way. And above all I remember
how kind she was to me, and what a loyal friend. Oh,
what saintly generosity, worthy of eternal memory! How
we, the poor, wept for her! Was there any among us who
could not recall a thousand good turns she had done?

Inés. Tell us, good mother, why are you here?

Fabia. How many among us were orphaned by her untimely death! The flower of all that ever bore the name
of Catalina. To this day my neighbors mourn her death.
Oh, no, they have not forgotten her. As for myself, was
there any kindness she did not do me? Oh, death snatched
her before her time, so soon, she had not reached fifty.

Inés. Do not weep, good woman, do not weep.

Fabia. How can I be comforted when I see Death take
the best of us and I remain alive? Your father, may God
keep him, is he at home?

Leonor. He went into the country this afternoon.

Fabia [*aside*]. Then he will be late home.—Since we
are speaking of the truth—you are young and I am old—
Your father, Don Pedro, once confided in me some secrets
of his youth. I, out of respect for her who now lies rotting,
kept his confidence—as was my duty. If there were ten
girls, five were not enough for him, he would have made
love to them all.

Inés. Virtuous father!

Fabia. Ah, your father in his day was like a madman,
all he saw, he loved. If you are of the same nature, then
I should be surprised if you are not in love, at least with
one gallant apiece. Do you never, in your prayers, ask
to be married soon?

Inés. No, Fabia, whenever that may happen, it will be
soon enough.

Fabia. A father who is tardy about such matters only
lays up trouble for himself. Freshly ripe fruit is a wonderful thing, my children, and it is foolish to wait until the
shortness of days wrinkles it. Of all things in the world,
I can think of only two that are good when they are old.

Leonor. And they are . . . ?

Fabia. Wine and a friend, my daughter. You see me
now? Well, I can assure you that there was a time when
my beauty and elegance kept many more than one young
gallant enthralled. Was there any that did not praise my

youthful spirits? He was considered a lucky man that I deigned to look upon! Oh, the silken dresses I wore, the money I spent, the exquisite feasts! I traveled in litters and was acclaimed on every side. I could have had any gift I wished from nobles far and near. But the springtime has passed, now never a man enters my house; for as time passes, so beauty fades.

Inés. Stay a moment. What have you there?

Fabia. Trifles I sell to earn my bread, that want may not force me to turn to evil means.

Leonor. May God help you in that, good mother.

Fabia. And there are my rosary and missal, nothing more, and now, ladies, time presses and——

Inés. Come back, just a moment. What is this?

Fabia. Papers containing camphor and sublimate, precious secrets for the cure of common sicknesses.

Leonor. And this, what is it?

Fabia. That you must not look at, though you were dying with curiosity.

Leonor. Tell me, Fabia, what is it?

Fabia. There is a certain girl who wishes to marry, but a man from Saragossa has deceived her. She has put herself in my hands. . . . I have pity. . . . It is but a work of charity, that they may live in peace.

Inés. What is this?

Fabia. Tooth powder, soap for the hands, pastilles, and various other curious and beneficial things.

Inés. And this?

Fabia. A few prayers. If dead souls could only repay what they owe me.

Inés. Here is a letter.

Fabia. You went straight for that as if it were meant for you. Put it back. You must not see it . . . you are too curious and inquisitive.

Inés. Let me see it. . . .

Fabia. There is in this town a gallant and educated young gentleman who is in love with a lady; he has promised me a golden chain if I deliver this letter to her, discreetly, in such a way that will not injure her honesty, modesty, and good reputation. Although his intentions are honorable, I dare not give it to her. Lovely Doña Inés, perhaps you can help me in this business, for I have an idea which may prove both effective and discreet.

You answer this letter for me and I will tell him it is from his lady.

Inés. It will certainly be beneficial to you, if you mean to win your gold chain by it. I will do it for you.

Fabia. May heaven lengthen your years to the span of a thousand gold chains. Read the letter then.

Inés. I will go to my room and read it, and then bring you the reply.   [*Exit* INÉS

Leonor. This is an excellent device!

Fabia. Oh, fire of love, prepare to burn the breast of this proud maiden.

Enter RODRIGO *and* FERNANDO.

Rodrigo [*to* FERNANDO]. I fear there are many obstacles to be overcome before I marry her.

Fernando. The lover always suffers.

Rodrigo. Here is your lady.

Fabia [*aside*]. Oh, untimely fools, what brings you here?

Rodrigo. But instead of mine, what a specter is there!

Fabia [*to* LEONOR]. It would be a great mercy to me, for I am in sore need.

Leonor. I will see that my sister pays you.

Fernando. If anything has taken your eye, madam, or if you can see any trifle you like, for though I would give you rich jewels, I hardly think this venerable woman brings any such with her, allow me to buy it for you.

Leonor. We have bought nothing. This good woman comes to the house merely to wash linen.

Rodrigo. Where is Don Pedro?

Leonor. He went into the country. He should be back by now.

Rodrigo. And Doña Inés? . . .

Leonor. She was here a moment ago. I think she is making the list for this good woman.

Rodrigo. I fear she saw me through the window and is avoiding me. Can the sight of one whose only desire is to serve her be so hateful to her?

Leonor. Here she is.

Enter INÉS *with a letter in her hand.*

Leonor [*to* INÉS]. See, Fabia is waiting here for the laundry list.

Inés. Here it is. You may give it to the boy to return.

Fabia. Oh, happy the water, Doña Inés, that is to wash the linen that has enclosed such a treasure of crystal. [*She pretends to read.*] Six chemises, ten towels, four tablecloths, two embroidered cushion covers, six gentlemen's shirts, eight sheets . . . et cetera; they will all come back to you as clean as the eyes in your head.

Rodrigo. My friend, give me the paper and allow me to pay the account, for I would dearly treasure any word written by that cruel hand.

Fabia. I should be conducting my business very well to be sure, if I were to give it you! Farewell, dear daughters.

[*She goes*

Rodrigo. That token should have stayed here and not left the house.

Leonor. Run after her, then, and bring it back if you wish to check the list.

Inés. Father has returned. You should leave the house at once, or else go and pay your respects to him, for though he never reproaches you, I know he does not like us to receive you alone.

Rodrigo. I pray constantly that Love or Death may grant me the strength to suffer your contempt. To Love that it might temper your cruelty, or to Death that it might end my life. But Love cannot and Death will not. Trapped at the crossroads of Love and Death, I cannot choose which path to take! Since Love transfixes me and yet decrees that I may win no favor from you, Love itself decrees my death! So kill me at once, ungrateful lady, kill him that adores you: for you must be my death, lady, since you will not be my life! All things that live are born of love, and live by love; all things that die, do so at the hand of a relentless power that undoes our lives. If my suffering is not strong enough to satisfy the demands of love, nor yet great enough to kill me, then indeed I must be immortal, since neither life nor death can do me good or ill.   [RODRIGO *and* FERNANDO *go*

Inés. What a bundle of foolishness!

Leonor. Your own was no less.

Inés. If you are referring to the laundry list, Leonor, have you ever known love to be discreet?

Leonor. Does love oblige you to write to a man without knowing who he is?

Inés. I suspect it to be an invention of the handsome stranger, to test whether I would write to him or not.

Leonor. I guessed as much myself.

Inés. If it was so, then he was discretion itself. Listen! I want to read you some verses [*She reads*]:

> "Phoebus, in all his courses round the sphere
> From Dawn's pale smile to his last western ray,
> Never beheld a shepherdess so fair
> As she that in Medina walked today.
> She moved, a crystal column, unaware
> That all eyes followed and were drawn away
> After two scarlet shoes whose dainty snare,
> Without restraint, was victor of the day.
> Though Love is said to dwell within the eyes,
> A slipper held me in complete surrender,
> And now, enmeshed within its soft green ties,
> Love's captive, and your slave, I only wonder:
> If with your feet you slay me, sweet Inés,
> What power is in those dark eyes' loveliness?"

Leonor. Your gallant must want you for a dancing partner if he is in love with your feet!

Inés. Say, rather, he starts with the feet because he next wants to ask for my hand.

Leonor. What did you reply?

Inés. That he should come tonight to the railing in the garden wall.

Leonor. What madness is this?

Inés. I do not mean to talk to him.

Leonor. Then what do you want?

Inés. Come with me and I will tell you.

Leonor. I fear your plan is rash and foolish.

Inés. When was love otherwise?

Leonor. You should flee from love at first.

Inés. Who can flee from first love, Leonor, when all know it is decreed by nature?   [*They go*

Enter ALONSO, TELLO, *and* FABIA.

Fabia. Four thousand blows, on my old back, have I suffered in your service.

Tello. I gather you handled the transaction very well.

Fabia. If you think you can do better . . .

Alonso. It was madness for me to aspire to heaven.

Tello. And with Fabia for your guardian angel, who has fallen into a hell of a beating to raise you up . . .

Fabia. Ay, poor Fabia!

Tello. And who were the cruel priests that used your shoulders as their lectern?

Fabia. Two lackeys and three pages. I left my cloak and hat there—ripped to ribbons.

Alonso. That would be of no account, good mother, if they had not presumed against your venerable person. Oh, what a fool I was to put my trust in those treacherous eyes, those false diamonds, that signaled to me only to deceive and lead me to my death! My punishment is just. Take this purse, good woman, and Tello, saddle the horses. We return to Olmedo tonight.

Tello. How can we, sir, when it is getting dark already?

Alonso. Why, would you have me kill myself?

Fabia. Do not torment yourself, Fabia has the remedy for you. Look!

Alonso. A letter!

Fabia. A letter.

Alonso. Do you deceive me?

Fabia. It is from her. A reply to your verses.

Alonso. Onto your knees, Tello.

Tello. Wait until you have read it first. They say the pen is mightier than the sword.

Alonso [*he reads*]. "Anxious to know if you are who I believe you to be, and hoping that you are, I entreat you to come tonight to the garden railing of this house, where you will find tied the green ribbon from my slipper, and then to put it in your hat in the morning, that I may know you."

Fabia. What does she say?

Alonso. How can I pay you or praise you enough for so great a deed?

Tello. Well, we shall not have any more madness about saddling and riding to Olmedo tonight. Do you hear that, my friends, you ponies? You can relax, we're staying in Medina.

Alonso. The day is dying. Come, Tello, we must prepare ourselves. Who knows, Inés may come to watch me take the ribbon.   [*He goes*

Tello. And I, Fabia, with your leave, will go and dress my master up in his night watchman's finery.

Fabia. Wait.

Tello. I would if I thought he was capable of getting dressed without me.

Fabia. Let him go alone. You are to come with me.

Tello. With you, Fabia?

Fabia. With me.

Tello. I?

Fabia. Yes; what we have to do concerns your master.

Tello. What do you want?

Fabia. I will trust my secret with you. I need a tooth from the head of that highwayman they hanged yesterday.

Tello. But didn't they bury him?

Fabia. No.

Tello. Why, what are you going to do?

Fabia. Get the tooth, and you alone shall accompany me.

Tello. Why should I get myself mixed up with you in such a business? What are you thinking of?

Fabia. Chickenhearted. You dare not go where I, an old woman, dare to tread.

Tello. You converse with the Devil, Fabia.

Fabia. Come.

Tello. Bid me fight ten armed men together, and I will do it, but do not make me meddle with the dead!

Fabia. If you do not come, I will send him to fetch you.

Tello. I must obey. Are you a woman or a demon?

Fabia. Come, you are to carry the ladder, for you are yet unskilled in such matters.

Tello. He who rises by such steps, Fabia, must expect the same end himself.   [*They go*

*

Outside the garden wall of DON PEDRO'*s house. It is night*

Enter RODRIGO *and* FERNANDO.

FERNANDO. Why do you come to gaze at this house in vain?

Rodrigo. My hope, Fernando, finds some consolation here. Sometimes these iron bars are graced by her crystal hands, and where she puts her hands by day, I place my soul by night. The more Inés pierces me with cruel contempt, the more I burn for her. See, Fernando, even these bars soften to see my sorrow; surely an angel such as she cannot remain unmoved by one who can melt hard iron? Look! What is here?

Fernando. A ribbon is tied to the railing.

Rodrigo. Doubtless the souls of rejected lovers are tied to these bars as a punishment for their presumption.

Fernando. It is a favor from Leonor. Sometimes she speaks to me here.

Rodrigo. I dare not think that Inés left it here, and yet, against all reason, my hope persuades me that her cruel hands have tied this knot. Give it to me.

Fernando. It is not mine to give, for if Leonor sees me tomorrow without it, she may think that I care nothing for her.

Rodrigo. Let us divide it then.

Fernando. Why?

Rodrigo. So that they will see us both wearing it, and by that token they will know that we came here together.

They halve the ribbon. Enter ALONSO *and* TELLO.

Fernando. Who's that? There is someone in the street, Rodrigo.

Tello [*to his master*]. Go quickly to the railing, master; Fabia is waiting for my help in some very important business.

Alonso. Fabia has business with you!

Tello. It is very elevated business.

Alonso. How?

Tello. I am to hold the ladder, and she . . .

Alonso. What will she hold?

Tello. The pincers.

Alonso. What are you going to do?

Tello. Take a lady out of her house.

Alonso. Have a care what you do, Tello. Do not enter a place from whence there is no escape.

Tello. It is nothing, I swear.

Alonso. Is the abduction of a lady nothing?

Tello. No, master, it is the tooth from that thief who was hanged yesterday.

Alonso. Hush, Tello! Look! There are two men here.

Tello. Maybe they are on guard.

Alonso. Is this why she told me to come for the ribbon?

Tello. It's a trick, master.

Alonso. If I had been too bold would she not seek some

other way to punish me? If that was her intention, she
was deceived. She little knows Alonso, the Knight from
Olmedo. By God, I swear I will teach her to punish by
other means the knight who serves her.

Tello. Take care!

Alonso. Gentlemen! No man lives that loiters here.

Rodrigo [to FERNANDO]. Who is this?

Fernando. I do not recognize his figure or his voice.

Rodrigo. Who dares to speak so arrogantly?

Alonso. One whose tongue is in his sword.

Rodrigo. Then here is one that will chastise his presumption.

Tello. Close with them, master. This is better than
drawing teeth from corpses. [RODRIGO *and* FERNANDO *are
driven back.*]

Alonso. Do not follow them.

Tello. They left this cloak behind.

Alonso. Take it and come this way. There are lights in
the windows.   [*They go*

Enter INÉS *and* LEONOR *above.*

Inés. When at last the April dawn brushed with ivory
feet the bright enameled flowers, after a whole long night
which I passed sleepless, fearing he should not come, I
could wait no longer: I crept out to look—and found the
ribbon had gone.

Leonor. The stranger took it secretly and went away.

Inés. Leaving me still in doubt, still in fear.

Leonor. I can hardly believe it is you, Inés, you who
were as cold as ice! How can you have changed in so
short a time?

Inés. I only know that heaven is punishing me for it
now. Either it is Love's vengeance or his victory over me,
for my heart is consumed with fire to think of the gallant
stranger. I cannot put him from my mind for a moment.
What can I do?

Enter RODRIGO *with the green ribbon in his hat.*

Rodrigo. Never did I imagine that my love could be
overcome by fear. But take heart and live again. [*To*
INÉS.] I have come to see Don Pedro.

Inés. You have come too early. He is not up yet.

Rodrigo. It is urgent business.

Inés [aside to Leonor]. Did you ever see such a fool?

Leonor. The man you love always seems wise and the man you despise, a fool.

Rodrigo [aside]. Is there no way to please this cruel creature? Can I find no place in her thoughts?

Inés [aside to Leonor]. Leonor! I see why he has come! I wrote to him myself telling him to come for the ribbon.

Leonor. Fabia has tricked you!

Inés. I can tear up the letter, but I will be revenged for having kept it so near my heart.

Enter Don Pedro, *and* Fernando *with the green ribbon in his hat.*

Fernando. Rodrigo sent me to broach the matter with you.

Don Pedro. Very well, I am prepared to discuss the proposition.

Fernando. But here he is. Love's clock is always fast.

Don Pedro. I assume that Inés has already shown some favor to him.

Fernando. Rather, he regrets, the opposite.

Don Pedro. Don Rodrigo . . .

Rodrigo. I am at your service. [Don Pedro *and the two young men talk softly together.*]

Inés [to Leonor]. It was all a trick of Fabia's.

Leonor. How?

Inés. Do you not see that Fernando is wearing the ribbon too?

Leonor. It would seem that the two of them are in love with you.

Inés. I only need you to be jealous of me now! This is too hard to bear.

Leonor. Why have they come?

Inés. Do you not remember what father was saying yesterday?

Leonor. About your being married?

Inés. Yes.

Leonor. Then if it should be Fernando, that is good-bye to him for me.

Inés. Perhaps they have both come bent on marriage, since they have divided the ribbon between them!

Don Pedro. This matter demands privacy and time. Let us go in where we may discuss it more freely.

Rodrigo. I have no more to say but that I hope to be your son-in-law.

Don Pedro. I can see you love Inés, and I am glad of that, but out of respect to me, we must discuss it a little further.   [*They go in*

Inés. How vain was my hope! How wild my thoughts! That I should have written to Rodrigo! And made you jealous for Fernando! Oh, treacherous stranger! Oh, lying Fabia!

Enter FABIA.

Fabia. Hush now, Fabia is listening.

Inés. False enemy, what web is this you've spun?

Fabia. No, the web was yours. You wrote to your stranger that he should come to your wall for a ribbon of hope and then set two men there to kill him. If they had not retreated when they did, I think they would have paid for their rash attempt.

Inés. Oh, Fabia, I must declare myself to you, even though I disregard the good name of my father, my position, and my honor. Tell me. Is it true what you say? for if it is so, then Rodrigo and Fernando took the ribbon and kept it for a favor for themselves. Good mother, I can find no peace except in thinking of him who sent you to me.

Fabia [*aside*]. My charms and spells have done their work! I foresee my victory in this.—Do not despair, my daughter. Take heart, soon you will be the wife of the noblest knight living this day in all Castile, and that will be no less than he whom they call, for his great valor, the Knight of Olmedo. Don Alonso saw you at the Feria, a peasant Venus, your eyebrows Cupid's bows, and your bright eyes his arrows. Who can blame him for following you? For wise men say that beauty dwells in the eyes and the understanding those eyes convey. You drew him after you, ensnared by the green ribbons on your slippers, for love has subtler holds than by the hair. He would serve you. You esteem him. He adores you. You have killed him. He writes to you. You answer him. Who could find fault with love so innocent? He will inherit, for he is the only heir, an income of ten thousand ducats; and, although he is young, his parents are already old. Love and be loved by the noblest knight in all Castile.

Handsome figure, handsome mind. The King has shown
great favors to him, for he it was most honored with his
presence the celebrations of the royal wedding, using his
sword like a Hector in the bullring there. He won thirty
prizes in the tourneys, all of which he gave to the ladies.
In his armor, he looks like Achilles eyeing the walls of
Troy. Dressed for the court, he looks like Adonis. . . .
May God grant him a better end. How happy you will
be with so wise a husband! How unfortunate is the woman
who is married to a fool!

Inés. No more, good mother, you will drive me mad!
But how can I be his if my father betroths me to Rodrigo?
Even now, he and Fernando are discussing the wedding
with my father!

Fabia. The two of you must annul the sentence!

Inés. But Rodrigo is there now.

Fabia. Have no fear. He is only a party and not the
judge.

Inés. Leonor, have you no advice to give me?

Leonor. You would not hear me if I had.

Inés. Let us go in.

Fabia. Leave it all to me. Alonso shall be yours. May
you be happy with a man who in all Castile is the jewel
of Medina and the flower of Olmedo.

ACT TWO

1

Enter TELLO *and* ALONSO.

TELLO. Master, this secret love of yours will soon be known
to all the world! And there are some I might name who
will not be well pleased when it is.

Alonso. Better to die, Tello, than to live without seeing her!

Tello. Who speaks of dying? All you need do is to guard
your tongue and use discretion when you visit her. Three
days you have known her, and you have traveled backward
and forward between Olmedo and Medina every day. Anyone with half an eye can see you have caught love's fever.
Perhaps you have it in a tertian form, it is so fierce today.

Alonso. My fever, as you call it, Tello, never cools. My
love is an ever-burning flame which needs no fanning, for

it never dies. My love is a lion, with a tyrant's strength, that overwhelms my heart and makes my soul his slave. This absence from her is merely a lull in love's action, for were I within her sight, my soul would be a salamander.

Tello. But do you never tire, never weary, of all this coming and going?

Alonso. What is it that I do, Tello, in riding from Olmedo to Medina? Leander crossed a sea each night and all the waters of the Hellespont could not temper his ardor. There is no sea between Olmedo and Medina, Tello, so it is a slight service I do Inés by making that short journey.

Tello. Strong swimmer you may be, but there is a tricky current that may yet sweep you away, one that Leander did not face. Rodrigo is as well aware of your love as I am, thanks to that cloak he left behind him in his haste. One day, not knowing then whose cloak it was I had earned that evening, I wore it as my own, and——

Alonso. You fool!

Tello. As I was saying, I went out one day with this cloak and who should I see but Rodrigo. He said to me, "Tell me, sir, who gave you that cloak? For I recognize the cloth." I replied, "If it is of any use to you, I will gladly make one of your servants a present of it." He went pale when I said that, and stuttered, "One of my lackeys foolishly lost it the other night, but it is better employed on you. Look after it well." And off he went with a nasty look in his eye and one hand on his sword. He knows I serve you, and he knows that he lost his cloak to you and me. For God's sake, master, have a care; the people here are proud and dangerous. What's more, they are in their own land, and cocks will always crow on their own dunghill. And another thing, it scares me to see your love for Inés mixed up with witchcraft. Honest folk should not put their trust in spells and conjurations. I had to go with her—though I swear it was against my will—to pull out a tooth from a hanged man. I put the ladder up at the side of the gallows, feeling just like Harlequin. Fabia climbed up, while I stood trembling at the bottom. Suddenly the corpse's mouth moved. The dead man spoke to me! "Climb up, Tello, don't be afraid. Come up, or I'll come down to you." Holy Saint Paul! I went out like a light, and fell to the ground in such a swoon that it is a wonder I ever came round to tell the tale. I could have sworn I saw him coming for me, and when I regained my senses, the sweat was pouring off me. I was wet through, as if I had been left out in a thunderstorm.

Alonso. Tello, true love fears no tale of danger. It is my misfortune that I should have a rival—and one that already seeks to marry Inés. What then am I to do—jealous and desperate for her love as you see me? I have no faith in witchcraft; it is mere foolishness. Perseverance and merit have more power to sway the will than old wives' spells. Inés loves me. I adore Inés; for her I live, and anything that is not Inés I hate, abhor, reject. I am her slave. I shall ride between Olmedo and Medina, because whether I live or die, Inés is ruler of my soul.

Tello. All that remains now is for you to say as much to her. I pray God some good may come of it!

Alonso. Knock on the door. It is time.

Tello. Very well, master. [*He knocks on the door of* DON PEDRO's *house.*]

Ana [*off*]. Who is there?

Tello. That was quick! It is me. Is Melibea at home? Calisto is here.

Ana. Wait a moment, Sempronio.

Tello. Now all we need is La Celestina herself.[1]

Inés [*off*]. Is it he?

Ana [*off*]. It is, madam.

The door opens and ALONSO *and* TELLO *enter the house.*

Inés. My lord! . . .

Alonso. Lovely Inés, this is to live at last.

Tello. Now is the time for those fine speeches you have been practicing on me.

[1] La Celestina is the most famous bawd in Spanish literature, and her name came to replace the original title of the book in which she appears (*The Tragicomedy of Calisto and Melibea*). This late fifteenth-century work, attributed to Fernando de Rojas, is Lope's source for much of the intrigue concerning the use of Fabia as a go-between (including the part played by witchcraft), and frequent verbal echoes would have continuously recalled his model to the contemporary audience. At this point, the parallel is made explicit by using the names of the hero and heroine for Alonso and Inés, that of Celestina for Fabia, and that of Sempronio (Calisto's servant) for Tello.—ED.

Inés. Tello, my friend! . . .

Tello. My queen!

Inés. My dear Alonso, how your absence tortured me! Rodrigo has been here again.

Alonso. Although obedience to your father may compel you to marry him, I will not abandon hope until I hear the sentence pronounced. I told Tello, even as he saddled our horses, that my heart was troubled and that my melancholy sprang from some new misfortune which as yet I had not heard. And now that I am with you, you tell me that it is so. Alas for me if it prove true!

Inés. Do not believe it, dear my lord, for I will say no to all the world, having given my word to you. You alone are master of my life and my will. There is no power on earth, Alonso, that can force me from my course, which is to be your wife. In the empty hours of yesterday, I beguiled the time by walking in the garden alone, even without the companionship of Leonor, who is still vexed because Fernando wore my ribbon. As I wandered, I told my love to the fountains and to the flowers, and as I did so the tears ran down my cheeks. "Fountains and flowers," I said, for so I spoke in my loneliness, "you enjoy a happy life, for although the night may come to shroud you in cold and darkness, yet each day you see your sun." I fancied a lily moved its yellow tongue and answered me —such is the trickery of love—saying: "When the sun that you adore, Inés, shines on you at night, when all other suns are spent, is not that a greater fortune?"

Tello [aside]. Thus did a Greek philosopher once answer a blind man who bemoaned his lot: "The night brings its own pleasures," so what has she to complain about?

Inés. I come as a moth to a candle, longing for your light. . . . No, not as a moth, but as a phoenix, for in the flame of this passion, I burn and die, and then am born again.

Alonso. Thrice blessed be the coral of these lips. The delicate petals of a rose whose scent in loving words gives me both life and strength. I too, when Tello is not there to hear me, tell my love, my hopes, my fears, to the flowers.

Tello [aside]. I've even seen him in Olmedo talking to the radishes. Lovers are all the same, they'll talk to the stones or the wind.

Alonso. My thoughts cannot endure either to be alone

or silent. They must be with you, sweet Inés. Oh, if I could only say now all that I say to you in your absence! But when I am with you, I forget even to live. As I ride here, Inés, I recount to Tello all your graces, all your charms, your wit, your understanding. The mere sound of your name is so sweet to me that I gave employment to a serving woman simply because she bore your name. In addressing her all day, I imagine that I speak to you.

Tello. Madam, your power over us is so great that you have turned my master into a poet and made a musician of me. Here is a song he has composed in your honor. [*He sings.*] [1]

> When Inés walked in the valley,
> The sky offered all its stars
> In exchange for the pale primroses
> That were gathered by hands like hers.
> As I walked alone in the valley,
> The dew fell in tears to see
> How I offered my heart with the flowers,
> But she scorned to pluck it from me.
> She gathered the flowers in the valley,
> But mocked the heart I gave.
> The only hands that will welcome it
> Are the pale hands of a grave.

Inés. You belie me, Tello. I would not banish my lord's heart to the grave.

Alonso. No, Inés, it is my love that is belied in the song, for no verses could ever convey such depths of meaning as lie in my love for you.

Inés. Someone is coming! My father!

Alonso. Will he come in here?

---

[1] The original is a complex and highly stylized *glosa* on a popular song which runs roughly as follows:

> I left Inés
> laughing down in the valley.
> If you should see her, Andrés,
> tell her I am dying,
> and hardly may rally.

This is "glossed" in accordance with the rules of this typically Spanish form, being developed in such a way that each successive stanza of the *glosa* culminates in one of the lines of the basic text.—ED.

Inés. Hide.

Alonso. Where?

They hide, and DON PEDRO *enters.*

Don Pedro. Inés, I thought I heard music. Why are you up so late?

Inés. I have been praying, sir, concerning what you said yesterday, and asking for God's help to do the best thing.

Don Pedro. I can think of no better husband for you than Rodrigo. Nothing could make me happier.

Inés. Everyone agrees that he deserves his great reputation, and if I were to marry, there is no man in Medina equal to him in merit.

Don Pedro. How, *if* you were to marry?

Inés. Because I cannot marry Rodrigo. I already have a husband.

Don Pedro. A husband! What news is this, Inés? Who is he? What is his name?

Inés. It is a name familiar to you. I intend to be a nun. It has always been my wish. Now I have confessed, Father. I beg you, if you love your daughter, have me a habit made tomorrow, that I may be rid of these unnecessary fineries, for so I should like to be dressed while I prepare myself for my future vocation. You still have Leonor. She, I am sure, will gladden your heart with grandchildren. For my mother's sake I beg you, do not gainsay me in this, but rather seek a wise and holy woman to give me lessons suitable for a novice, and also a tutor to teach me Latin and singing.

Don Pedro. Is it you that speaks, Inés, or who?

Inés. It is my voice, and my will, that speaks, Father.

Don Pedro. One half of my heart melts to hear you, Inés, and the other half has been changed into marble by your words. I had hoped that your green youthfulness would cheer my dotage with grandchildren. But if this is your true vocation, then God forbid that I should stand in the way. Do your will, although it is far from mine; but mine, I know, need not be God's intention. But since our human frailty is often vain and full of change—particularly is it so in women, who are readily persuaded—and since saying is far from doing, and women are never more like themselves than when they change their minds, do not, I beg you, exchange your pretty dresses for dismal

black. Your dress need not prevent you from reading Latin
or learning to sing, or from doing what you please. So
continue to dress as befits your youth and beauty, lest you
become a laughingstock when Medina marvels one day to
see you a holy woman and the next to see you turned
human again. I will engage a woman to teach you Latin,
for, after all, you must obey a greater father than I. And
now, good night, and God be with you; for me, I must go
and weep; I should not wish to cause you distress by the
sight of an old man's tears.

He goes, and ALONSO *and* TELLO *enter.*

Inés. Forgive me, my lord, if I have angered you.

Alonso. No, Inés. I am not angry. You have found a
way to lead us both to death. Oh, Inés, could you find no
other remedy than this, which kills even as it cures?

Inés. Even at our life's eclipse, my lord, love's light can
lead us out of danger.

Alonso. How, out of danger?

Inés. Now, at least I have made an end to Rodrigo's
hopes, and time makes an end of all evils, so unless some
second sentence is passed upon us, we need not give up
hope.

Tello. She is right, master. While Inés is studying and
singing, the pair of you may be making plans how you may
enter the Church together. Apart from that, Rodrigo's
cause is lost, for he cannot now persuade Don Pedro to
keep his word to him. It is no affront to him that Inés
should leave him for the reason she has given. Besides, it
provides an easy means for me to come and go at liberty
in this house.

Alonso. At liberty?

Tello. She is going to study Latin. What could be sim-
pler than that I should become her tutor? I will teach her
to read your letters!

Alonso. How cunningly you have devised my salvation!

Tello. And Fabia may come disguised as a holy woman
to teach her.

Inés. Very well, Fabia shall be my tutor in holy usages
and virtues.

Tello. I can well imagine what virtues she will teach!

Alonso. My sweet Inés, love is so dear a subject that
lovers do not feel the hours flying. I fear that dawn may

soon be upon us unawares and that I may be recognized
as I leave the house, or else I shall be forced to stay.
Forced! What delightful imprisonment! But stay I cannot,
for tomorrow Medina, as you know, is to celebrate the
Feast of the Finding of the Holy Cross. I must leave you,
for success with the bulls is not his who is too idle to
practice the art. And here in Medina I mean to do you
honor. Besides, I have heard that the King himself, Don
Juan, will honor the town with his presence during the
festival. The Constable requested this honor and it has
been granted, for at this time the King will be traveling
between Valladolid and Toledo. Our noblemen must strive
to do him honor, and since I am determined not to be
outdone in this, I must leave you and prepare myself.
Farewell, and may God be with you.

Inés. Wait. Let me go first to open the door.

Alonso. Why must the dawn come so soon? Does she
envy our love?

Tello. You said we had to go before it was light.

Alonso. How, Tello?

Tello. Dawn is breaking, master, and at this rate, the
sun will be up before we are in the saddle.   [*They go*

Enter RODRIGO *and* FERNANDO.

Rodrigo. Indeed, he has often given me cause to wonder, Fernando, and surely I have reason to be jealous of
so proud and elegant a rival.

Fernando. You have all the symptoms of the true lover:
that as soon as you see a handsome man of your own age,
you fear at once that if your mistress sees him she will fall
in love with him.

Rodrigo. But his renown is such that popular applause
acclaims him wherever he goes. As I told you, I met that
young fellow wearing my cloak in the streets here. Wearing it boldly in broad daylight. That cloak I lost together
with my honor! I accosted him and he insulted me, so
confident he was. I made certain inquiries and soon discovered the reason for his daring. His master is indeed
Alonso, the Gallant Knight of Olmedo, the great swordsman, feared alike by men and bulls. If such a man should
love Inés, what can I do? And if she returns his love, how
can I ever hope for her to look upon me with human eyes?

Fernando. Are you so certain she will return his love?

Rodrigo. She will. I know it, and who can deny that he is worthy of her love? What else am I to think, when I know she despises me?

Fernando. Jealousy, Rodrigo, is a chimera, given form by envy, wind, and shadows, so that the yet uncertain but constantly imagined consequence becomes a fearful phantom in the night. A hideous ghost that draws a man to madness, and a lie that takes the name of truth.

Rodrigo. Then why does Alonso come so often to Medina? And why does he only come at night, using the darkness as his cloak? Come, Fernando; I mean to marry her: you are a discreet and honorable man: what advice can you give me, if not to kill him?

Fernando. I should first ask myself why, when Inés has never loved you, should you assume that she loves him.

Rodrigo. Because he is luckier—or more handsome.

Fernando. Is it not an insult to Inés to suppose that she necessarily wants a husband?

Rodrigo. By all the saints, I swear that I shall kill him! In loving her he has dishonored me—made me the object of her hatred and contempt. Because of him I lost my cloak. Soon I shall lose my mind.

Fernando. We should not have left him the cloak; I think it spurred him on. But you have Don Pedro's consent. Arrange for the wedding, Rodrigo; let Alonso keep the cloak and his glory. You will have the final victory.

Rodrigo. My love is overpowered by jealousy. Anger chokes me!

Fernando. Ride gallantly to the fiesta, and I will go with you; the chestnut and the bay whinny for their saddles. Remember, the King is coming. Seek entertainment there, and you will find ease from torment in action.

Rodrigo. If Alonso comes, what hope has Medina against Olmedo?

Fernando. Despair is madness!

Rodrigo. Love has driven me to it.

They go. Enter DON PEDRO, INÉS *and* LEONOR.

Don Pedro. If you love me, Inés, do not persist in this folly.

Inés. You cannot change my mind.

Don Pedro. Daughter, what do you intend, that you administer this poison to me? You have time——

Inés. What difference does it make if I wear the dark habit now, since I have vowed it shall be mine forever?

Leonor. You are foolish, Inés.

Inés. Hush, Leonor.

Leonor. At least go to the fiesta looking your best.

Inés. These clothes have no delight for me. I long for black and a life dedicated to God.

Don Pedro. Is it nothing to you that I desire it?

Inés. Very well, I must obey you, Father.

Enter FABIA, *with a rosary, staff, and spectacles.*

Fabia. Peace be within this house.

Don Pedro. And with you.

Fabia. Which of the ladies is Doña Inés, that is to be the bride of the Lord? Which is she that has chosen her bridegroom and takes this step to win his love throughout eternity?

Don Pedro. Holy mother, you see her here, and I am her father.

Fabia. May you continue so for many years to come, and may she soon see her lord that you see not yet. As I trust in the Lord, I hope he will grant you grace in all piety to accept such a bridegroom for her, for indeed, he is a noble gentleman.

Don Pedro. Yes, indeed, mother, he is as you say.

Fabia. I hear that you seek a tutor to guide your daughter's green years, one to show her the ways of the Lord, and lead her, a beginner, into the paths of love. I prayed to the Lord, and it was revealed to me that I should come and offer myself, great sinner though I am.

Don Pedro. Here is the woman you need, Inés.

Inés. This indeed is the one I need. Good mother, embrace me.

Fabia. Careful, mind my hair shirt.

Don Pedro. Never have I seen such humility.

Leonor. What she has in her heart is written in her face.

Fabia. Oh, what grace, what beauty! May your sweetness obtain all that I desire for you. You have an oratory?

Inés. Mother, I begin to feel better already.

Fabia. As I am a sinner, I fear your father may prevent the happiness you seek.

Don Pedro. Have no fear. I shall not stand in the way of such a divine vocation.

Fabia. In vain, Satan, you sought to devour her! Inés shall never be married in Medina, while there is a convent in Olmedo: Domine, if it is within my power, ad juvandam me festina.

Enter TELLO, *wearing a scholar's cap.*

Tello [*off*]. If he is here with his daughters, then I am certain he will be glad I have come to offer my services. [*He enters.*] You see here, Don Pedro, the tutor you seek to teach your daughter Latin, and sundry other subjects which will appear in the course of time. I learned at the church that you seek a student of Latin, for the honest intention of this lady is already known. And so, although I am a stranger in these parts, I have come to be of service to you, if I may, to teach her.

Don Pedro. Now I do believe, and hold it as certain, seeing how all things have come together, that it was indeed the will of heaven. You, holy mother, may reside in my house, and you, young gentleman, may come to give her lessons. I will leave you together now to arrange all things needful. [*To* TELLO.] Where do you come from, young man?

Tello. From Calahorra, sir.

Don Pedro. What is your name?

Tello. Martín Peláez.

Don Pedro. You must be related to the Cid. Where did you study?

Tello. In Coruña, and received my degree there.

Don Pedro. Are you ordained?

Tello. Yes, sir, a very short while ago.

Don Pedro. Good. I shall return presently.   [*He goes*

Tello. Is that Fabia?

Fabia. Can you not see it is?

Leonor. And are you Tello?

Inés. Dear Tello!

Leonor. Was there ever such roguery!

Inés. How is Alonso?

Tello. Can I trust Leonor?

Inés. You can.

Leonor. My love for Inés would feel insulted if she kept her thoughts hidden from me.

Tello. Madam, my master, Alonso, is well and ready to serve you. He is preparing for the Fiesta. His sword and lance are impatient to do you honor. I think the bulls are trembling already for fear of him. But fate will decide and you will see it all in good time, at the Fiesta.

Inés. Did he not write to me?

Tello. I am a fool. Here is the letter, madam.

Inés. I stamp it with a kiss, and read.

DON PEDRO *returns.*

Don Pedro [*off*]. If the sorrel is still unfit, prepare the coach. [*Enters.*] Well, is the matter settled?

Tello. Here is your father. Read this, and I will pretend to be teaching you Latin. Dominus . . .

Inés. Dominus . . .

Tello. Go on.

Inés. What next?

Tello. Dominus meus.

Inés. Dominus meus.

Tello. You will soon read Latin as well as I do.

Don Pedro. What! At your lessons already, Inés?

Inés. I am eager to learn, Father.

Don Pedro. Leave it for the moment, Inés. I have word from the council that I must attend the festival myself.

Inés. They have acted wisely, for I hear the King is coming.

Don Pedro. But I will go only on one condition; that you will come with Leonor.

Inés. Mother, tell me: May I go to the Fiesta without sinning?

Fabia. Have no fear, my daughter. Only the overscrupulous would consider it a sin, people who imagine they offend God every time they breathe, and forget they are only human, like everybody else. They consider any entertainment that takes the mind from work to be a monstrous excess. Although such pleasures should be taken in moderation, I give you license, at least for this once, to go to the Fiesta, for after all it is jugatoribus paternus.

Don Pedro. Come, then, for I must pay your tutor for his pains, and give the reverend mother something for a new mantle.

Fabia. May the mantle of heaven cover us all. And you, Leonor, will you not soon be like your sister?

Leonor. Yes, mother, indeed, it would be hard not to follow such a holy example.   [*They go*

✦

Enter the KING, DON JUAN, *with courtiers and the*
CONSTABLE.

KING [*to* CONSTABLE]. Why bring us business to despatch just at the moment of setting out?

Constable. It is only a matter of signature, there are no questions for you to hear, my lord.

King. Tell me briefly then what they are.

Constable. Shall I bring in the messengers?

King. Not now.

Constable. His Holiness, the Pope, has granted your request concerning the Order of the Knights of Alcántara, sir.

King. I think the new dress will be much more suitable.

Constable. The old style was very ugly, sir.

King. Now they may wear a green cross. We are most grateful at his favor to us.

Constable. Here are two writs, both excellent.

King. What matter do they contain?

Constable. The conditions you have imposed upon the Moors and Jews living in Castile.

King. Concerning this matter, Constable, we wish to comply with the desires of Brother Vicente Ferrer, who so ardently desired that it should be so.

Constable. He is a holy and learned man.

King. I resolved with him yesterday that wherever the races dwell together in my kingdom, the Jews should wear a tabard with a sign on it, and the Moors should wear a green hood. Thus the Christians will be able to distinguish them and behave with suitable decorum and avoid them so as not to be corrupted.

Constable. In the second writ, Your Highness favors Don Alonso, whom they call the Knight of Olmedo, with a knight's habit.

King. He is a man of great honor and renown. I remember him well. He graced the wedding of my sister with his presence.

Constable. I believe he intends to be at your service in the Fiesta at Medina tomorrow.

King. Bid him continue to win ever more fame, for we intend great honors for him, both in estate and rank.

[*They go*

Enter ALONSO.

Alonso. Oh, hard condition, when absence is my enemy! Absence that divides my soul in two and soon, I fear, may take my life! Truly you are called a living death, for you give life to desire and death to sight. Had you known pity, you would have taken my life at the same moment as you robbed me of my soul, when I left Medina. Ah, happy Medina, where lives divine Inés, your finest treasure, the honor of the court. Her praises are sung by the fleeting waters, the birds who hear the still sweeter sound of her own voice, and the flowers who emulate her beauty. The bright sun envies her, for he sees no beauty to compare with hers as he twines his golden ribbon round the world. Nothing so lovely comes within his view, neither when he shines in glory over Spain, nor when he sinks beyond the Indies. And I have dared to love her! Oh happy daring! And yet, the need for secrecy prevents my dearest wish, which is to see her, to adore her, and to serve her. When I left Inés, she was weeping, and her tears were as seals of truth upon her words. That night well knows that she might have been mine. Oh, coward love! Why do you wait, Alonso? Why stand on ceremony? Oh, God, what agony it is to part a soul and divide a life!

Enter TELLO.

Tello. Do I merit a welcome?

Alonso. How can I say yes to that when you have kept me waiting so long?

Tello. It was for your own good, master, so you cannot blame me.

Alonso. Who in the world can do me good except Inés? Has she written to me?

Tello. She has. I have a letter for you.

Alonso. Then you may tell me later how well you have served me. [*He reads.*] "My lord, since you left me I have not lived an instant. You have departed from me and I am left in darkness."

Tello. Will you not read further?

Alonso. No.

Tello. Why not?

Alonso. It is too rich a diet for a starving man. Let us talk of her instead, Tello.

Tello. I arrived wearing a short gown and gloves, looking like a poor scholar that tries to prove his learning by a scrawny neck and mean clothes. I made up a flattering greeting, full of tangled verbosity. I thought it a clever speech for a Bachelor of Arts, perhaps too clever, for they rarely have two thoughts to rub together in their heads! Then I turned around and saw Fabia standing there——

Alonso. Wait, Tello. I must read further. [*He reads.*] "I have done all that you desired. There is only one thing which I cannot do, and that is to live without you. But that you did not command."

Tello. Are you listening now?

Alonso. Tell me, how did Fabia behave?

Tello. So wisely and with such discretion, such bigoted opinion, such hypocrisy, that some folks I know who spend all day with their heads bent in prayer will have to look to their laurels. Now I know how far a scheming woman, or a hypocritical religious, can go. Well, if you had seen me, with my airs and graces, with my face drawn into a pious expression, you would have said I had been transformed into a reverend Moslem priest. The old man believed us both, and yet to look at him, you would think him the living image of Cato himself.

Alonso. Wait! Stop for a moment. It is a long time since I read any of my letter. [*He reads.*] "Make haste to come, so that you may know how wretched I am when you are away, and then how I am changed when you return to me."

Tello. Is that the end of the paragraph?

Alonso. So, you were allowed to enter and to speak to her?

Tello. Her only study was you, master. You were all her Latin and the only lesson she would hear.

Alonso. What was Leonor doing all this time?

Tello. She envied Inés her love for you. I could see that she thought you deserving of her sister's love. I think Leonor loves you too! For, to say true, many women love an object simply because they see it loved by another.

When a man is greatly loved by one woman, they imagine there must be some secret attraction about him. They are wrong, of course; it is all a matter of your stars.

Alonso. Oh, lovely hands, let me read the last line you write: [*He reads.*] "They say that the King is coming to Medina, and they speak truly, for you are coming, and you are my king." There the letter ends.

Tello. Everything in the world ends somewhere.

Alonso. Good things last but a short while.

Tello. You have managed to make a four-act play out of it.

Alonso. Wait, here are a few words more in the margin. [*He reads.*] "Hang this sash about your neck. I would I were the sash."

Tello. You would look a fine sight riding into the plaza with Inés hanging around your neck.

Alonso. Where is the sash?

Tello. They gave me nothing.

Alonso. How?

Tello. Let me put it another way. What have you given me, master?

Alonso. Ah, I understand you. Take any one of my suits that you need.

Tello. Here is the sash.

Alonso. It is exquisite.

Tello. So were the hands that embroidered it.

Alonso. Give orders that I leave at once. Oh! Tello!

Tello. What now?

Alonso. Last night I had a dream.

Tello. Do you believe in dreams, now?

Alonso. No, Tello, and yet . . . the image was so strong, it has made me fearful.

Tello. Dreams are lies, master.

Alonso. It is said they are revelations from the soul.

Tello. What misfortune can befall you now? All you hope for is to marry Inés. There is no danger in that.

Alonso. Not only the dream has made me fearful, Tello. Just as dawn was breaking, I rose from my bed after a troubled night. I opened the window and as I looked at the flowers and the fountains that adorn the gardens, a linnet fluttered down and settled on a broom bush. Its yellow enameled wings added bright flowers to the green branches. The song from his small throat rose into the clear air in untaught cadences of love. Suddenly a hawk flew out from an almond tree, and since their arms were so unequal the flowers were soon tinted with blood and the air was full of falling feathers. The dawn gave back weak echoes of the linnet's sad chirruping, and close by his mate lamented, watching the tragedy, helpless, from a jasmine. These warnings from the soul have mingled with my dreams, and now they haunt my mind, and although my reason tells me they are meaningless, I can barely raise my spirits, and I have lost all hope, and even lack the heart to live.

Tello. This is a poor reward for the heroic firmness with which Inés bravely faces fortune's blows. Come to Medina, and pay no heed to dreams or omens. Both are against the Faith. Ride with your accustomed spirit, master. Let your prowess, your elegance, your valor, kill all the men with envy and all the women with love. Inés shall be yours, despite all those who seek to divide you.

Alonso. You speak well. Inés expects me. Let us ride to Medina joyfully, Tello. They say the coward suffers many deaths before he dies, and none but Inés can decree my death.

Tello. She shall see us in the plaza making bulls kneel down before her windows.

ACT THREE

1

There is a sound of drums, and Rodrigo *and* Fernando *enter with lackeys bearing lances.*

Rodrigo. Fortune has cursed me, Fernando.

Fernando. We have no luck.

Rodrigo. My sword, give up all hope of serving Inés.

Fernando. What can we do?

Rodrigo. Nothing, except despair.

Fernando. Let us try again.

Rodrigo. It is useless, Fernando. Fortune is on the side of the man from Olmedo.

Fernando. He made not a single mistake.

Rodrigo. He will, I promise you.

Fernando. A man favored by fortune can achieve anything, Rodrigo.

Rodrigo. Love opened the door to him and left me outside. A stranger is always attractive to women.

Fernando. You have just cause for anger, Rodrigo. A gallant knight he may be, but not so great that he need put all the men in Medina to shame.

Rodrigo. The town itself is like a fickle woman. I am scorned because I am familiar to them.

Fernando. It has always been so, since the times of Greece and Rome. [*A clash of armor and shouts are heard off.*]

A Voice. There was a stroke!

Second Voice. What a piece of luck!

Third Voice. Did you see the grace with which he broke that lance? [1] What skill! What elegance!

Fernando. Why do we wait here, Rodrigo? To horse!

Rodrigo. Come.

Voice [off]. He has no equal in the whole world.

Fernando. Do you hear what they are saying?

Rodrigo. I hear! Every word is a sword between my shoulders.

Second Voice [off]. Victor seven hundred times over, the Knight of Olmedo!

Voices [off]. The Knight of Olmedo! Bravo!

Rodrigo. What can my fortune be now, Fernando? You hear those voices?

Fernando. Why listen to the shouting of peasants?

Voices. God be with you! Bravo! God keep you!

Rodrigo. Could they say more if he were the King himself? But let them shout, let them stop at nothing. There is nothing we can do.

Fernando. Do not overrate their applause. It is always the way of the vulgar to acclaim what is new to them.

Rodrigo. He is coming for a fresh horse.

Enter TELLO *with lance and livery, and* ALONSO.

Tello. By heaven, I never saw such luck as you are having.

Alonso. Saddle the gray, Tello.

---

[1] In the Spanish, *quebró el rejón*. The *rejón* is a short lance with a detachable blade which is meant to stay in the bull, hence *quebrar el rejón* means to plant the blade in the bull, thereby detaching it from the shaft, which remains in the rider's hand.—ED.

Tello. They are all on our side. I think they will acclaim us victors of the day.

Alonso. Both of us, Tello?

Tello. Yes, both of us, you on horseback and me on foot. We have done well.

Alonso. Yes, Tello, you deserve their praise.

Tello. I played and hamstringed six bulls as if their legs were radishes.

Fernando. Come, Rodrigo, let us go back. They are waiting for us, although you think yourself forgotten.

Rodrigo. Maybe they wait for you, Fernando. They have no wish to see me—unless it be to see the bull kill me or drag me around the ring, so that they may jeer and laugh.

Tello [*aside to* ALONSO]. Those two men are watching you, master.

Alonso. I have seen them. They are jealous of my fortune, and angry to see me look upon Inés.

[RODRIGO *and* FERNANDO *go*

Tello. She has granted you so many smiles, and indeed smiles are the best of favors, for they are soundless words that tell better than any others what is in the heart. Every time you passed her window, she looked as if she was ready to throw herself down from the balcony.

Alonso. Oh, Inés, if it should be fortune's will that my parents should inherit such a daughter to succeed them!

Tello. You will soon achieve that wish, master, for Rodrigo's hopes for Inés are at an end. No man could mistake her looks today.

Alonso. Where is Fabia? I have not seen her. Hurry to her, Tello, while I take a turn through the town, and tell her to warn Inés that I must speak to her before I go; tell her I must ride back to Olmedo tonight, for if I do not go back, my parents will be certain that the bulls of Medina have killed me. I cannot inflict such fear upon them and I will not rob them of their sleep.

Tello. You are right, master, let them sleep in peace.

Alonso. I must return now to the plaza, Tello.

Tello. Heaven keep you. [ALONSO *goes.*] And now for my own plans: I mean to win that gold chain from the old woman for all her cunning. Circe, Medea, and Hecate all put together did not know the half of what she knows; and I warrant the key to her heart has thirty turns, but when I tell her I love her . . . for that is the certain

remedy with old women. All they need is a couple of
words of love whispered in their ear and they think they
are young again and believe themselves eternal. [*He goes
to the door of* DON PEDRO's *house.*] Here is the house.
I will knock. Fabia . . . And yet, Tello, you are an ass
to think you can fool her. She knows you are only after
the gold, and that you hate old women. Old goat-foot will
have whispered that in her ear, too.

Enter FABIA.

Fabia. Tello! What are you doing here? Is this the way
you serve your master? What is it? What do you want?

Tello. Remember you are still in Don Pedro's house.
A holy woman. I bring a message from Alonso.

Fabia. How has he fared with the bulls?

Tello. Like a god. Of course, I was with him.

Fabia. Words are not deeds, Tello.

Tello. You ask the King which of us excelled. He could
hardly sit still when I went past. Why, he almost jumped
down from his balcony.

Fabia. A rare favor!

Tello. I would prefer yours.

Fabia. What is this?

Tello. For you, Fabia, I would become a Hercules. Bulls
of Medina! Fabia, you should have seen me! I pricked
them with such an air, and the crowd shouted and ap-
plauded so wildly that in the midst of it all one of the
bulls said to me: "Enough, Tello, enough!" "No, no!"
I cried, and dealt him such a stroke that one of his legs
flew clean off and landed on a roof nearby.

Fabia. Did you? And how many tiles did it bring down?

Tello. Ask the owner. I did not care to know. Fabia,
tell your mistress that Alonso is coming to take his leave;
he must return to Olmedo, or his parents will fear he has
been killed. That is the message from my master. Now I
must return to the plaza or the King will miss me, his
private taurine executioner. But before I go, give me a
favor.

Fabia. A favor?

Tello. Reward my love.

Fabia. What, am I your inspiration? Is it for my sake
you have done these deeds? What is it you like most about
me?

Tello. Your eyes.

Fabia. You can take my glasses then.

Tello. That is no favor for a knight.

Fabia. The nearest you'll ever be to a knight is a horse.

Tello. Yes, a chestnut stallion.

Fabia. Mind how you go, galloping around the bulls, or I shall be surprised if the biggest entertainment of the day is not to see you chased by a bull wearing your own shirt and breeches on his horns.

Tello. I know my business as a bullfighter, Fabia.

Fabia. Tell that to the bulls, I dare you.

Tello. I am not afraid of any bull.

Fabia. The bulls of Medina have a taste for lackeys from Olmedo.

Tello. Lackeys or bulls, this Spanish arm of mine fears none of them.

Fabia. Be careful, or by this time tomorrow you will not be on the end of it.   [*They go*

Noise and shouting is heard from the plaza.

Voice. Rodrigo has fallen!

Alonso. Get back!

Voices. Oh!

Second Voice. Look! Look at Alonso! He has gone to his aid!

Third Voice. He has reached him!

Voice. He's dismounting.

Second Voice. What a stroke! Did you see it?

Third Voice. He has killed the bull!

Cheers from off. ALONSO *enters supporting* RODRIGO.

Alonso. Take heart, sir.

Rodrigo. You saved my life. I did not think to breathe again after that fall.

Alonso. I do not think you should go back into the plaza today. If you will excuse me, I will leave you in the care of your servants. Forgive me. I must go and retrieve the horses. They bolted in fear.

ALONSO *goes and* FERNANDO *enters.*

Fernando. Rodrigo! What happened?

Rodrigo. I was unhorsed! And, worst of all, I owe my

life to the man whose success fills me with jealousy, and
who I wish was dead.

Fernando. Before the King! And Inés, who saw her gallant knight kill the bull to save you.

Rodrigo. I shall go mad. No man on earth suffers as I
do! Injuries, affronts, insults, jealousies, slights, and evil
omens dog my path! I looked up for one moment to see
Inés, whom, like an abject fool, I still adore, to see if her
eyes held one spark of sympathy for me. She might have
been Nero surveying burning Rome from the Tarpeian
rock, for all the warmth there was in her look for me. She
turned her head away and smiled on Alonso! And as she
smiled I glimpsed the pearls between her crimson lips; and
saw one bright carnation of a blush grow on her jasmine
cheek when she saw me in my misfortune, cast down and
humiliated before the favored knight. I swear by heaven
that smile of hers will be changed for mourning before
Apollo gilds the dawn! Let me but meet Alonso between
Medina and Olmedo!

Fernando. He is well able to defend himself.

Rodrigo. You do not know the power of jealousy.

Fernando. I know that it is a fiend. But acts of consequence should not be undertaken without thought.

[*They go*

Enter the KING, CONSTABLE, *and train.*

King. The celebrations have ended late, but I have never
witnessed such a display.

Constable. I said that you were in haste to leave tomorrow, but Medina is so eager for you to stay and see the
tourney with which they desire to honor you, that they
have begged me, sir, to persuade Your Highness to remain
a second day. I beg you, grant this favor to Medina.

King. For your sake I will, although I must then make
haste to reach Toledo by the appointed day.

Constable. The Knight of Olmedo proved to be gallant
and skillful beyond imagination.

King. Let us admit, Constable, that his good fortune
was astounding.

Constable. Indeed, I cannot tell which is the more remarkable, his luck or his valor, but I know I have never
seen so valiant a fighter.

King. He is consummate in all things.

Constable. Your Highness does well to favor him.

King. He deserves favor, as much as he merits the praise you give him.   [*They go*

Enter ALONSO *and* TELLO.

Tello. It is late, master. We have stayed too long. You cannot travel home tonight.

Alonso. I must, Tello. Whatever the time, I must go. For my parents' sake.

Tello. If you intend to speak with Inés before you go, it will be broad daylight before you leave her balcony.

Alonso. No, Tello, my soul will give me stern warning when it is time to go.

Tello. Hark, I can hear Leonor's voice.

Alonso. I can feel the sun's brightness, despite the starlight.

Leonor. Is that Alonso?

Alonso. It is.

Leonor. My sister will be here in a moment; she is talking with my father. Tello may come in. Inés wishes to give you a present. [*She goes in from the window.*]

Alonso. Go in, Tello.

Tello. If by chance I should be delayed, master, ride ahead without me. I will overtake you on the road.

The door of DON PEDRO'S *house opens.* TELLO *goes in, and* LEONOR *reappears at the balcony.*

Alonso. Oh, Leonor, when shall I be able to enter here as freely as my servant?

Leonor. It will not be long, I think. Our father was so impressed by your conduct today that he is already well disposed toward you. His chief desire is that Inés should marry, and so as soon as he learns of your mutual love, he will welcome you with open arms, and rejoice in so valiant a son-in-law.

INÉS *appears on the balcony.*

Inés. Who are you talking to?

Leonor. Rodrigo.

Inés. No, it is my lord.

Alonso. Your slave, I swear, as heaven is my witness.

Inés. My lord.

Leonor. I will leave you now. Only jealousy or foolishness would wish to disturb lovers.   [*She goes*

Inés. My lord, my life!

Alonso. I have come at last, near to death at so long an absence.

Inés. The sadness of this parting tempers the joy I have felt in watching you today, my lord. You were the complete knight, an example to all the men and a tormentor of all the women. I am jealous of everyone that looks upon you. I want them all to praise you, and then I am fearful when they do, lest I lose you. How many praises you have earned, how many titles I have heard you given for your valor, out of envy and out of admiration! Even now, my father desired that you should marry Leonor, so that you should be his son-in-law, and my love blessed him for wishing it, even as my heart filled with fear and jealousy. My soul cried out: "He is mine, mine alone," although my tongue denied it. But why am I so happy, when you have come only to leave me once more?

Alonso. Care for my parents is the only cause, Inés.

Inés. You do right, my lord, and yet deprive me of all joy.

Alonso. I go to Olmedo leaving my soul in Medina. Yet how can I both go and remain at once? Love fears absence, absence begets jealousy, and jealousy fears every wind that blows. What can I say to you, one foot already in the stirrup? [1] Madam, I spend my days amid a host of terrible imaginings, mingling joy in all my sorrow and sorrow in all my joy. Sometimes my mind presents me so

[1] This speech is a *glosa* (see note on p. 199) on a *copla* beginning

> "One foot already in the stirrup,
> I feel the very hand of death."

In her edition, Miss Macdonald argues that the use of these lines "with the idea that they are a final farewell" is meant to recall Cervantes' allusion to the same *"coplas antiguas,"* in his valedictory dedication to *Los trabajos de Persiles y Sigismunda.* If so, this play must have been written after the publication of the *Persiles* in 1617. Such topical references are as characteristic of Lope's many-sided appeal to his contemporary audience as his autobiographical passages (see note to *Peribáñez,* p. 42).
—ED.

cruel a vision of losing you that I seem to feel the very hand of death upon me. I am so fearful of the envy of my adversaries, that although it is within my power to overcome them all, I spend hours together torn between thoughts of love and fear. Sometimes I imagine that I may never see you again, and, supposing myself still to be alive, I hear myself saying: "Madam, as I write to you . . ." To feel that I may already claim the title of your husband is a favor and token of love beyond imagination. And yet I am troubled that these dark fears still haunt a man so fortunate and so beloved as I. But though the shadow of death itself pursues me as I go, and though death may take me ere I come again, there can be no parting, for my soul remains forever in your keeping.

Inés. My lord, you trouble and frighten me with your fears, and yet you belittle my love if you imagine you have cause to doubt my faith. Trust in my love, Alonso. I understand your troubles, but as yet you do not understand the steadfastness of my love for you.

Alonso. My imaginings are merely the fretful motions of an unhappy soul, Inés, not jealousy. I should insult you dearly were I to doubt your faith. These illusions proceed from dreams and fantasies, not from suspicions of you.

Inés. Leonor has returned. [LEONOR *appears on the balcony.*] What is it?

Alonso. Is it time I went?

Leonor. It is. [*To* INÉS.] Father has asked to see you before he goes to bed.

Inés. Alonso, you must go. Do not protest, my lord. You must. Farewell.

Alonso. Oh, Inés, when will God grant that we may be together? My life ends here, for I must leave you. Farewell. Tello has not returned. He must have been detained within the house. I will ride ahead and let him follow me.

INÉS *and* LEONOR *go in.* ALONSO *walks away. A dark figure enters wearing a black mask and hat and stands in front of* ALONSO *with his hand on the hilt of his sword.*

Alonso. Who is that? He pays no heed! Who is it? Speak. Why do I fear one man, who have not feared many? Is it Rodrigo? Will you not answer me? Who are you?

Figure. Don Alonso.

Alonso. Who?

Figure. I am Don Alonso Manrique.

Alonso. It cannot be! I am Don Alonso Manrique. If you lie, then draw your sword. [*The* FIGURE *vanishes.*] He has gone. Vanished into air! Which way? Stay, Alonso, to follow would be madness. What man dares to follow his own shadow? My shadow? No, it cannot be, a shadow possesses no power over words and he spoke my name, "Alonso." It is the very action of my sorrow that drives my mind to such wild imaginings. And yet, what may this vision portend? To fear without cause is base. This is Fabia's trickery, one of her wiles to keep me from going to Olmedo. Always she has warned me to take care and told me not to travel at night. Why, for what reason? Only that envy treads my heels wherever I go. Surely Rodrigo can bear me no ill will? Why, he owes his life to me, and the honor of a knight as noble as Rodrigo would forbid him to forget his debt. No, rather we shall become friends, if God wills, for ingratitude has no place in noble blood, and resides only in the basest creatures. And the quintessence of baseness is to return ill for good.   [*He goes*

Enter RODRIGO, FERNANDO, *and two servants.*

Rodrigo. His life and my jealousy shall have an end tonight.

Fernando. You are resolved?

Rodrigo. Nothing can dissuade me now. Only his death can atone for her breaking faith with me. What deceit! To say she wished to be a nun! And all the while his servant, Tello, was teaching her so-called Latin, which was soon translated into love letters written in plain Romance! And a fine tutor Don Pedro welcomed to his house in the shape of Fabia! Wretched girl, I cannot blame your innocence if it is the hell-fire of her witchcraft which inflamed you. How could Inés be so deceived? I cannot believe she knows of the trickery. How often have noble houses been dishonored by bawds and witchcraft! Fabia, who can move mountains; Fabia, who can stop rivers in their courses, and who rules the black ministers of Acheron as a lord his servants; Fabia, who can cause a man to fly through the air from these shores, over the seas, beyond our horizons

to the burning equator, to the poles, or where she will—
that she should give Inés her lessons! I could almost laugh
at the bitter irony of the jest.

Fernando. For that very reason, Rodrigo, persist no more
in vengeance.

Rodrigo. By Heaven, Fernando, do you beg me to play
the coward?

Fernando. Inés has never loved you, Rodrigo. She is not
worthy of revenge.

Rodrigo. If you can bear such craven baseness, I cannot.

Servant. Sir, a rider is coming. Telltale echoes from the
hillside give news of his approach.

Rodrigo. If he has his servant with him then we shall
know he is afraid.

Fernando. No such thing. He is as brave a man as I
ever saw.

Rodrigo. Hide, all of you. Keep silent. You, Mendo,
over there! Stay behind a tree with the flintlock.

Fernando. How full of change is fortune, how fickle and
inconstant! He who rode before the King today and heard
the plaudits of the cheering crowd is menaced now by a
cruel, inglorious death.

They hide, and ALONSO *enters.*

Alonso. Until this moment, fear was a stranger to me.
But now as I travel to Olmedo, I know fear. All things
seem sorrowful. The gentle sound of the stream and the
soft swaying of the branches in the wind augment my
melancholy. And as I travel forward, my troubled thoughts
fly back. Love and obedience to my parents persuade me
to go on, and besides, this simple journey is but a petty
test of my valor. Yet it was harsh of me to leave Inés so
soon. How dark it is. This night is all horror until dawn's
gilded feet once more touch Flora's carpet of the world.
There is someone singing. Who can it be? It sounds far
off. A peasant going early to the fields and singing as he
goes. It is nearer now. That is no rustic accent—he has
an instrument, and the song is sweet and sonorous. How
melancholy music sounds when one's own thoughts are sad!
[*The sound of singing comes gradually closer.*]

Singer. They killed him in the darkness,
　　　　The noble knight,

The glory of Medina,
The flower of Olmedo.[1]

Alonso. What words are these? If this is Heaven's warning to me, why warn me now, since the moment is upon me? I will not return. This is a trick of Fabia's, who at my love's entreaty seeks to dissuade me from returning to Olmedo.

Singer [*off*]. Shades warned him
He should not go,
They counseled him
He should not go,
The noble knight,
The glory of Medina,
The flower of Olmedo.

Enter a PEASANT.

Alonso. Hello there, good man, singer!

Peasant. Who calls me?

Alonso. A man. One who is lost.

Peasant. I'm coming.

Alonso [*aside*]. All things alarm me.—Where are you going?

Peasant. To my work.

Alonso. Who taught you that song you were singing so sadly?

Peasant. I heard it in Medina, sir.

Alonso. I am known as the Knight of Olmedo, and as you see, I am alive.

Peasant. I cannot tell you more about the song or its history than that I learned it from one Fabia. If it concerns you, I can do no more for you; you have heard me sing it. Go back. Do not pass this stream.

Alonso. It would be base cowardice to return to Medina now.

Peasant. Your valor is foolish. Go back, go back to Medina.

Alonso. You come with me.

Peasant. I cannot.   [*He goes*

Alonso. What shadows fear invents! What tricks it

---

[1] This snatch of an anonymous popular ballad probably gave Lope the idea of writing the play, which is based on an elaboration of its mood and constructed to provide a fitting explanation for the tragic ending (see Introduction).—ED.

plays! Listen, good man—— Where did he go? Already I can scarcely hear his footsteps in the road. Hey, peasant, listen! Wait! Only the echo answers "Wait." He sang of my death! But it must be a lament composed in Medina for some other man from Olmedo who once was killed on this road. I am halfway now, what would people say if I turned back? Someone is coming. I am not sorry to hear them. If they are on the way to Olmedo, I will accompany them.

Enter RODRIGO, FERNANDO, *and servants.*

Rodrigo. Who goes there?

Alonso. A man. Do you not see me?

Fernando. Stop.

Alonso. Gentlemen, if it is necessity that drives you to this extremity, my house is but a short way off; once there you shall not want for money. I willingly give to all who do me the honor of asking alms of me, by day.

Rodrigo. Hand me your sword.

Alonso. My sword! Do you know to whom you speak?

Fernando. To the man from Olmedo, the great bull-fighter, who comes as a foolish braggart to affront the men of Medina, who dishonors Don Pedro's house with his infamous bawds and tricksters.

Alonso. If you were noble, you would have found occasion to challenge me before—there was time enough. Not now, when I am alone. You could have challenged me that night when you left your cloak behind you in your haste and fear. There was time. Not now, at midnight, like a gang of thieves. But even now is time enough to prove you cowards, for though you are many in number, you are but few in valor. [*They fight.*]

Rodrigo. I came to kill, not to compete in fencing matches. [*To servant.*] Shoot. [*The servant shoots.*]

Alonso. Treacherous dogs! Yet without firearms you could not kill me. Oh, God! [*He falls.*]

Fernando. Well shot, Mendo.

[RODRIGO, FERNANDO, *and servants go*

Alonso. How little credence I gave to Heaven's warnings! Belief in my own valor deceived me and delivered me to the foul hands of treachery and deceit. Envy and jealousy have killed me. Alas, what shall I do in this wild country-side alone?

Enter TELLO.

Tello. Why were those men riding in such furious haste toward Medina? I shouted to them, asked them had they seen my master, Don Alonso, but they did not reply. Why did they not reply? I fear for my master.

Alonso. Oh, God, have mercy! Ah, Inés! God knows my love for you was honorable.

Tello. What was that? The sad echo of a cry! From over there. A man in mortal anguish. All the blood has drained from me, my hair, not my head, supports my hat. Ah, sir!

Alonso. Who is it?

Tello. Oh, God! Why do I doubt what I can see? It is my master, Don Alonso!

Alonso. Tello, welcome.

Tello. How am I well come when I have come so late? How welcome, when I find you a river of blood? Traitors, villains, dogs, come back, come back and kill me too! Infamous traitors, you have killed the noblest, most courteous, and most valiant knight that ever wore a sword in Castile!

Alonso. Peace, Tello, peace. I am dying. There is no time to think of anything but the soul now. Put me on your horse and take me to my parents.

Tello. What good tidings I bring them back from the Fiesta of Medina! What will your noble father say? What will your mother and your country do? Oh, vengeance, pitiful Heaven!   [*He goes off carrying* ALONSO

Enter DON PEDRO, INÉS, LEONOR, *and* FABIA.

INÉS. Is it true that the King has granted you so many favors?

Don Pedro. He has indeed shown his magnanimity with a liberal and royal hand. Medina is grateful to him, and in thanks for what I myself have received from him, I have brought you, my daughters, to kiss his hand.

Leonor. Is he preparing to leave already?

Don Pedro. Yes, Leonor, he travels to Toledo today. I am overwhelmed with joy that he has shown such favor to me, chiefly on your behalf, for you are the ones who will benefit from his generosity.

Leonor. You have good reason to be pleased, Father.

Don Pedro. I am created Warden of Burgos, and you must kiss his royal hand.

Inés [*aside to* FABIA]. I fear more absence, Fabia.

Fabia. Fortune still frowns upon you.

Inés. Since my lord Alonso left me, my heart has been full of sadness. I fear I know not what.

Fabia. If my old eyes can still see clearly then I fear a greater evil yet awaits you. Who can say? No one, not even Fabia, can see with certainty into the future.

Inés. What greater misfortune can befall me than separation from my love? That alone is worse than death.

Don Pedro. Inés, if you were to abandon your resolve, I should wish for no further happiness. I would not compel you to do so, but nothing could delight me more than to see you married.

Inés. I need no persuasion, Father. I am only astonished that you have not guessed before.

Don Pedro. I do not understand you.

Leonor. Let me explain for you, Inés. Father, you wanted to marry her to a man she could not love. That is all.

Don Pedro [*to* INÉS]. Inés, why did you not confide in me? Had I known the true state of your feelings, I should not have persisted for all the world.

Leonor. Inés is in love with a gentleman whom the King has honored with the cross of knighthood. Her love is honorable, and it will be a worthy match.

Don Pedro. If he is a gentleman of quality and you are in love with him, what more is there for me to say? Marry him, Inés, and the best of fortune go with you. But may I not be told his name?

Leonor. Don Alonso Manrique.

Don Pedro. Oh, happy name! The Knight of Olmedo?

Leonor. Yes, Father.

Don Pedro. He is a man of great honor. Your choice is wise, Inés, and I am delighted. I never thought it was your vocation to be a nun. Speak, Inés, do not be shy.

Inés. Leonor exaggerates. . . .

Don Pedro. There is no need to hold an examination of the case. I am satisfied at your good sense and that you wish to marry him. Consider him your husband, Inés, and I shall be only too pleased to have so distinguished a son-in-law, and one so rich and well-born too.

Inés. I kiss your hand a thousand times. Fabia, I shall
go mad with happiness.

Fabia. I congratulate you. [*Aside.*] I only pray I shall
not soon be giving my condolences.

Leonor. Here comes the King.

Enter the KING, CONSTABLE, *and train, also* RODRIGO *and*
FERNANDO.

Don Pedro [*to his daughters*]. Go and kiss his hand
now.

Inés. With happiness I obey you, Father.

Don Pedro. Your Highness, my daughters and I kiss
your hand in gratitude for the honor you have shown me
in creating me Warden of Burgos.

King. We are more than satisfied, Don Pedro, of your
nobility and of your service to us.

Don Pedro. I desire to do yet more in your service.

King. Are you married?

Inés. No, sir.

King. What is your name?

Inés. Inés.

King. And yours?

Leonor. Leonor.

Constable. Your Highness, Don Pedro deserves two
gallant sons-in-law, and they are present. I beg leave to
speak on their behalf, that they may marry Don Pedro's
daughters.

King. Who are they?

Rodrigo. I, sir, with your permission, aspire to the hand
of Inés.

Fernando. And I would offer to her sister, Leonor, my
hand and will.

King. Don Pedro, I ask you to accept these two gallant
gentlemen as your sons-in-law.

Don Pedro. Sir, I cannot grant Inés to Rodrigo, for she
is already betrothed to Don Alonso Manrique, the Knight
of Olmedo, to whom you have already shown great favor
and honor.

King. I promise to do yet more for him.

Rodrigo [*aside to* FERNANDO]. What paradox is this?

Fernando. Take care.

King. For he is a man of great merit.

Tello [*off*]. Let me in.

King. What voice is that?

Constable. A man, sir, a squire; he demands entrance from the guard.

King. Let him come in.

Constable. He is weeping and demanding justice.

King. The administration of justice is our sacred duty, and the meaning of our scepter.

Enter TELLO.

Tello. Great King, who, despite the cruel envy of lesser men, guards with an invincible hand the peace and safety of Castile: I have come to Medina in the company of Don Alonso's aged father to demand justice upon two infamous murderers, but the sad exertion of the journey has caused the old man to stay outside fainting, if not already dead for sorrow. And so I, who serve him, have dared to push past your guards and venture into your royal presence. I beg you, hear me, since Heaven has placed in your hands the wand of justice, and entrusted you with discretion to chastise what is evil and reward what is good. Last night, after the fiesta known as the Feast of the May Cross, which is celebrated here by the knights of Medina—and it is certain knowledge that where there is a cross there is passion—my master, Don Alonso, that illustrious youth who merited your praise as few have done, set out from Medina to Olmedo, a simple journey with honorable intent, to assure his noble parents that he had suffered no harm from the bulls. They were less vicious than his enemies. I stayed behind in Medina, to look after the horses and their trappings, as was my duty. As I left Medina, disheveled night lolled between the poles and gave to murder a sword, and a cloak to violence. I passed a stream, which is a crossing and a landmark on the road, when I saw six men fleeing towards Medina, obviously in alarm and disorder, although they rode together. The moon shone meanly and with a blood-stained face, but its pale light was enough for me to recognize two of them, for sometimes Heaven will plunge a candle of light into the darkest haunts of silence that men may see the authors of evil deeds and heavenly eyes not be the sole guardians of their secrets. I went a little farther, where, alas, I found my master, Don Alonso, dying, enwrapped in his own blood. Great King, I cannot keep back my tears, sorrow chokes my words. I put him on my horse, at which time he showed such spirit that if his enemies had seen him they might have doubted if they had killed him. He reached Olmedo with just enough life left in him to hear the blessing of his grief-stricken parents. Oh, God! They washed his wounds with tears and kisses. Now his house and lands are covered in mourning. His funeral will be the burial of the phoenix, sir, to live again though dead, in the tongues of fame, which yet are stronger than man's frailty and time's forgetfulness.

King. A strange tale, indeed.

Inés. Alas!

Don Pedro. My child, my child, control your grief, if you can.

Inés. Father, what I asked you without meaning it before, I now ask sincerely. And, generous King, I beg you for justice upon these cruel murderers.

King [*to* TELLO]. Tell me, since you say you recognized them, who are the two murderers? Where are they? By Heaven, we shall not leave Medina until they are brought before us.

Tello. They are here, great King. Rodrigo is the one and Fernando is the other.

Constable. Their guilt is manifest. Their confusion shows it.

Rodrigo. My lord, hear me——

King. Arrest them, and tomorrow in a public place their heads shall be struck off in payment for their most notorious crime. Let justice be done before we leave Medina!

JUSTICE WITHOUT REVENGE

(El Castigo sin Venganza)

CHARACTERS

The Duke of Ferrara
Count Federico, *his illegitimate son*
Cassandra, *who becomes* Duchess of Ferrara
Carlos, Marquis Gonzaga
Albano
Rutilio
Floro
Lucindo
Aurora
Lucrecia
Batín
Cintia
Febo
Ricardo
Servants

The action takes place in and near Ferrara.

JUSTICE WITHOUT REVENGE

ACT ONE

1

Night

Enter FEBO *and* RICARDO, *servants.*

FEBO. A rare device!

Ricardo. A night for revels!

Febo. And who would recognize the leader of our sports as the lecherous Duke?

Ricardo. Hush, here comes Ferrara!

Enter the DUKE.

Duke. No man must recognize me.

Ricardo. All things are licensed behind a cloak, my lord. What else is the dark which nightly hides bright heaven from our sight? Naught but a jeweled cape studded with silver stars and pricked with the bright medal of the moon.

Duke. Will you start your rambling now?

Febo. Ricardo's was an original metaphor, my lord. None of your modern poets—divine, they call themselves —has thought of it.

Ricardo. I might quote them and speak worse. Why, I heard one name the moon the cottage cheese of the sky.

Duke. You are right, for poetry these days has sunk so low that it is nothing but conjuring tricks, all sleight of hand and little brain. Just so many colored ribbons drawn from the conjurer's mouth. But to turn to matters of more interest, that woman is not unattractive.

Ricardo. Not unattractive? She is an angel! But there is one intolerable snag, sir.

Duke. What is that?

Ricardo. Her wretched husband, who needs must keep her to himself.

Febo. Take care you are not recognized, my lord.

Duke. Such is the stupidity of the poor.

Febo. He whose wife receives gifts of jewelry, clothes, and gold should pity, not envy, the man who buys them, for if the wife should die, then the husband inherits his share, while the giver gets nothing.

Ricardo. Indeed, such people have little charity. They will share nothing.

Duke. They are a sort of friends that first entice and then prevent the continuation.

Ricardo. I might call here, but much talk would be needed.

Duke. Why?

Ricardo. A holy old woman lives here praying and scolding two girls—a lovely pair, halfway between bud and blossom, as they say. One is like silver, the other is a pearl.

Duke. I never trust external appearances.

Ricardo. Not far off there lives a lady like sugar of the Indies, dark and sweet.

Duke. Is she passionate?

Ricardo. As you would expect from her dark complexion. She lives with a curious, melancholy man, who sniffs around her visitors to find out all about them, and never gives her a moment's peace.

Febo. I know that sullen ox.

Ricardo. There is a woman close by who has a lively wit. She would have made a fine advocate, had she studied.

Duke. Let us go there.

Ricardo. But she will not let us in at this time of night.

Duke. If I tell her who I am?

Ricardo. That, of course, is a different matter.

Duke. Knock then.

Ricardo. She will answer to two kicks.

Enter CINTIA, *above.*

Cintia. Who is there?

Ricardo. It is I.

Cintia. Who may "I" be?

Ricardo. Friends, Cintia; come, open, for the Duke is
with me, lured here by my praises of you.

Cintia. The Duke?

Ricardo. Do you doubt me?

Cintia. Not that he should be with you, but that such
an exalted gentleman should visit me, and at such an
hour as this.

Ricardo. He is come in disguise, to make a fine lady of
you.

Cintia. Ricardo, had you told me this of the Duke a
month ago, I should have believed you, for it is well
known among the vulgar that he has been a libertine and
spent his youth in riotous excess, and that he did not
choose to marry so he might live as freely as he pleased,
never caring that a bastard should be his heir—not that
I would speak ill of Federico, he is a gallant young
gentleman. As I say, a month ago, I should have believed
you if you said the Duke had come to see me, but now
that he has reformed and arranged to marry Cassandra,
and has already sent his son to Mantua to bring her here,
we shall no longer see him at night on his wild errands in
these streets. He is at home in his palace waiting and preparing for her arrival. It would be a liberty in Federico at
this moment, but how much more so would it be in him.
If you were the loyal servant you pretend, you would not
discredit him and slander his good name with your tales.
For I know the Duke your master is at this moment in
bed and asleep. So tell me no more of your lies and leave
me in peace. Good night to you.

Duke. This is a fine bawdyhouse you have brought me
to!

Ricardo. It was not my fault, sir.

Febo. Shall I break the door down?

Duke. So that is what they think of me.

Febo. Ricardo is to blame. But sir, the sure way for
one in authority to find out how he is regarded, whether
with love or fear, is to leave the tender adulation of
sycophantic servants and go out disguised at night. Kings
and emperors often do so.

Duke. Then they are fools. The eavesdropper always
hears ill of himself. The common herd is no judge of
truth, and they are fools that base their good name

on what crude minds believe. Common opinion is inconstant and variable, not ruled by reason, but by the personal jealousies of those that will tell any lie to satisfy their thirst for news and gossip. And those that are so base that they have no entry into palaces and great houses to know the truth, murmur against that which they may not know. I confess I have lived riotously and have not married because I would not be bound, and that I wished Federico should be my heir although a bastard; but now that Cassandra comes from Mantua, I will put it all behind me.

Febo. Marriage will be the remedy.

Ricardo. If you would like some entertainment, listen at this door awhile.

Duke. They are singing?

Ricardo. Can you not hear them?

Duke. Who lives here?

Ricardo. An actor-manager.

Febo. The best in Italy.

Duke. They sing well. Are his plays good?

Ricardo. That depends on the audience. A friendly audience applauds and it is called a good play. Enemies will hiss and report it a bad play.

Febo. They cannot all be good.

Duke. Febo, for the wedding, prepare the best rooms and engage the finest players in Ferrara to entertain us. Let them play no vulgar works, mind. Only good ones.

Febo. We will inquire which the gentlemen and writers commend and these we will bring you.

Duke. I think they are rehearsing now.

Ricardo. Listen, a woman is speaking.

Duke. Can it be Andrelina? Her fame is great. What timbre! what passion!

Voice[*off*]. Leave me, my thought. Return, memory, no more, for you turn my past glory into torment. I would have no memory, only forgetfulness. For memories of happiness that is lost are like sad tales, only fitting to recall in happy hours.

Duke. What depth of feeling!

Febo. She is most rare.

Duke. I would stay to hear more, but that I am become melancholy. I will go home to bed.

Ricardo. At ten o'clock?

Duke. All things weary me.

Ricardo. But this woman is unparalleled.

Duke. I fear what I might hear.

Ricardo. But how could it concern you?

Duke. Do you not know, Ricardo, that a play is a mirror in which the fool, the sage, young men and old, the warrior, the courtier, king, governor, maiden, wife, may all learn by example, concerning life and honor? Our customs are portrayed for what they are, fickle, or severe. Truth is mingled with the mockery, and censure is in the wit and the tragedy that entertain us. I have heard enough already that concerned my reputation. And will you now persuade me to hear more? Remember, dukes are not used to hearing the truth unveiled.   [*They go*

Enter FEDERICO *elegantly dressed in traveling clothes and* BATÍN, *his servant.*

BATÍN. I know not what ails you, sir. You must stop and admire the view every time we come to a clump of broken-down willow trees. Have you forgotten we are on business?

Federico. My displeasure in this journey prevents my taking more trouble and making more haste. I would spin out this opportunity of being away from court, and rest from my troubled thoughts beneath the green canopy of these trees which listen to the sleeping ripples of this river, and watch the swaying of their own green boughs in its cold, pure, sonorous crystal. Here I may retreat even from myself and still the voices of my thoughts, which ever debate within my mind my father's marriage, when I had thought I was his heir. For though I show an outward pleasure, as courtesy demands, my soul is full of deep displeasure. I go unwillingly to Mantua, for when I bring my stepmother, I bring home with me my own death potion. But there is no remedy.

Batín. Your father, after much disapproval both from his own family and others, of his libidinous way of life, has finally come to the feet of virtue, and would turn to quiet and honorable ways, and there is no rein like marriage to keep a man quiet and honorable. Once a vassal of the King of France presented him with a lively, beautiful steed, Swan by name, and swanlike in appearance. Its coat was like untrodden snow and when it tossed its proud head the mane waved and rippled like the sea, from the delicate ears down to the elegant feet. Among its many graces, nature endowed it with that pride and disdain that the most beautiful women have, so that it held it as an injury to allow even the bravest and most skillful trainer to mount upon its back. Seeing such beauty and such ill behavior, the King ordered the steed to be put into a pit together with a fierce lion which he kept there. When the sensitive creature saw the lion, all its hair stood on end all over its body, and its mane, no longer softly flowing, stood up like a curve of white lances down its head and neck. The proud horse was become as a meek and cowering hedgehog that shivered and sweated a drop of gall from every hair. A dwarf sat quietly on its back, and the proud beast, that before would not obey a trainer, from that time would suffer even a child to ride him.

Federico. Batín, there is no need for you to tell me by way of metaphors that marriage is the best cure for my father's licentiousness, but surely he might understand how I feel, when I have lived so long in the false belief that I should be his heir. I know that a woman can tame the wildest and the most arrogant man, and that the fiercest giant of a man is softened by his first child's tender babbling, and will take it in his arms and let it pull his beard. A married man regards his family with more love than the peasant has for his ripe grain, and for its sake gives up all former vices. But why should I rejoice that my father is to reform and abandon his former pleasures, if he is to have new sons to inherit his estates, and I must become a base squire. So must I bring home a lion that will tear me to pieces.

Batín. Sir, when wise and discreet men find themselves in the midst of irremediable ills, they use patience, and pretend to be contented and even happy, so they should not seem to be envious or harbor vengeful feelings.

Federico. Am I to suffer a stepmother?

Batín. Did you not suffer many more before, when you had a new one every night? Now you will have but one, and she a great lady.

Federico. I hear voices.

Batín. There are people down there on the riverbank.

Federico. They are women. I will go and see what ails them.

Batín. No, wait.

Federico. Batín, you are a coward. I must show them courtesy, must I not? [*He goes*

Batín. To keep out of danger's way is true valor. Lucindo! Albano! Floro!

Enter LUCINDO, ALBANO, FLORO.

Lucindo. The Count calls.

Albano. Where is Federico?

Floro. Do you want us to bring the horses?

Batín. He heard a woman shout, and was off like a shot —or like a fool—to see what the matter was. Call the others up, while I follow him. [*He goes*

Lucindo. Where are you going? Wait.

Albano. It is some foolery.

Floro. Yes, you are right. Although I think someone is coming along the riverbank.

Lucindo. Federico already shows little inclination to obey his new mother, although he is on the way to fetch her.

Albano. He shows his sorrow in his eyes.

Enter FEDERICO, *carrying* CASSANDRA.

Federico. I fear necessity only imposes the sweet duty of carrying you this far and here I must put you down.

Cassandra. I thank you, sir, for your great courtesy.

Federico. And I thank my good fortune that brought me to this wood, though it be off my path.

Cassandra. Sir, who are these people?

Federico. They are my servants and travel with me. Do not fear them, madam, they are all at your service.

Enter BATÍN, *carrying* LUCRECIA, *a servant*.

Batín. They say that women are light to love. They are anything but light of weight.

Lucrecia. Where are you taking me, sir?

Batín. Somewhere out of the way of all this loathsome sand that the river leaves behind it on the shore. I think it was a plot: the river stretched out an arm and overturned your coach on purpose, because it wanted to catch you for a nymph. It would have, too, you know, if I had not been near.

Federico. Madam, so that I may speak to you with the respect that your person clearly deserves, tell me who you are.

Cassandra. There is no cause to hide my name. I am Cassandra, sir, the new Duchess of Ferrara, and daughter of the Duke of Mantua.

Federico. Then how is it you are here alone?

Cassandra. I am not alone—that would be inconceivable; the Marquis of Gonzaga is some way off. He was accompanying me, but I asked him to leave me for a while to walk down this lane and spend the burning siesta beside the river. I wished to come to the water's edge, which seemed to have more trees and more shade; but the ground was treacherous, the coach tilted over, and we might have been borne away on the water and drowned had you not come to the rescue. But let me know, sir, who you are, though from your appearance there is no question of your valor and nobility. For not only must I show my gratitude for your kindness, but the Marquis and my father will wish to express their gratitude as well.

Federico. First let me kiss your hand, and then you shall know who I am.

Cassandra. Do not kneel, sir, that is too much courtesy, for it is I who am in your debt.

Federico. Madam, it is just and needful, for I am your son.

Cassandra. How foolish I was not to guess it! Who else but you could have come to my aid when I was in such danger? Let me embrace you.

Federico. Madam, I scarcely merit your hand.

Cassandra. Count Federico, I owe you my life.

Federico. My soul is at your service.

Batín. Since we have been so fortunate that this is indeed the same lady for whom we were going to Mantua, it remains for me to learn if you are an excellency or a ladyship, that I may know whether to address you with as much reverence as your beauty demands.

Lucrecia. I have served the Duchess since I was a child. I am her lady's maid. I dress and undress Her Grace.

Batín. Are you not her head waiting woman?

Lucrecia. No.

Batín. Then you have been overlooked. I know many such chits as you. They are everywhere. Neither maidens nor old maids, but something in between, both all and nothing to their mistresses. What is your name?

Lucrecia. Lucrecia.

Batín. Not the Roman Lucretia?

Lucrecia. Oh, no. I come from Mantua.

Batín. Thank heaven for that. Every time I hear her story it gives me nightmares. All that forced chastity and frantic retribution. Did you ever meet Tarquin?

Lucrecia. Who?

Batín. What would you do if you did meet him?

Lucrecia. Are you married?

Batín. What?

Lucrecia. Have you a wife?

Batín. Why?

Lucrecia. I should like to ask her advice.

Batín. Do not worry. I am no Tarquin. Do you know who I am?

Lucrecia. How could I?

Batín. Is it possible you have not heard of Batín in Mantua?

Lucrecia. Why, are you famous? I think you are one of those fools who think that theirs is the only famous name in the world when nobody has ever heard of them.

Batín. May God forbid that I should be such a one, or that I should ever be one to mutter enviously against other men's virtues. I was only joking, Lucrecia. I am not really smug or arrogant. I admit that I should like to be famous among wise men, men of science and letters, for fame among the ignorant herd is not true fame, but a harvest where those who sow senseless acts reap worthless praise.

Cassandra. I cannot rate too highly the pleasure of meeting you. All the good I had heard of you is but a little now that I see you in person. Speech and action show truly the greatness of the character, and your action, my lord—my son—shows clearly what a noble soul dwells in your noble body. It was a fortunate misfortune that led me along this path, for it has allowed me to know you the sooner. As after a dark and driving storm at sea, the light that breaks through shines more brilliantly than before, so has my fortune been: my mistake was the dark night; the river the sea; the coach a ship; I was the pilot and you my star. From this day, Count Federico, I will be your mother, and I beg you to regard me so. I am most content with you, and my soul rejoices so greatly to have such a rare treasure, that I find more joy in having you for my son, than in my new position as Duchess of Ferrara.

Federico. Most beautiful lady, I know not how to answer you. I am confused by so much honor. This day the Duke, my father, divides my being in two, for my body alone was born before, and today my soul takes life from you. Therefore you are most truly my mother, for the greater part of me is born today. For although it is God that gives the soul, I have never felt in which part of me it dwelt until I saw you, and you have made me anew, for till now I lived without a soul. Therefore, since I am your son, then I am that first-born that the Duke hopes for. And do not think it strange or impossible that I should be born though already a man, for I have a precedent in the sun that has burned in the heavens for six thousand years and is newborn each morning.

Enter MARQUIS GONZAGA, RUTILIO, *and servants.*

Rutilio. This was where I left them, sir.

Marquis. It would have been a great misfortune had not the gentleman you tell me of arrived in time to save her.

Rutilio. She bade me leave her, as she wished to add pearls to the water by bathing her snow-white feet in its smiling waves. And so I was some distance off, and though I hurried to where I heard her cries, I could not have reached her, but arrived in time to see this gentleman carrying her to safety in his arms. When I saw that they were all safe on the bank I did not stay but ran to fetch you straightaway.

Marquis. There is the coach, half in the water and half on the sand, but no one is with it.

Rutilio. The Duchess is over there with the gentleman's servants, but these willows prevented us from seeing her before.

Cassandra. Here come my people.

Marquis. Madam!

Cassandra. Marquis!

Marquis. We have all been greatly troubled until this moment that we see you in safety, madam. I thank God you are safe, my lady.

Cassandra. And after God, thank this gentleman, whose kindly courtesy bore me from the water's edge.

Marquis. My lord Count, who else but you could honor this lady whom I may already with just cause call your mother.

Federico. My lord Marquis, I would I were Jupiter to turn myself at once into an imperial bird, and, like Phaëton, risk my feathered wings in the light from that bright sun which we see here, and fly with her between my golden claws. I would bear her as if she were the golden fleece to where my father's people would see her and rejoice.

Marquis. Sir, the heavens have ordained your meeting to be thus, so that Cassandra should owe a debt of love to you, and that a stepmother and her stepson should for once be so closely bound by mutual love that all Italy may wonder at the example.

Cassandra [*aside to* LUCRECIA]. While Federico talks with the Marquis, tell me, Lucrecia, what you think of him.

Lucrecia. I would tell you my opinion if you will give me leave, madam.

Cassandra. Speak, though I suspect already what you will say.

Lucrecia. I think. . . .

Cassandra. What do you think?

Lucrecia. I think you would be happier if fortune had given you the son and not the father.

Cassandra. You are right, Lucrecia. My fate has erred. But it is done now. I am tempted to return to Mantua on some pretext, but if he knew my feelings, my father would kill me in his anger. Or even if he did not, the news would soon fly throughout Italy of my madness. And even then I could not marry Federico. Therefore I cannot return to Mantua, but must go on to Ferrara, where the Duke awaits me, though I go with a heavy heart, for I have heard fearful tales of his wild and libidinous way of life.

Marquis. Here come the rest of our company, so let us gladly leave this dangerous wood. Rutilio, go ahead to

Ferrara, and take word to the Duke of this happy meeting, if the news has not already speeded there; as may well be, for good news is always slower of foot than bad. Come, madam, and let the Count's horse be brought, for he will ride with us.

Floro. The Count's horse.

Cassandra. Your Excellency would fare better in my coach.

Federico. I will travel however Your Grace chooses.

The Marquis *leads* Cassandra *off by the hand.*

Batín. The Countess is a most elegant and noble lady.

Federico. What do you think of her, Batín?

Batín. I think she is like a lily that, with its snow-white courteous tongues, offers the dawn the gold upon its stamens in exchange for its gift of drops of pearl. I have never seen such a lovely and charming woman. By heaven, sir, if there was an opportunity . . . but no, they are already getting into the coach and you cannot stop her . . . otherwise I should have said . . .

Federico. Say nothing, Batín, for with your shrewdness you have seen my soul in my eyes, and you flatter my taste by saying what I would like to hear.

Batín. But would not this bright carnation, this fresh budding spray of orange blossoms, this golden, amber-scented fondant of a woman, this very Venus, or this Helen, would she not suit you far better than your father? A curse upon the laws of the world.

Federico. But we must give no suspicion of our thoughts, and I will be the first stepson who ever thought his step-mother beautiful.

Batín. Then, sir, you must show great patience. But it would be easier if you found her ugly. [*They go*

✦

Enter the Duke of Ferrara *and* Aurora, *his niece.*

Duke. If she left Mantua when this letter says, Federico should have met her on the road.

Aurora. He was slow to start, for he was unwilling to set out to accompany Her Grace.

Duke. I think some private sadness put off his parting.

And it may well be so, for, until now, Federico had no cause to doubt that he was my heir, for he is the dearest thing I have, and I will confess, Aurora, that to marry was a decision taken much against my liking. It was my vassals that persuaded and convinced me that I should now betray his trust by marrying. They say that although they would like to have him for their lord—either because they know my love for him, or because they too love him, I know not—those other kinsmen who had hopes of succeeding me would hasten to press their claims, and if they should take up arms to force a settlement, they would lay the dukedom waste, to the great harm of all my vassals, for the peasants are always the greatest sufferers from wars. And so for their sake I agreed to marry. I had no choice, Aurora.

Aurora. Sir, you are not to blame, the fault is with fate. But the Count is a wise young man, and will be calm and patient. Although, sir, if I might, I would suggest a remedy. Forgive me if I am too bold, but trusting in the love you show me, I will bravely speak my thoughts. Invincible Duke, I am your niece, and the daughter of your brother, who in his youth fell to inexorable death as the almond blossom falls before the north wind's blast. Then, when my mother shortly followed him, you brought me to your house, where I have lived till now. You alone have been as a dear father to me, and in the confused, blind labyrinth of my sad fortunes, you have been the golden thread of light that led me. You gave me Federico for a brother, and we, two cousins born, grew up together trustingly and in sweet friendship. We loved each other with equal love, living one life together. One law, one love, one will, one faith, governs us both, and if we were married all these would be one eternally, for I am his, and Federico is mine, so surely that even death would scarcely dare to break so strong a bond. Since the death of my loved father, my estate has ever increased, and there is not to be found in all Italy a more suitable match for Federico, both by nature and position, than myself, among all the ladies there are. I know not of Spain, and think not of Flanders, but of Italy I am sure. If you will marry him to me, you can be sure that he will have no need to fear Cassandra's bearing you an heir, for I have lands enough to protect Federico from any want. Think if this advice of mine does not solve your problem.

Duke. Aurora, let me embrace you, for you are the true light of dawn and brighten the dark recesses of my troubled mind. The sunlight of your thought shows clearly what must be done. You give me back my life and honor, and most willingly I betroth you to Count Federico —certain as I am that he justly returns your honest love, for that is the least of your deserts, Aurora. And so, since I am sure your wills are one, I give you my word that your wedding shall be celebrated together with mine. When the Count comes, you shall see what great rejoicing I shall cause throughout Ferrara.

Aurora. Sir, I am your daughter and your slave. I can say no more.

Enter BATÍN.

Batín. Your Grace, great Duke, give thanks equally to the wind and to myself for the news we bring, for I know not which of us has borne the other here, whether I rode on his back or he on mine, whether he used my feet, or I his wings. My mistress, the Duchess, is coming, safe and well, and if by chance the news has reached you of the river's rash daring that tried to snatch Her Grace, it was nothing. The coach overturned, that is all, for the Count arrived at that moment, picked her up in his arms, and brought her back to dry land. Thus they silenced at their first meeting that common saying that stepsons and stepmothers never love each other. And now they ride home together so happily that you would say that they were true mother and son.

Duke. I give you grateful thanks for this happy news, Batín, my friend, and rejoice to know that Federico is contented with Cassandra. I pray God that their love shall ever increase.

Batín. So do we all, sir.

Aurora. Have you no news for me, Batín?

Batín. Oh, Aurora, may Heaven's own glorious light sing your praises. What do you wish to hear?

Aurora. I should like to know whether Cassandra is beautiful.

Batín. That question comes not from you, but on behalf of the Duke. I think you have both heard tell of her

famous beauty—which I may not repeat now, for here
they come.

Duke. Batín, wear this chain for me.

Enter RUTILIO, FLORO, ALBANO, LUCINDO, *the* MARQUIS
OF GONZAGA, FEDERICO, CASSANDRA, LUCRECIA, *accompanied with great pomp and color.*

Federico. Here, lady, in this orchard, a pavilion has been
prepared for you, so that the Duke may welcome you
while all Ferrara prepares for your triumphal entry into
our city, which, though it be the greatest procession that
this age has seen, will still fall short of your deserts.

Cassandra. I confess, Federico, that the lack of any
greeting or welcome had somewhat saddened me.

Federico. Here come the Duke and Aurora to receive
you.

Duke. Lovely Cassandra, to whom I gladly offer my
soul together with my estates, may heaven keep you the
mistress, honor, and glory of my house.

Cassandra. My lord Duke, I come as your loving slave,
your title and renown bestow greatness on my house,
honor on my father, and glory on the state of Mantua,
whose deserts have made me worthy to enter your house
and country.

Duke. My lord Marquis, let me embrace you, to whom
I owe the possession of this jewel.

Marquis. I am happy to have played a part in this joyful
union, and shall continue in that service until the ceremony is over.

Aurora. Cassandra, I am Aurora and your servant ever.

Cassandra. One of the greatest joys among so much
happiness is to have you, Aurora, for my friend.

Aurora. Madam, my only answer will be to serve you
faithfully and love you as the mistress of all that I am or
possess. Ferrara is fortunate indeed, Cassandra, that you
should come to add luster to its fame.

Cassandra. To enter with so many favors and good
wishes is, I am certain, an augury that all my actions here
shall come to good.

Duke. Pray you be seated, madam, that my kinsmen and
my household may pay you their homage.

Cassandra. I obey, my lord.

The DUKE, CASSANDRA, *the* MARQUIS, *and* AURORA *sit
under the canopy.*

Cassandra. Will not the Count be seated?

Duke. No, madam, he must be the first to kneel and
kiss your hand.

Cassandra. Forgive me, sir, I would not have him kneel
to me.

Federico. Madam, it is my duty.

Cassandra. No, Federico!

Federico. Do not forbid me, madam. I kiss your hand
three times, once for you, to whom I humbly subject myself to be yours as long as I live, in whose service I shall
be the example that all the rest must follow. Second for
the Duke, my father and my lord, whom I respect and
obey, and third for myself, neither as a duty nor as an
example, but out of my own desire to pay you homage—
and obedience which comes from the heart, madam, is the
truest of all forms of loyalty.

Cassandra. Come, Federico, rise. Let me embrace you.

Duke. Federico shows a most politic courtesy.

Marquis. I have long desired to see you, fair Aurora, for
your beauty is famed even in Mantua, and now I thank
my good fortune that has brought me to your presence.
And now, although my wish to meet you is fulfilled, my
desire to serve you is stronger than ever, since I see how
beautiful you are.

Aurora. My lord Marquis, I had heard that you were a
great soldier—reports of your deeds in battle resound
throughout Italy—but did not know you were a courteous
gallant as well.

Marquis. Madam, fired with such favor, from this day,
I name myself your knight, and in these coming celebrations I swear to maintain against all the knights in Ferrara
that none has so fair a mistress.

Duke. You must rest, Cassandra. I would not weary you
with too much ceremony as some foolish husbands do, and
after so long a journey I should be doubly foolish to detain
you further. Love shall not say of me that I do not truly
value you or take due care of his beautiful gift.

They all go, with great ceremony, leaving
FEDERICO *and* BATÍN.

Federico. Oh, heaven help me!

Batín. Why, what is this?

Federico. They say that life is a dream and all men's actions nothing more than fantasy. They say well, for not only when we sleep, but also when we wake, imagination soars beyond the bounds of reason.

Batín. Yes, sir, you are right. Why, sometimes, when I am with a group of gentlemen, suddenly I have a great urge to hit one of them, or bite him in the throat. Or, if I am on a balcony, sometimes I feel I might throw myself off and kill myself. Or in church, during the sermon, I imagine myself shouting out and telling the priest: "I've already read that!" Often I want to burst out laughing at a funeral. Or when I see two men earnestly gaming together and oblivious of all else, I long to pick up a candlestick and throw it at them. If I hear anyone singing, I want to sing myself, and when I see a woman with her hair piled up in a coil, I fancy myself grabbing it, and then blush as though I had done it in reality.

Federico. Oh, God, defend me from my waking dreams. How can I think it, how can I imagine it? She is my father's wife! I swore obedience so little time ago and now my savage thoughts betray my words.

Batín. What is it? Secrets unknown to me?

Federico. No, none at all, Batín—just thoughts, not deeds. And so, since thoughts without deeds are formless fancies in the air, not to tell you what neither is nor shall be is to hide nothing from you.

Batín. If I tell you what your trouble is, will you deny or admit it?

Federico. Flowers will open in the sky and stars bloom in this garden before you guess, Batín.

Batín. Listen, see if I do not answer you at once. Cassandra, your new-found stepmother——

Federico. Do not say it, Batín, it is so. And yet how am I guilty, since thought is free?

Batín. It is, so much so that they say the soul's immortality may be seen in its flight as in a mirror.

Federico. The Duke is fortunate.

Batín. He is.

Federico. Although it is impossible in nature, I envy him.

Batín. I do not wonder, sir: Cassandra would be a better match for you than for your father.

Federico. Do not say it, Batín; my love may never be spoken, although I betray my jealous thoughts to you.

ACT TWO

1

Enter CASSANDRA *and* LUCRECIA.

LUCRECIA. Your ladyship has astonished me.

Cassandra. "Your ladyship"? What means this title?

Lucrecia. I call you by the title your high rank demands, madam.

Cassandra. I am not high in happiness, Lucrecia, nor am I highly esteemed. I would I were a peasant so I might wake in the morning beside a loving laborer rather than dress in crimson and gold and be spurned by a great lord. Oh, I would God I had been humbly born, for then I would have found a man to value me for myself alone, a man to love me in return. There is as much contentment in a lowly life as may be found in royal beds, for all love is equal in the night, whatever its lineage. When the morning sun looks in through crystal windowpanes it does not find a sweeter rest enjoyed, nor see a happier embrace under gilded ceilings, than when by chance it slips through ill-fitting boards to find two bodies with but one soul. How fortunate is she who at dawn rises happily from her husband's side! Who goes to the spring and laughs as she sees her reflection, and lifts her hands to her face to wash in its cool water, and not in grief to wipe away the tears, as does the woman whose husband loves her not, though he be the Duke of Ferrara. One night alone in the past month have I seen him in my arms and since that time I have enjoyed only his contempt. Yet how can I complain, for I should have known from all I had heard about his way of life that nothing would make him reform. It seems it passes for freedom in a man that he should live as he chooses and not come home till dawn. Who can prevent him? But he that forgets he is married, and treats a noblewoman with such scorn, must either be a fool or one that seeks his own disgrace. The Duke regards me, his wife, as nothing more than a trophy to adorn his house, as if I were a piece of furniture, a table or a desk in his drawing room. That he loved me not would be a misfortune enough. But his discourtesy is beyond bearing. And if gossip should arise, he would find it better to give no occasion to wrong than to right it afterwards.

Lucrecia. Your words fill me with pity and wonder, that you should suffer such a monstrous injustice. Who would think the Duke would continue his former ways now he is married? Or, as you say, though he shows no love he might at least show courtesy and due respect to you. Then you would have just cause for anger at his wild behavior still, but that would be a worthier passion than your present humiliation. If he were your lover and a young gallant, then one might suppose he employed those common tricks that lovers use: to pass by laughing with another, praise other women, and show scorn to you simply to make you jealous and your love more strong. But what husband ever used such wiles? Have you written to your father of your grievances?

Cassandra. No, Lucrecia, only my own eyes know of my sorrows.

Lucrecia. Oh, madam, it would have been more natural and more just that the Count should have won you, and that his son should have become heir to the Duke. Besides, the Count is melancholy of late.

Cassandra. Does he still envy me my position, Lucrecia? Does he still fear that I might give him brothers? If he regrets my presence here, he could not regret it more than I.

Enter the Duke, Federico, *and* Batín.

Duke. Federico, had I thought that by my marriage I should cause you so much sorrow, I would have died before undertaking it.

Federico. Sir, it would be most wrong of me to resent your marriage. I know that you love me no less because of it. And be assured that if your marriage were the cause, I should not be so churlish as to show my feelings, but out of respect for you and Cassandra should put on a good show of pleasure. My sickness may be seen in my face, but not the cause.

Duke. The best doctors in Mantua and Ferrara have given much thought to your melancholy, and marriage, they declare, is the best remedy for such a sadness.

Federico. They treat me as if I were a young girl. If I

were, their remedies might have some effect, but a man of my age and condition is not to be cured so.

Cassandra. The Duke scarcely acknowledged me! I will not suffer his discourtesy!

Lucrecia. Perhaps he did not see you, madam.

Cassandra. Negligence is a fine excuse for cruelty. Come, Lucrecia. If I am not mistaken, he will have cause to regret his scorn one day. [*They go*

Duke. Therefore, it is my wish to propose a marriage for you, with one who I believe is close to you in love.

Federico. Is it Aurora?

Duke. Yes, Aurora. I have consulted the oldest and wisest among our counselors, and they all agree that such a match would more than compensate for your just grievance.

Federico. They know nothing of me, and they judge wrongly. They know I have never opposed your marriage.

Duke. I believe you, Federico, and I know your loyalty, and therefore will I tell you that already I repent of my marriage.

Federico. Sir, to prove my love and that I am not unreasonable first let us know if my cousin Aurora is willing. If she is, then I will do as you bid me.

Duke. Her wish is already signed and sealed by her own lips to me.

Federico. But I have certain knowledge of a new development, for the Marquis has remained in Ferrara in order to serve her.

Duke. But what is that to you, Federico?

Federico. Should it not trouble a man about to marry that another gallant has courted his lady? Why, to marry her then is to write on paper that is already smudged.

Duke. If men are to concern themselves over everyone that looks with pleasure upon a woman, then they had better lock their women up in towers from birth. If you see yourself in a mirror of purest crystal, your breath will mist it, but one wipe renders it clear and bright as ever.

Federico. Sir, your wit and determination urge me cleverly, but when a blacksmith throws water on the coals of his fire that roars and spits out sparks, the flames die down for an instant only to leap up again with fiery tongues that lick the water that was to have quenched them. So does a husband at first dampen the blind ardor of the lover, but

soon the flames of his desire spring up more violently than
before. Therefore, I am wise to fear the man that loves her,
for I would not be the water that rouses him to set my
honor in flames.

Duke. Count, you speak foolishly. Your language is un-
couth, your manner, importunate.

Federico. Wait, sir——

Duke. There is no more to say.

Federico. Sir, wait——   [*The* DUKE *goes*

Batín. That is a fine way to curry favor with His Grace!

Federico. His displeasure completes my misery; now my
despair is such that only death can crown it. But to die
once is nothing: death cannot satisfy me; I should need
to die a thousand times before my suffering would cease.
And if I do not prove my own murderer, it is because my
misfortunes are greater than any death might deal me.

Batín. Then, sir, you would seem to be a hermaphrodite,
since you hesitate between life and death, as the hermaphrodite does between male and female. Your sorrow
must be great indeed. But, sir, I can do nothing unless you
tell me the cause of your melancholy; if you will not then
I must find an equal sorrow in leaving you. Give me your
hand.

Federico. Batín, if my trouble were limited, subject to
reason, and such that I could tell it to you, then its nature
would be other than it is, but when I hope to solace my
spirit with words, I find there is more distance between
the soul and the tongue than between earth and heaven.
If you so choose, do go, Batín, and leave me here alone, so
that no shred of pleasure may be left in me.

Enter CASSANDRA *and* AURORA.

Cassandra. Do not weep, Aurora.

Aurora. Madam, have I not cause, since Federico hates
and despises me? He accused me and said that I loved the
Marquis of Gonzaga. Carlos! How could I! Who told him
so? When did I ever give them grounds to say so? When?
How? I can only think that, enraged by his father's marriage, he has determined to flee from this court and go to
Spain, putting all memories of us behind him, for before
his father married, Federico could hardly bear to look on
any other thing but me, I was so dear to his eyes. Now he

shuns the very sight of me as if I were loathsome to him. Once no dawn spoke upon the world but it found Federico sleepless and sighing with longing for me, whom he called the light of his heart. Every jasmine flower and every rose that bloomed in all the gardens of the court was to him my forehead or my lips and to it he whispered his love. He told me so. And every instant he spent away from me was death to him, for he swore I was his life's blood, his soul. And our trust grew, through the loving converse we had together, until those two souls which God had given us were become as one. Our love had its beginning in our earliest years, I think it was born with us, and now his falsehood has put an end to it. Such is the power of thwarted ambition.

Cassandra. It grieves me, Aurora, that I should have been in part the cause of it. But calm your troubled heart while I speak to him on your behalf. Yet I know it is a hard task to reason with jealousy.

Aurora. Why jealousy?

Cassandra. The Duke says it is the Marquis Gonzaga . . .

Aurora. I think his grief comes from some other source, and although I know not what it is, I am sure it is neither love nor jealousy.   [AURORA *goes*

Cassandra. Federico!

Federico. Madam, your slave kisses your hand.

Cassandra. Rise, Federico. Do not humiliate yourself by kneeling to me.

Federico. Give me your hand, else you offend my love. I will not rise until I have kissed it.

Cassandra. Then I must raise you in my arms, my son. What is the matter? Why do you gaze at me? Federico, you are trembling. Do you not know that I love you?

Federico. My soul divined it and told it to my heart, whose swift report has caused my telltale face to betray my secret hopes.

Cassandra. Leave us, Batín. I wish to speak to the Count alone.   [BATÍN *goes*

Federico. Oh, heavens, I die at every moment, and live on like the phoenix! Put out the flames, merciful God, and give me peace.

Cassandra. Federico, I have heard from Aurora that you no longer wish to marry her since the Marquis Gonzaga

came to Ferrara. I wonder that you should so belittle your
own merits as to think that he should be a rival for her
hand, the more so because jealousy and envy are censorious
judges, and are quick to see the faults in their adversaries.
Surely you can see that, handsome as the Marquis is, he
has more of the soldier about him than of the gallant courtier? Or do you fear that since the Duke has married me
another son may disinherit you? Is not this the reason for
your melancholy? If it is, then I can soon put your mind
at peace. You will have no brothers, Federico, for the
Duke, your father, made this marriage merely to comply
with the wishes of his vassals. And his nightly sports, not
to give them a worse name, have only allowed him time
to come to my bed on one occasion, which, it seems, in
his opinion should suffice me for a year or more. After our
wedding night, he broke straight from the check of my
embrace to return with more fury than ever to his former
delights. As a proud horse bolts at the sound of a drum,
scattering the fragments of its harness and trappings like
foam before the wind, the bit flashing through the air on
one side, the reins and the halter on the other, so did the
Duke burst asunder the vows to which holy matrimony
bound him, and now consorts with the whores of the city,
scattering the pieces of his broken honor on all sides,
tossing away the fame, laurels, titles, and good name
which his great forebears won. Thus he wastes his valor,
his health, and his time, making days of his nights with
his unworthy rioting. And so, Federico, you may be assured
that there will be none but you to inherit his estate, for I
shall write to my father and tell him that this is no husband, but a tyrant, and ask him to rescue me from this
palace, which to me is no better than a Moorish prison, if
death does not first put an end to the suffering that has
come upon me in so short a time.

Federico. Your Grace began by reproving me, and now
you end in sorrow which would move the hardest rock to
pity. I fear you must look unkindly upon me as the son of
him who has abused you. But, madam, I would never seem
to be the son of such cruelty as that which he has shown
you. You injure me when you impute my melancholy to
base greed and jealousy. Do I need land or riches to be
what I am? Are not my cousin's estates enough, if I
should marry her? Or if I choose to draw my sword against

some neighboring prince, could I not soon regain more than I had lost? My melancholy does not spring from greed for wealth and power. I tell you, madam, my life is more full of sorrow than that of any mortal man since love first loosed his deadly shaft upon the world. There is no remedy for me. My life burns slowly out like a candle, and in vain I beg Death not to wait until the wax has melted and the flame gutters, but that with a short sigh my days may be lost in night.

Cassandra. Noble Federico, cease your tears. Tears are women's realm, who, though their hearts may be full of courage, lack the power to right their wrongs. Men should show a firm resolve and weep for one cause alone, the loss of their honor. Oh, cruel Aurora, to disdain a knight so handsome, wise, noble, and so worthy to be loved.

Federico. No, it is not Aurora.

Cassandra. Then who?

Federico. The sun itself. Why, Aurora is but the pale dawn's light, and, like the dawn, one such may be seen every day. There is but one sun.

Cassandra. Do you not love Aurora?

Federico. My thoughts fly higher.

Cassandra. Is there any woman who, having seen you and spoken with you, and heard you say you love her, could help loving you in return?

Federico. If you knew the horror that is in my mind, you would say I must be made of marble, that my griefs have not killed me, or else hold it a miracle that I still live in the midst of them. Phaëton dared to take the golden chariot of the sun, Icarus soared into the heavens upon wings of feathers bound with weak wax, until the waves saw them break and flutter downwards like a flock of birds till they lay in the salt waves' lap. Bellerophon, astride the winged horse Pegasus, saw the world as a bright distant speck among the circling stars; Sinon, the Greek, placed that fatal horse inside the walls of Troy where it gave birth to fire and armies of warriors; and Jason yoked the pines and canvas of Argos to carry him boldly across the unknown seas—yet none of these were as foolhardy as I.

Cassandra. Federico, do you love some bronze image, or nymph, or goddess shaped in alabaster? Women's souls are not clothed in ice or jasper. Only a fragile veil conceals a woman's thoughts. Love so deserving never knocked at any breast but the soul replied: "Here I am, but enter silently." Tell your beloved, whoever she may be, that it was not without example that the Greeks so often portrayed the goddess Venus in the arms of a satyr or faun. Though she be high, yet the moon is higher, and Diana came down from her silver disk a thousand times for love of Endymion upon Mount Lathos. Take my advice, Count: however chaste and guarded be the fortress, you will find the door is made of wax. Speak your love, do not die in silence.

Federico. To catch the Indian pelican, the industrious huntsman builds a fire around the nestlings. The parent bird sweeps down from the tree to protect its chicks, and as it beats its wings in alarm, it fans the fire it seeks to kill. At last when the pelican's wings are burnt so it can no longer fly, the hunter catches it easily upon the ground. My thoughts, the children of my love, which I keep safe in a nest of silence, are consumed with fire, madam. The wings of love fan the flames. The fire grows, and bird, chicks, and nest will all be burned. You deceive me, and I burn, you incite me, and I am lost. You urge me, I am fearful, you encourage me, I am troubled, you free me, I am entangled, you teach me the way, I am confounded, for the danger I am in is such that I think less evil would ensue should I die in silence.   [*He goes*

Cassandra. Why did heaven give man the power of imagination? It confounds reason and turns our firmest resolve to ashes. Imagination turns fire to frost and transforms all things to the shapes desire would have them be. It turns war to peace, and storms into calm weather. It is a kind of spirit that deceives more than it enlightens. Federico's meaning shone clearly through his veiled words, and he has left me full of contending thoughts that twist my will into as many directions as a forest takes beneath a raging tempest. The fiercest storms in the world are those within the mind. When my imagination boldly affirms that the Count loves me, my reason cries out that it is impossible. When my conscience reminds me of my marriage, imagination ever conjures impossible worlds in which all things are possible. I fear I shall go mad. Already I see myself avenged upon my cruel husband, although I know that so to sin could bring no good reward. And even now the shadow of his sword falls across the image of that pleasure. The Count is good, gentle, and honorable, but I should be most evil, savage, and bereft of honor if I should permit so unlawful a passion to overcome us. Merciful Heaven, drive all such thoughts from my mind. I have not yet offended, for if unspoken thoughts could give offense, there is no man on earth whose honor goes unscathed. I have only consented to the thought of wrong, which, though it be sinful in the sight of God, offends not our human code, for God knows all our thoughts, but honor sees them not.

Enter Aurora.

Aurora. You spoke long with the Count, madam. What did he say?

Cassandra. He is glad that you love him, Aurora; he is jealous, that is all. Give him no cause for jealousy and all will be well.   [CASSANDRA *goes*

Aurora. A cold consolation for my ardent fears! To think that ambition could so change a man. Love, your power is great indeed. Life, honor, and souls themselves give way to you. And now Federico, who once loved me, is dying of sorrow to see Cassandra here. Now must I try love's strength. Since Federico has feigned jealousy of me as a cloak for his true passion, I will try to reawaken his sleeping love: I will favor the Marquis.

Enter Rutilio *and the* Marquis.

Rutilio. To hope for success against such a rival is to hope in vain. You aspire too high, Carlos.

Marquis. Hush, Rutilio, here comes Aurora.

Rutilio. I know not whether you yourself are here, or whether a mere airy spirit accompanies me. A spirit with but one purpose and many changing moods.

Marquis. Beautiful Aurora, since I came from Mantua I have served you faithfully, but, alas, with no reward, although you are the light that brings warmth and color into my dark world. But all my admiration has only served to make you weary of me. The dark night of absence is all I have received, though I sigh for the dawn of your presence. But do not imagine that I consider myself unfortunate, for to have seen a heavenly light, though unattainable, I count a blessing. My regret is that my love should have aroused in you nothing but forgetfulness and neglect.

I am ready to depart, for that is the only remedy. I must
flee your stony looks and seek strength in the cruel cure of
absence and thwarted love's revenges. Madam, give me
your hand and your leave to go.

Aurora. No lover that gave up after the first rebuff ever
died of sorrow. The sweetest favors are never granted at
the first approach. They are reserved until love is tried and
trusted. You love little, therefore you suffer less. But since,
by asking my leave to go, you give me an undeserved authority, I will use that authority and beg you to remain.

Marquis. Madam, so great a favor as your command to
stay binds me with such a bond of love that I will wait,
not ten years as did the Greeks in their relentless siege of
Troy, nor yet the seven that the shepherd Jacob endured
when Laban promised him his fairest jewel, but for immortal centuries. I will wait as long as Tantalus, ever torn
between doubt and certainty of your good will or bad. I
am most happy in my love and in my hope.

Aurora. While one's desire is yet in doubt, there is some
merit to be found in suffering.

Enter the DUKE, FEDERICO, *and* BATÍN.

Duke. I must leave for Rome. This letter from the Pope
commands my presence there.

Federico. Does he not say the reason?

Duke. My only answer, Federico, must be to go without
delay.

Federico. If you would not confide in me, I will ask no
more.

Duke. When have I ever hidden my thoughts from you,
Federico? I can only tell you what I guess to be the truth.
He is preparing his great army for the wars in Italy and
intends to appoint me as the Church's general. Furthermore, I think he expects some financial help from me if
my election is to be effected.

Federico. You would truly hide your thoughts from me
if you were to go alone, Father. You could not find a
better squire to bear arms at your side than myself.

Duke. That may not be, nor would it be right to leave
my house unguarded. It is my pleasure that you should
stay and rule my estates while I am away.

Federico. I have no wish to displease you, sir, but what
will be said of me in Italy if I remain at home?

Duke. They will say that these are affairs of state and that their importance forbids even the presence of my son.

Federico. It is a severe trial of my obedience to bid me stay behind.   [*The* DUKE *goes*

Batín. Sir, while you talked with the Duke, Aurora has been in close conversation with the Marquis. She has not observed your presence.

Federico. With the Marquis?

Batín. Yes, sir.

Federico. And what importance do you attach to that?

Aurora. Let this ribbon be the token of my first favor.

Marquis. Madam, it shall be as a chain around my neck, a manacle upon my wrist, that I may never part with it. Should you put it on, your favor would be redoubled.

Aurora. No, sir, you must put it on yourself, for it has passed from the lesser hand to the greater in being given to you.

Batín. It was a wonderful device in nature to make women false. Had they been true, those men that adore them now would worship them as idols of perfection. Do you see the ribbon?

Federico. What ribbon?

Batín. Ha! What ribbon? Why hers, sir. The sun itself, so you described her. She that shone alone in the heavens while the circling planets paid homage to Her Grace's beauty. But now that sun is in eclipse, a tiny star in the tail of the heavenly dragon. I remember a time when that ribbon would have been the seed of as great a discord as the golden apple Paris gave to Venus.

Federico. That was one time, Batín; now is another age.

Aurora. Come with me into the garden.

                           [AURORA, *the* MARQUIS, *and* RUTILIO *go*

Batín. See with what liberty he takes her hand and leads her into the garden.

Federico. What would you expect, since their souls are in harmony?

Batín. I never thought to hear that answer from you.

Federico. How else should I answer?

Batín. Why, sir, a swan will not suffer another to come near it, but will rise up with his mate and fly to other waters. A barnyard cockerel, if a strange cock ventures among his hens, attacks his rival, looking like a wild Turk, his turban standing high, his red beard flaring. In rage and jealousy he will peck and claw, never abandoning the fight, not even with the dawn, but crowing his challenge to his adversary anew. How, then, can you suffer the Marquis to take from you a treasure that you loved so well?

Federico. Because the sweetest revenge upon a woman is to let her have her way. That way her honor is at the mercy of her own changefulness.

Batín. Oh, then give me a copy of your rules of knighthood that so dictate and I will learn them by heart. No, Count, forgive me, there is some deeper mystery in your present mood. Thoughts of love are like buckets of a water wheel. As one bucket empties the water out, the next scoops it up. You leave Aurora for some new love. What else can you do but tip the other out?

Federico. Batín, you are a fool and a chatterer. You take great pains and trouble to wring from me something I do not understand myself. Go in! Discover when the Duke plans to depart, that I may ride with him some part of the way.

Batín. You call me fool, but I should be more foolish if I flattered your humor.   [*He goes*

Federico. Why do I place my life in danger, flying in thought beyond the wildest reaches of the winds? Be still, my whirling thoughts; your madness carries me to death. Let me rest and do not bring me to a wretched end. Yet all things are attainable to the lover that attempts them; only you were born to be eternally beyond my reach.[1]

Enter CASSANDRA.

Cassandra. My faithless hopes spring up to choke my honor, seeking to feed themselves on things impossible. My soul inclines to evil. The Duke has used me ill, and now I dream of mingling pleasure with revenge, accepting Federico's love. So would I be avenged upon my husband through his son. Federico was troubled, and came near to telling me his thoughts, then showed his nobility by keeping silent, which often proves the most moving form of speech. The sorrow I saw in him delighted my soul: a voice within me whispered that if it be true love, then it is no

[1] In the original, this speech takes the form of a sonnet, which is subtly linked to the play's emotional structure both by verbal echoes and by a complex network of associations. See Peter N. Dunn, in the article referred to in the note on p. 12.—ED.

treachery, since the Duke has abused me so shamefully.
And if in desperation I should become Federico's mistress, I should not be the last to fall in love, nor the first
to be unfaithful. Daughters have loved their fathers, brothers loved sisters. My sin would be less inhuman, since he
is not related to me by blood. But if one sins, one has no
cause to take example from the sins of others. Here is the
Count. What shall I do? But since my mind is resolved
what have I to fear?—Are you yet melancholy, Federico?

Federico. My sorrow is eternal, madam.

Cassandra. That cannot be. It is some sickness of the
body.

Federico. My sickness is of the soul, not of the body.

Cassandra. If I can help you to a remedy, then trust me,
Federico. Tell me what troubles you. Do not doubt that
I will hear you lovingly.

Federico. I would trust you, madam, but fear forbids it.

Cassandra. You told me your sorrow was due to love.

Federico. That is so.

Cassandra. Antiochus, enamored of his stepmother, fell
sick with sorrow and despair.

Federico. He was fortunate if he died of it.

Cassandra. The King, his father, was troubled by his
malady, and called all the doctors of the realm together,
but their time was wasted, because Antiochus dared not
reveal that love was the cause of his illness. But Erasistratus
was wiser than Hippocrates and Galen, and diagnosed the
trouble at once, and saw that the poison was already between the lip and the heart. He held his pulse and ordered
that all the ladies in the place should come into the room.

Federico. And then some spirit spoke . . .

Cassandra. When his stepmother entered the room, he
knew by the speeding of the pulse that it was she for whom
he pined.

Federico. A strange experiment.

Cassandra. Indeed, it was acclaimed throughout the
world as most ingenious.

Federico. And was he cured?

Cassandra. Do not deny it, Federico, for I have seen the
same symptoms in you.

Federico. Would you be angered if it were so?

Cassandra. No.

Federico. And would you pity me?

Cassandra. Yes, a thousand times.

Federico. Madam, my love has driven me beyond fear of God, beyond dread of my father's wrath, to such a point that I am in despair. I am bereft of God, myself, and you: of God because the love I have for you is forbidden by his laws; of myself because my soul is lost to you; of you because I possess you not. And lest you should misunderstand my meaning, I will plainly demonstrate how you are responsible for my guilty passion. Death is said to be man's greatest misfortune, yet I would gladly die if not to be would release me from my misery. Since I lost my soul to you I have endured such anguish that I am no longer the man I was. So changed am I that now I dare forget that my life, which I unlawfully and unrepentantly give to you, belongs to God. In loving you I lose the love of God. We two are both to blame for my forgetfulness of my true nature. To lose my soul to you is nothing, for without you my life is nothing. But what life can there be without God? Oh, what barbarous presumption it is for a man to plunge himself into such a blind abyss that he is bereft of God, of you, and of himself. I fight a losing battle, desperate in the knowledge that I cannot win, nor can the struggle end.

Cassandra. Federico, when I think of God and of the Duke, I confess I tremble, for I see the wrath, both human and divine, that would fall on such a wrong. But love has always found an excuse in the world. Many have erred before, taking example from those who have fallen, not those who repented. If there be any remedy, it is to flee from the sight and speech of each other, for without meeting or speaking, either our lives would end, or else our love would die. Go from me, I beg you, for I could sooner kill myself than leave you.

Federico. I will leave you, madam, and go to seek my death. But first give me your hand to kiss, give me the poison that has killed me.

Cassandra. To do so would put fire to the powder. Go, Federico, go, and God be with you.

Federico. This is treachery. [*He takes her hand.*]

Cassandra. I must not stay, but the poison rises from hand to heart.

Federico. You were a siren, Cassandra, that by your singing drowned me in deep waters.

Cassandra. I shall be lost forever. Oh, where is honor now?

Federico. Let such sweet poison kill me.

Cassandra. My senses flee from me.

Federico. This is madness.

Cassandra. And it will lead to death.

Federico. Though we should die, there will be joy in immortality: my soul will spend eternity in love with you.

ACT THREE

1

AURORA. It is true, I swear it is.

Marquis. You cannot persuade me to believe it.

Aurora. I had to tell you. I need your advice.

Marquis. Speak lower. We may be overheard. How came you to see Cassandra with Federico?

Aurora. I shall tell you. I confess I loved the Count, and he returned my love. But then he proved a more cunning liar than Greek Ulysses. Time nurtured our love, and when he left to bring Cassandra to the palace our marriage was arranged and agreed. Federico went to Mantua to fetch her, whence he returned so sorrowful that when the Duke proposed our marriage to him, he made a paltry excuse— that he was jealous because of you. Hearing this, and knowing that love's best trick to arouse a tardy lover is to pique him by favoring a rival, I pretended to give him true cause to be jealous of you. But it had as much effect as it would upon a diamond, for where there is no love, jealousy makes no mark. So, seeing how he scorned me, I began to seek out the reason, and since an unrequited love is lynx-eyed and sees through rough walls, I soon discovered why he neglected me. In Cassandra's bedroom, there are two closets which have their walls covered not in tapestries, but in mirrors and portraits. Suspicion counseled me to tread stealthily, and, to my horror, I saw reflected in a mirror the Count Federico measuring the roses of Cassandra's lips with his own. I stayed no longer, but fled, shaken to the soul, and wept for my sorrows and for theirs, living so blindly in the Duke's absence. It seems they compete in love and take pleasure in their offense, not caring if it be published to the world, though their offense is blacker than any vileness naked savages may practice. As I watched, I fancied that the mirror's silver clouded so that it should not see their lust. But love was not so coy; he did not hide his face, but with my eyes followed every embrace. I know all that has passed between them. They say that the Duke is returning home a conqueror and that a wreath of holy laurel circles his brow. Tell me, Carlos, what am I to do? For now I find I am afflicted with fear of the terrible outcome if he should know their treachery. And also, since one betrayal may be followed by another, I fear that you may prove like Federico and deceive me. Did you speak truly when you swore your true love to me?

Marquis. I spoke truly, sweet Aurora. Tell the Duke that you wish to marry me, and we will go to Mantua, where you will be beyond the reach of any vengeance that may ensue. It is said that the tiger, bereft of its cubs by the cruel huntsman, in its anguish, hurls itself into the sea. What will the great Achilles of Ferrara not do when he sees the rape of his honor and good name? So foul a stain will not be cleansed without such bloodshed as will never be forgotten, unless Heaven chooses to chastise their lechery, striking them down with thunderbolts before he comes. Therefore, Aurora, I counsel you to leave for Mantua with me.

Aurora. My troubled thoughts are glad of your advice.

Marquis. The mirror in which you saw her will be as Medusa's glass to this new Circe.

Enter FEDERICO *and* BATÍN.

Federico. Would he not wait until any could be sent to welcome him?

Batín. He had barely reached the borders of his lands when he spurred his horse, saying he would ride ahead and that none was to inform you of his coming. Such is his love and the impatience of his desire to see you. For although he would be glad to see the Duchess, all know that his love for you surpasses any other passion. You are the very light of his eyes, and he has borne with little patience these last four months' eclipse. Count, you must prepare a triumphal welcome for him. The army that he led will soon enter the city, bearing golden crests and the many trophies they have won.

Federico. Aurora, must I ever find you accompanied by the Marquis?

Aurora. Do you jest, Count?

Federico. Is that all you can say, after your many infidelities?

Aurora. I am amazed my friendship with the Marquis Gonzaga should now offend you. It seems you have awakened after four months' slumber.

Marquis. Sir, I did not know you bore such feelings as you now imply. I wooed Aurora believing that I had no rival or competitor, especially yourself, to whom in all humility and service I would render anything, except my love. I have never known you serve her, but since it is your pleasure, it becomes me to depart. I am sure you are more worthy of her great worth than I.   [*The* MARQUIS *goes*

Aurora. What is it that you want? What madness has seized upon you? How often have you seen me talking with the Marquis since this mysterious melancholy came upon you? And far from seeking to attract me, you never even spared a glance for me. And now, suddenly, you are jealous. Now that I am to marry him? Count, I guess your motives. Let me marry and do not seek to hinder me, for I would sooner kill myself than have a hand in your deceits. Return to your melancholy, Count. For my soul does not forget how you rejected me. It is too late to come to me for aid.   [AURORA *goes*

Batín. What have you done?

Federico. I swear I know not.

Batín. You are like the Emperor Tiberius, who had his wife murdered and then sat down to the table and called her to come and eat with him. Or Messala, the Roman who forgot his own name.

Federico. I have forgotten that I am a man.

Batín. Or the peasant who, after he had been married for two years, said one day to his wife, "Why, you have brown eyes!"

Federico. Oh, Batín, I am troubled.

Batín. You remind me of the old man from Biscay who gave his horse its hay but forgot to take off the bridle. When he found the horse would not eat, despite his coaxing, he fetched a horse doctor to see what was the matter with it. When the quack saw that the horse still had its bridle on, he turned the Biscayan out of the stable and took off the bridle and bit. When the old man returned, there was hardly a wisp of hay left in the manger, for once the bit had been removed, the horse ate so quickly that it almost ate the manger as well. "Vet," said the Biscayan, "you are better than a doctor, I swear. Next time I am ill, I shall come to you myself." What bridle is it that prevents you from eating, sir, if I may presume to be your vet?

Federico. Oh, Batín, I am a stranger to myself!

Batín. Then tell me nothing. But do not expect me to cure you.

Enter CASSANDRA *and* LUCRECIA.

Cassandra. He is coming then?

Lucrecia. Yes, madam.

Cassandra. And with so little warning?

Lucrecia. He rode ahead in his haste to see you.

Cassandra. Do not believe it, Lucrecia. I would sooner welcome my death than the Duke's return. Federico, I hear the Duke my husband is returning. Is it true?

Federico. They say he is already near. His love for us ever draws him closer.

Cassandra. I shall die if we must meet no more. What shall we do?

Federico. Die.

Cassandra. Is there no other remedy?

Federico. No other. To lose you is to die.

Cassandra. My life ebbs from me at the thought. But must I lose you because he is returned?

Federico. From this time I shall appear to love Aurora. I will woo her and ask the Duke to arrange our marriage. Thus he will suspect nothing and disregard any murmurings he might hear against us.

Cassandra. No! Jealousy I could bear, but not that naked insult! Marry! Are you out of your mind?

Federico. Sweet Cassandra, I must. Think what danger we are in.

Cassandra. How little you know of me, Federico. Dare you mock me so—you, the sole cause of my undoing? By Almighty God I swear I will shout aloud. All the world shall hear our story.

Federico. Cassandra . . . !

Cassandra. I will not suffer it.

Federico. Someone will hear you.

Cassandra. Let the Duke kill me a thousand times over. You shall not marry her.

Enter FLORO, FEBO, RICARDO, ALBANO, LUCINDO, *followed by the* DUKE, *dressed very gallantly as a soldier.*

Ricardo. Even now they are making ready to welcome you.

Duke. But my love traveled faster.

Cassandra. My lord, you find us unprepared. What persuaded you to come so soon, unheralded?

Federico. Sir, the Duchess is distressed by her unreadiness to meet you. I hope you will not conclude it was my usage of her in your absence has brought her to this state.

Duke. My son, the love of a father for his son, his own blood and image, never ceases. My love for you made light of the journey, for neither weariness nor hard travail can subdue him who has suffered long absence from those he loves. And you, madam, share equally in the love that bore me here, unresting. Do not take offense that I place you as an equal with Federico in my affections.

Cassandra. Your blood and your virtue, sir, which dwell in him, make it an honor for me, and I thank you.

Duke. I shall return your loves. I hear that Federico has governed my estate so wisely in my absence that not one of my vassals has had reason for complaint. This knowledge was a great comfort and reassurance to me in the midst of many battles. I give thanks to God that the enemies of the Holy Church quailed and fled before my sword. Rome received me with triumph as though I were the great Spaniard Trajan, and there, crowned with laurels, I kissed the hand of the Pope. From that time, I resolved to change my way of life, renounce my vicious ways for virtue. For I have earned such fame abroad that it would ill become me to belie the praise I have received with infamy at home.

Ricardo. Here are Carlos and Aurora, sir.

Enter the MARQUIS *and* AURORA.

Aurora. Your Grace is more welcome home than words can tell.

Marquis. Sir, may I kiss your hand and declare my love to you.

Duke. It is a great sorrow to be parted from those we love, but how much greater is the joy of returning to their embrace. And now, my precious jewels all, I would rest from my journey, and since the hour is late, let us tomorrow celebrate this happy homecoming.

Federico. Great sir, may heaven grant you a hundred years of happy life.

They all go with the Duke, *leaving* Batín *and* Ricardo.

Batín. Ricardo, my old friend.

Ricardo. Batín.

Batín. How did the wars go, eh?

Ricardo. As justice ordained, since heaven was on our side. Lombardy is subdued and our enemies all put to ignominious flight. A single roar from the lion of the Holy Church was sufficient to dash all their arms to the ground. The Duke has won such renown that his name echoes throughout Italy, as in those far-off days when the women sang that Saul had killed his thousands and David his tens of thousands. But the Duke is so much changed by his experience that he seems another man. There are no more women, no more feasts, no more thought of swords or shields. He thinks only of Cassandra, and has no love for any but Cassandra and his son. The Duke is become a very saint.

Batín. I can scarcely believe my ears.

Ricardo. Just as good fortune causes some to turn to vice, the acclaim of the vulgar making them arrogant so that they imagine themselves immortal, and all other people as but dust under their feet, so has the Duke's triumph made him humble. He seems to despise his victor's laurels. Why, he hardly noted the banners that waved in his honor.

Batín. I hope to heaven that his humility will not prove as the cat to that Athenian who sacrificed to Venus, begging her to change a certain black-and-white cat into a woman. The goddess did as she asked. One day the woman who had been a cat was sitting in her room, in her fine skirts, and with her hair coiled and braided on top of her head, when she saw a little animal run across the room, one of the poets of the animal kingdom, the consumers of paper, a mouse. She leapt lightly off her stool to catch it,

showing that nature is unchangeable—cats will be cats,
dogs will be dogs, for ever and ever, amen.

Ricardo. Have no fear. The Duke will not revert to his
wild ways. Certainly he will not, should Cassandra bear
him children, for they always have leave to comb with
their soft fingers the manes of the fiercest lions of men.

Batín. I shall be heartily glad if you prove right.

Ricardo. God be with you, Batín.

Batín. Where are you going?

Ricardo. Febo is waiting for me.

He goes. Enter the DUKE *with letters.*

Duke. Are any of my servants here?

Batín. Yes, sir, the humblest of your household.

Duke. Batín!

Batín. God keep you, sir. I kiss your hand in welcome.

Duke. What were you doing here?

Batín. Ricardo was telling me of your noble deeds. According to his chronicle, you are the true Hector of Italy.

Duke. Did the Count govern well in my absence, Batín?

Batín. He might be said to have equaled in peace your
deeds in war, my lord.

Duke. Did he behave kindly toward Cassandra?

Batín. To my knowledge, sir, there has never been a
stepmother so happily disposed toward her stepson. She
is most wise, discreet, and virtuous.

Duke. I am certain nothing is closer to her heart than
to deserve his love. But as Count Federico is, of all things
I have, the dearest and the most esteemed, and since I
knew his melancholy when I left for the wars, I am most
happy that Cassandra should have treated him with prudence and kindness. That they should live in peace and
friendship together is the greatest blessing that my soul
could ask of heaven. And so, Batín, there are two victories
to be celebrated in my house, my victory in war, and fair
Cassandra's conquest of Federico. From this day, I shall
love no other but her in the world. I am weary of my
foolish ways.

Batín. The Pope has wrought a miracle, sir, that he took
the Duke of Ferrara to the wars, and returned him to us
a hermit. The next thing we shall hear is that you have
founded a nunnery.

Duke. Let my household know that I am another man from that I was.

Batín. But sir, you went to rest, how is it you are still up?

Duke. As I was on my way to bed, I was brought these letters, and, fearing that they might contain complaints from my vassals, I prefer to set my mind at rest by reading them at once. Go, Batín, leave me. Those who govern must give their full attention to their office.

Batín. May Heaven, that rewards those who work for the public good, crown you with many victories, and eternal fame.   [*He goes*

Duke [*reading*]. "Sir, I am Estacio. I work in the gardens of your palace, and, being an expert in planting seeds and growing fruit, I have reared six fine sons. I beg you to give the two eldest . . ." Enough, I understand. In future, I shall give alms with more care than before. [*Reading.*] "Lucinda, widow of Captain Arnaldo . . ." This, too, begs. [*Reads.*] "Albano, who has lived for six years . . ." So does this. [*Reads.*] "Julio Camilo, arrested for taking . . ." Again the same style and content. [*Reads.*] "Paula de San Germán, an honest maiden . . ." If she be honest, what can she want, unless she wants me to find her a husband? This one is sealed, and was given to me by a man dressed in rags. I would have talked with him, for he looked troubled, but there was no time. [*Reads.*] "Sir, look carefully to your house, for in your absence the Count and the Duchess . . ." My thoughts did not prove traitors, they governed ill. But I will have patience. [*Reads.*] ". . . have offended with infamous boldness your bed and honor." What, shall I bear this? [*Reads.*] "If you are circumspect, your own eyes shall prove it to you." What is this? Do these letters really spell out such words? Do they not know that I am the father of him who they say robs me of my honor? You lie! It cannot be. Would Cassandra betray me so? The Count is my son. But already the letter replies that he is a man and she a woman. Oh cruel, lying letters that spell these words. And yet there is no evil so base that human weakness cannot compass it. Or is this the wrath of Heaven upon me? This is Nathan's curse upon David. So God punished him. Federico is my Absalom. Yet if this be Heaven's anger against me, I suffer more than David, for they were but

concubines, Cassandra is my wife. My past excess has
brought this grief upon me, although I did not enjoy
Bathsheba, nor take Uriah's life. Oh, treacherous Federico!
Can it be true? I cannot believe that a son would commit
so ugly a crime against a father. But if it be so, I would
that Heaven might grant me, after I have killed you, to
return to life again that I might a thousand times beget
you and kill you again. How truly it is said that a father
cannot trust his own son in his absence! How can I pru-
dently discover the truth? For no man would dare to reveal
this horror to me. I must tread warily, since any whispered
reports against my son dishonor my name also. But why
inquire? None would dare speak so of a son if it were not
true. To punish him is no vengeance, for he who chastises
does not take revenge. I will have no inquiry, for honor
is so frail that no act need be committed! Mere words that
report an imagined infamy are enough to destroy it forever.

Enter FEDERICO.

Federico. Father!

Duke. God keep you.

Federico. I have come to ask a favor of you.

Duke. My love grants it, Federico, before you ask.

Federico. Sir, when you told me it was your pleasure
that I should marry my cousin Aurora, I was overcome
with joy. But at that time the Marquis of Gonzaga's jealous fury and his attentions to her gave me cause to disobey
you. Since then my love for her has overcome such
thoughts. We have made our peace, and I have promised
her that we should marry if you would grant me your permission, now you are free from military affairs. That is my
request.

Duke. You could not have given me greater pleasure,
Federico. Leave me now, for I must ask your mother's
opinion, for she too must be consulted. It would not be
right for you to arrange a marriage without her knowledge.

Federico. I am not of her blood. Why should I consult
her?

Duke. What difference does it make? Cassandra is still
your mother.

Federico. My mother was Laurencia, and she has long
lain dead in the earth.

Duke. Does it displease you to hear her called your

mother? And yet I had heard to my pleasure that you two were much in agreement during my absence.

Federico. God knows best concerning that. I assure you, sir, although I dare not complain, since you adore her, as well you might, that while she shows herself an angel to others, yet she has not been so with me.

Duke. I am sorry that they deceived me, for I was told that nothing so delighted Cassandra as your presence.

Federico. At times she favored me, but at others she proved that they cannot be loved as sons that are born of other women.

Duke. I do believe you. For her to love you is all I ask of Heaven. That would delight me more than that she should love me. Your mutual love might guarantee the peace of our realm. God be with you.

Federico. And with you, sir.   [FEDERICO *goes*

Duke. How glib he was, how double-faced with his guileful invention about Aurora! What care he takes to speak ill of Cassandra! Thus do criminals imagine they keep silence, while they proclaim their guilt to the house-tops. He refuses to call her mother. Small wonder! His father's wife is now his mistress: how could he call her his mother? And yet why should I believe so easily that he is guilty? Might not an enemy of Federico have invented this story, hoping to revenge himself upon the Count through me? It must be so. I am ashamed for ever having credited the tale.

Enter AURORA, CASSANDRA.

Aurora. I rely upon your help in this, my lady.

Cassandra. Yours is a worthy choice, Aurora.

Aurora. The Duke is here.

Cassandra. My lord, are you up so late?

Duke. I have been long away from the cares of my estate. Duty demands that I should pay them some attention now, however well you and the Count may have governed them in my absence. This letter here confirms it. All here shower praises on you both.

Cassandra. Sir, you owe your gratitude to the Count, not to me. For without flattery I assure you that he shows greatness and nobility in everything he does, and is as gallant as he is discreet. Indeed, he is the living portrait of yourself.

Duke. I have heard so much. I hear he has been in everything so much my image that you have treated him as if he were myself, for which you shall be fittingly rewarded, madam.

Cassandra. I come to you now with a petition from Aurora. Carlos has asked for her hand in marriage. She loves him and I beg you to agree to the match.

Duke. I fear that one far greater has superseded Carlos in his desire. Even now, the Count begged me that he might marry Aurora.

Cassandra. The Count asked for Aurora?

Duke. Yes, Cassandra.

Cassandra. The Count, you say?

Duke. I do.

Cassandra. I would only believe it from your lips.

Duke. I intend them to marry tomorrow.

Cassandra. Let it be as Aurora wishes.

Aurora. I beg your forgiveness, sir, but the Count will never be my husband.

Duke [*aside*]. What further assurance do I need? But Aurora, is not my son superior to the Marquis in every way? In courtesy, intelligence, and valor?

Aurora. I know not, sir. When I loved him and wished to marry him, he scorned me. Now that he asks for me, it is just that I should refuse his suit.

Duke. Do it for me, Aurora, not for him.

Aurora. Marriage must be made by free choice. I will not have the Count.   [AURORA *goes*

Duke. She is determined.

Cassandra. Aurora is right, although she was overbold in her speech.

Duke. She will marry him whether she will or not.

Cassandra. Sir, do not use force. Love cannot be coerced, love must be free. [*The* DUKE *goes.*] Woe is me. The faithless Count has wearied of me.

Enter FEDERICO.

Federico. Was not my father here?

Cassandra. Are you so shameless that you dare face me here?

Federico. Hush, Cassandra. We are in danger.

Cassandra. How can I think of danger? I am beside myself with anger.

Federico. Speak lower. All the house will hear.

Enter the DUKE, *who hides and watches them.*

Duke. Here I will learn the truth. I must hear that which I cannot bear even to imagine.

Federico. Madam, at the least remember your position.

Cassandra. What other man in the world would be such a coward? What other man would leave me so? Having taken so much pleasure in destroying my virtue with his love.

Federico. Madam, I am not yet married. I only wished to reassure the Duke. To ensure our safety, which cannot long continue thus, Cassandra. The Duke is not so base that he would see his illustrious name dishonored before his eyes and not avenge the insult. Love has blinded us. We must be satisfied. Ask for no more.

Cassandra. Are those tears, those entreaties with which you robbed me of my honor, now quelled by womanish fear? Coward! Was the soul I gave you not enough that you now rob me of my reason too?

Duke. To witness more I must needs be made of marble. They have confessed all without the rack. No, not without the rack, for they have me upon it. No more is needed. They have confessed. Now, honor, you must be the judge and execute both the sentence and the punishment. I must be cunning in my vengeance. For a man whose honor has been publicly avenged ever carries with him some trace of the foulness with which it was stained. No living soul must know that I have suffered this disgrace, and I must bury my dishonor as though it had never existed. Once the offense is known, nothing can erase it from the minds of men.   [*He goes*

Cassandra. Oh, unhappy women! O false, faithless men!

Federico. Madam, I swear I will do all that you wish. I give you my word.

Cassandra. Will your word be true?

Federico. Infallible.

Cassandra. Love calls nothing impossible. I have been yours and I still am yours. We shall not lack excuses to meet each day.

Federico. Then, madam, go to the Duke. Seem to take pleasure and be delighted in his company.

Cassandra. I will. In doing so, your love shall find no offense, for that which is pretended is not pleasure.

They go. Enter Aurora *and* Batín.

Batín. Fair Aurora, I have heard the good tidings, that the Marquis is to be your husband and that you are to return to Mantua with him. Therefore I have come to beg you to take me with you.

Aurora. Batín, you astonish me. Why do you wish to leave the Count?

Batín. To serve long hours and prosper little is a grievance that either kills or drives mad the wisest and most sensible of men. "Yes" today and "no" tomorrow, "perhaps," "later," "do this," "do that," what-not and I know not what. Madam, the Count is bewitched; I know not what is the matter with him. One moment he is happy and the next melancholy. Sane one moment and mad the next. What is more, the Duchess is as changeable as he. How can aught go well with one when all things are awry? The Duke imagines himself a saint and walks about the palace talking to himself, wandering everywhere like a man looking for something he has lost. Indeed the whole place seems full of lost souls, and I would leave it to go to Mantua with you.

Aurora. If I am so fortunate that the Duke grants my hand to Carlos, then I will take you with me.

Batín. Madam, I kiss your hands a thousand times; I will go and speak to the Marquis.

He goes and the Duke *enters.*

Duke. Honor, cruel enemy of mankind! Who was the first to impose your harsh law upon the world? Who first ordained that you should reside in women's keeping and not in men's? The worthiest man may lose you, though he commits no sin at all. A barbarous tyrant, and no man of discernment, invented this fierce stricture. To leave us such a legacy only proves that he who first lost his honor invented this inhuman code so that others should suffer also. Aurora!

Aurora. Sir!

Duke. I understand the Duchess wishes you to marry the Marquis Gonzaga. I have conceded her request,

for I would sooner please her than grant the Count his
wish.

Aurora. Sir, I am forever grateful to you, and yours to
command.

Duke. Tell the Marquis that he may write to his uncle,
the Duke of Mantua, and tell him the news.

Aurora. I will, my lord. I go now to tell the Marquis
these happy tidings.   [AURORA *goes*

Duke. Oh God of Justice, my house shall this day see
no more than you decree. Raise your divine rod to bless
my action. I do not avenge my injury. I will not invite
your divine displeasure by taking vengeance, for to do so
against my own son would be a double cruelty. This must
be Heaven's chastisement and nothing more. To win
Heaven's pardon, rigor must be tempered with moderation.
I must act as a father, not as a husband, and administer
punishment without revenge to a sin that was beyond
shame. The laws of honor demand that much; and secrecy
too, that nothing may be known in public, for he who
publicly chastises only doubles the dishonor to himself,
since the knowledge of his stained honor spreads irre-
trievably throughout the world. I have left the infamous
Cassandra bound hand and foot and covered in a silk
cloth, with a gag in her mouth, so that her cries shall not
be heard. So much was simple, for when I told her why
I had come to her, she fainted. Human pity might steel
itself against the pleadings of a faithless woman, but what
heart would not quail at the necessity of killing a son?
The very thought makes my body tremble and my soul
faint. My eyes flow with tears, my blood dies frozen in
my veins, I lose my breath, and my mind and will are
tortured on the rack of love and duty. Anguish stops the
flow of speech from my heart to my lips as the coldness
of a winter night stops the flowing of a stream. Why
must love hinder me? Does God not command that sons
should honor their fathers? Has the Count not broken
that commandment? Love, do not prevent me from
punishing one who scorns the sacred laws of God, for if
he takes my honor from me today, he will as surely take
my life tomorrow. Artaxerxes killed fifty upon a lesser
pretext. The swords of Darius, Torquatus, and Brutus
executed the laws of justice without vengeance. Love must

not stand against me, when honor, presiding in the court of reason, pronounces its implacable sentence. Truth is the prosecutor that has accused him. His guilt is plain; both eyes and ears have borne witness to it. Love and blood are powerful advocates in his defense, but they shall not prevail, for shame and infamy accuse him. The law of God reports the case, and his conscience is the scribe. Why, therefore, do I play the coward? Here he comes.

Enter FEDERICO.

Federico. Sir, the news goes about the palace that you are to marry Aurora to the Marquis Gonzaga and that she will go with him to Mantua. Am I to believe it?

Duke. I know not what they say. I have not spoken to the Marquis. My mind is occupied by weightier matters.

Federico. He that rules has little rest. What is it that troubles you, Father?

Duke. Federico, a certain nobleman, here in Ferrara, plotted against my life, but foolishly trusted a woman with his secret. She revealed it to me. How wise is he that praises women, how foolish he that trusts them! I called the traitor to me, saying I had some important business to discuss with him. Once before me, I told him I knew his treachery. So overcome with fear was he that he fainted. Thus, without difficulty, I bound him in the chair where he sat, and covered his body, so that he who came to kill him should not see his face, and so keep secret the traitor's name for the sake of public peace. Federico, I can best trust you with the deed, since none must know of it. Draw your sword boldly, Count, and take his life. I will watch from here to see with what valor you kill my enemy.

Federico. Do you seek to try my love? or has there in truth been a plot against your life?

Duke. When a father gives an order to his son, whether it be just or unjust, should he bandy words with him? Go, coward, or I will . . .

Federico. Hold your sword, my lord. I am not afraid. There is no cause, since your enemy is bound. I know not why, but I tremble to the very soul.

Duke. Stay then, traitor.

Federico. I go. It is enough that you command it. Oh, God!

Duke. Dog!

Federico. Stay, Father, I will go, and though I find Caesar himself, yet for you I will strike him a thousand times.

Duke. I shall observe you.—He is there. Now, now the sword pierces her heart. He who wrought my dishonor now executes my justice. Ho, there! Captains! My men! Guards! Knights of Ferrara! Come hither!

Enter the MARQUIS, AURORA, BATÍN, RICARDO, *and all those who have appeared in the play.*

Marquis. Sir, what means this summons? Why do you call so urgently?

Duke. The Count has killed Cassandra. His only reason is that she was his stepmother. She had told him that she was to bear me a son to disinherit him. Kill him, kill him. The Duke commands it.

Marquis. He killed Cassandra?

Duke. Yes, Marquis.

Marquis. I will not go to Mantua until I have his life.

Duke. Here comes the murderer, his sword still bloody.

Enter FEDERICO.

Federico. I uncovered her face. You told me it was a traitor.

Duke. No more. Silence. Kill him.

Marquis. Die!

Federico. Oh, Father, why do they strike at me?

Duke. In the tribunal of God, you will learn the cause. Aurora, with this example in your mind, go with Carlos to Mantua, for he deserves you, and I am satisfied.

Aurora. Sir, I cannot speak.

Batín. What you have seen has not been without a cause, Aurora.

Aurora. I will thank you, sir, tomorrow.

Marquis. The Count is dead.

Duke. Amid so much misfortune, still my eyes long to see him dead beside Cassandra. [*He opens the curtain.*]

Marquis. He has wrought justice without revenge. See, how he looks upon them yet again.

Duke. Just punishment is no vengeance. My grief is too great, my valor too weak, to hold back my tears. He has paid for that crime by which he hoped to be my heir.

Batín. Thus ends, wise jury, the tragedy of justice without revenge. Let that which was a fearful wonder to Italy be now an example to Spain.